Good Design in Soft Toys

Good Design in Soft Toys

Rudi de Sarigny

MILLS & BOON London
TAPLINGER PUBLISHING COMPANY New York

First published in Great Britain 1971 by
Mills & Boon Limited, 17–19 Foley Street, London W1A 1DR

First Published in the United States in 1971 by
Taplinger Publishing Co., Inc.
New York, New York

British ISBN 0 263 51396 3

American ISBN 0 8008 3570 0

Library of Congress Catalog Card Number 71 164671

To Derek.

Printed in Great Britain.

Contents

Introduction

A toy is a most suitable gift for a child. One may well ask why? The answer is simple. These small objects, pretty or ugly, clean or dirty, are a comfort to a child, often a best and closest friend and if one may call it so—an educator.

In play, a child relives puzzling situations created for him by the adult world. In that turmoil of feelings, in that chaos of newly-acquired knowledge, who is a better companion than a patient, silent Teddy Bear, a kind Rabbit or a pretty doll?

By understanding a child's mentality, either through direct contact, or by reading any of the many and excellent books on the development of children, one can get a very good idea of what is suitable and what will be wanted. Often from the heights of our adult status, we try to project our own ideas and tastes on the young and if they reject them, we feel hurt. Yet we must not forget that a child's conception of a plaything differs vastly from ours. The toy is ultimately a gift for a child, its role is to please the young. What we find amusing, a child may not. He often shows no interest in what we regard as a "good design" and what we think will be good for a child may become an unwanted toy put aside. So, by learning about children, we can appreciate more fully the function of a toy.

The Danish designers of wooden playthings perfected the art of supplying the child with what it needs. Take, for instance, their most excellently made sets of large wooden cubes, the largest measuring about 24″ × 24″ with one side open, so that the slightly smaller ones can be fitted inside each other. This type of toy is ideal in its concept because it serves several functions. It is educational; it helps a child's understanding of shape as he fits the cubes together. At the same time it is good for play because of the variation of ideas which children can project into these cubes. For a boy, they can become an engine and rolling stock, a car, or even a bicycle. For a girl, they can be transformed into dolls' cots, tables with working tops upon which to knead pastry, or they can even make a snug "hiding" bed for a small child, or a bench to sit on during a meal.

I have seen three-year-olds, immersed in their world of play, using these cubes as school desks for their assorted collection of soft toys, and instructing them in the rudiments of good manners.

With regard to soft toys, their appeal lies entirely in the expression and the realism of shape, also colour and feel. It is important for a child to be able to identify the toy as an object seen before, either in real life or in a book. A mask with comical grin or sad drooping features or a shape exaggerated in line and size, so often seen in modern soft toys, deprives a child of the fantasy it needs to express through play. Any little boy or girl will soon make the toy into a character they want it to be. One day Teddy will be a "naughty boy" punished for bad behaviour, to become later on, even the same day, a "poor darling" loved and nursed as only a sick child can be during an illness. This change of mood in play belongs to the child alone and is, in fact, the essence of play.

Judging by the play instinct in every child, we can safely assume that man has always made some form of toy to amuse and to educate his children. Whether this be a miniature spear, or a doll carved out of a piece of bone, these toys, although originally intended for play, would also have had their instructional side. Even today the primitive people of the Far East, South America, and Africa make toy boats to teach their little sons the art of building a boat, and they carve small arrows for them to use, first in play, but later on in the serious occupation of hunting.

When some years ago I was asked by a television director to do a few programmes on the history of toys, I had to turn from a toy designer into a toy historian. This entailed many months of hard work in libraries and museums, but once the pages of history started to unfold in front of my eyes, I became completely absorbed and enthralled. And I do hope that any of the readers whose appetite has been whetted by this very brief mention will follow it up by their own studies in museums or through books.

Between them, the museums in London have the largest and finest collection of toys in this country, but some of the provincial museums also have a good selection, notably Edinburgh and Brighton. As far as books are concerned, most of the County Libraries will be helpful in supplying the necessary literature. But by far the most exciting thing about research into the history of toys is to follow up the book reference by a visit to a museum where the toys can be seen in real life.

From experience, I know that designing, by which I mean making up one's own patterns, is the most thrilling and challenging part of toymaking. The problem of carving out from a dead piece of fabric a three-dimensional object with a life of its own, gives one a tremendous feeling of satisfaction and achievement. In spite of the trials and tribulations—needless to say many will be encountered on the way—the satisfaction of creating a toy, and the happiness on the face of the recipient, is ample reward.

And so the first part of this book is dedicated to the learning of design. We will make mistakes and we will learn how to correct them, we will be angry and frustrated but finally we will reach our goal—we will make a toy. When this happens, a feeling of joy and pride in one's efforts will be achieved.

The second part is arranged to introduce ready-made patterns for many toys to suit the age of the child and the skill of the worker. We start with the easiest toys, the baby and pram toys, then come the cuddly toys, and we end with designs applied to an older child and a more advanced worker. Assembling patterns and sewing the parts together is an exercise in logic and craft, whether using one's own or other people's patterns. The artistic touches are in the finishing. There are no two toys alike, because the character and personality bestowed upon them is the ''breath of life'' instilled by each individual worker. You will also be able to interchange the patterns and make different designs, because, by the time you reach the second part of this book, you will understand the basic rules of pattern making and you will know how it all began.

Since play is the most important factor in the development of a child and since toys are essential to play, it is hoped that this book will encourage many people to take up this ancient craft, and that the ideas and designs provided within these pages will benefit old and young alike.

Materials and Tools

Toymaking is one of the most inexpensive crafts. In nearly every home there are bits of various materials left over from dressmaking or from some outgrown garments which could be used for a toy. There is, however, one most important point to remember. These bits of fabric must be arranged so that they will look gay and attractive. A pair of old corduroy or flannel trousers can make a hare, a rabbit or a teddy bear, but do add a brightly-coloured waistcoat or a skirt to cover up the drabness of the body.

If you are a beginner in the art of toymaking there is no need to spend money on new materials; look first at the bits and pieces you can find at home. Of course, later on you can launch out and buy special fabrics for a special toy, but even then, the pieces needed are so small that it does not involve one in great expense. For some patterns included in this book, the cost of materials does not exceed —and often is well under—a pound.

Ginghams and cotton fabrics will be found in any draper's shop. They come in bright colours and patterns, 36" (91 cm) wide. These shops also keep a limited range of nylon fur fabrics which are 52" (1 m 32 cm) wide and the price depends on the thickness of the pile.

Handicraft shops will have most of the essential materials and accessories needed for toymaking. They will have a good variety of nylon fur fabrics and baizes (a fabric based on a cotton and rayon mixture) 48" (1 m 22 cm) wide and about the same price as the nylon, and also a selection of felts, sold in squares of 9" (23 cm) or by the yard (91 cm). Make sure when buying fur fabric that it is not jersey-backed material, because when the work is ready for stuffing it will pull into an odd shape due to the pliability of jersey. Also when choosing felts, it is wise to pay that bit extra, to get a good firm felt.

All in all, when purchasing or selecting material for toymaking always bear in mind that one of the processes of toymaking is stuffing, therefore your fabric must be firm enough not to distort the shape under pressure.

Handicraft shops also stock glass eyes in various sizes and colours from 5 mm to 13 mm. My tip is, always try to buy the larger size, as the large eye gives a toy a wide-awake and perhaps slightly surprised look. Nowadays, with the variety of imported buttons, it is worth while having a look at these first and use them instead of glass eyes. Extremely good results can be achieved by mounting buttons on felt discs to give the desired finish to the face.

Dolls' and animals' faces can be obtained, but I prefer to make my own because then I can get the expression I want for a particular toy, and it is great fun experimenting with the features and arranging them in various ways. While talking of materials, one must add the many and varied braids which can be used for finishing. Most drapers have a large selection of lampshade decorations and most of these can be used to enhance the look of a soft toy.

As for stuffing, after trying out many stuffing materials, I have decided that cotton flock is the best. It works extremely well, particularly when one is stuffing to shape. One of its merits is that, when packed firmly, it does not spring back as the foam plastics are inclined to do, and it is not fluffy. It does not creep into one's hair and nose and does not hang on to the material. Cotton flock is sold by Messrs. Dryads of Leicester in 2 lb, 7 lb and 14 lb bags.

Before purchasing materials it is always worth while to have a good look at local market stalls, because there I, and many of my student toymakers, have found very useful and inexpensive remnants.

In choosing your materials, make sure that they are washable. Felts are, of course, the exception; although they won't wash they are cheap and colourful to work with.

For machining I use No. 60 Super Sewing Cotton or a synthetic thread. This thread is also suitable for closing the stuffing opening by matching it to the colour of the body of the toy. For the eyes, one needs very strong and durable cotton, and I sew them on with Linen Button Thread No. 35. The hand-embroidered noses are made in black embroidery silk.

Needles used for toymaking will be found in any sewing box at home, except for one special needle which will be necessary for sewing on the eyes. A 3″ long darning needle will do the job well and it is thin enough to avoid tearing the fabric.

The tools required for toymaking are: an ordinary domestic sewing machine, wire-cutting pliers, also a pair of small round-nosed pliers for bending wire, a bradawl—a useful tool to help with inserting glass eyes and also removing fur pile caught in the seams during machining—and finally a stuffing stick, obtainable from Messrs. Dryads of Leicester. I must admit, I like working with the stuffing stick, but if you are making your first toy and do not wish to go out and buy any extra tools for your experiment, use an ordinary pencil (not sharpened) or a large wooden knitting needle, working with the blunt end, as the pointed end can tear the fabric. Should you need a longer stick, a piece of $\frac{3}{8}''$ dowelling bought from a local do-it-yourself shop will only cost you a few pence. Most households have a fine wire or stiff brush, used for clothes, which can be included in the list of tools. A fur fabric toy, when finished, must be brushed over, particularly along the seams. This treatment will cover up the joins in the fabric and will restore the somewhat flattened pile of the fur. A pair of tailoring scissors would be useful for cutting out fur fabric.

I have not used wire frames for the toys included in this book, as by careful stuffing one can achieve very good and lasting results. However, if you wish to use wire for some of the standing animals such as the camel or the giraffe, these are the suitable materials.

Make the frame of galvanised or coppered wire 15 or 16 S.W.G. which is about as thick as a match. You can buy this wire in hardware shops, or probably get one or two welding rods from a garage. These range in thickness from $\frac{1}{16}''$ upwards and being copper-plated, are not prone to rust.

The technique of wiring, if you wish to use it, is explained on page 50.

GLOSSARY FOR AMERICAN READERS

bradawl—a straight awl with chisel edge used to make holes
chemist—pharmacist
flock—cotton waste similar to kapok
moquette—a fabric having a velvety pile
Perle sylko—embroidery thread
plaits—braids
pound sterling   approximately $2.40
pram—baby carriage
scut—small, erect tail

Part 1: Design

1 Choice of design-A Profile Horse

There is an inherent fear in most of us to make a move into an unknown sphere of work. I have heard my students say: "I can't draw" or even "I will never be able to make my own patterns". Of course, I do not expect startling results straight away, and I advise everybody to have patience. Give yourself time, gain experience and then your results will surprise you. The two most important factors to remember are—patience and perseverance. And I must stress this again—don't ask of yourself the impossible. Start in a small simple way and then develop your acquired knowledge into more sophisticated toys.

To cheer up the doubtful and the frightened let me admit, here and now, that with my training and many years of practical experience even I have difficulty in producing a perfectly good pattern straight from the drawing. In some cases it takes me as many as six re-makes to get the overall line of the toy to satisfy me and the people who have commissioned the design.

But one must make a start somewhere, and even if the first effort is a disappointment, it is, at the same time, the first lesson on the way to improvement and to understanding the problems involved.

For your first experiment always use gay, colourful materials, as these will make the work much more amusing, and even if the toy does not come up to expectation, the charm of fabric and trimmings will soften the blow.

I remember an excellent designer, a director of one of the oldest
toy factories in this country and under whose guidance I learned
the practical side of designing, taking as long as three months to
finish a toy he was working on. But, believe me, at the end the
toy was perfect in every detail. Still, for an ordinary enthusiast,
a period of several months would be too long. Unless one is
specially dedicated, such perfection is seldom necessary, and one
would lose interest, get bored and give up toymaking never to
return to it again. The latter would be a pity indeed, because
making toys is great fun!

With regard to the actual designing, I have to quote the words of
my own teacher: "Designing is seeing". How right he was. Most
people—and I would even go further and say all people—can
design if they will only train themselves to picture the proportions
and the outlines of the toy they want to make. To learn how to do
just this, you will be carefully guided through these pages, starting
with the easiest type of toy, developing it further, to end with a
sophisticated toy made to your own design.

The question of being able to draw simply does not come into it!
This can be overcome by copying out shapes of various animals
from existing books. The "feel" for a good outline will come with
experience, and the more toys one is able to make the more
accustomed one will become to the various characteristic outlines
of animals—and in the case of dolls, of the human body.

It is advisable, however, to have some idea of the bone structure
of the creature you are going to make, as this will give your toy
an identifiable shape. Further, it is also very useful to have a
photograph or drawing in front of you while making up the
patterns and, later on, during the process of stuffing; most
important when finishing the face, positioning the eyes, ears and
nose. Also bear in mind that if you make a toy for a small child or
a baby, it is not the skill of the pattern which will attract the
attention but the colours and the feel of the toy.

Taking into consideration that one is a beginner, a horse is a good
toy to start on. Although easy to make into an elementary toy, in
later stages of development, it is by far the most difficult. To make
it well and true to shape, one will be able to learn the necessary
refinements in designing complicated patterns.

To avoid drawing a horse from memory, pay a visit to the local
Public Library. There, looking through books, don't miss the
opportunity of seeing some of the famous paintings by the greatest
English painter of horses, George Stubbs (1724–1806). He was
born in Yorkshire and was trained as an anatomist to become later

a lecturer on this subject. After a tour abroad he turned his attention to the horse and did many dissections of his own, often in horribly difficult conditions. Consequently, apart from their artistic value, his pictures are acknowledged as reaching the highest standard of anatomical accuracy, which, in itself, is of great value to a toy designer.

However, the best art work to choose for the purpose of making a toy, is one illustrated by simple outline and it must be a side view of the animal—a profile. Hence, the simplest toy to construct will be called the "Profile Toy". If a photograph is used, make sure that it is clear and without shadows. On the other hand, if an artist's impression is picked out, this too has to be clear, not in perspective and certainly not exaggerated in movement, expression or proportions. The best drawing suitable for splitting into patterns is simple and clear.

Plate 1 Profile Horse made in very small black-and-white check gingham. The brightening touches are added by tying a red ribbon round the body with a black bobble braid, red ric-rac and white braid round the hooves.

This basic illustration of the horse will then be used for making a profile toy. For a beginner this is a necessary step to learn the art of "seeing" the toy in three dimensions.

14

The more prototypes of profile toys you can make the better; particularly if each of them represents a different animal. This way you will gain experience and be prepared to launch on more advanced toys later on. Also, being quick to construct and make, these toys will give the student a feeling of achievement, and what is most important, they will build up confidence necessary for the timid and the frightened starters to get on with the job.

COPYING THE DRAWING FROM THE EXISTING ARTWORK

From the many books examined, I decided to select this simple artist's impression of a foal. The outline in this drawing (Diagram 1) is clear, simple, and distinct, and it is easy to make it into a pattern.

1 Outline drawing copied from a book and suitable for making a simple Profile Horse.

Diagrams 2 and 3 although attractive in movement and typical of a horse, will never make a toy. The prancing horse in Diagram 2 standing on two legs only with one front leg and one back leg suspended in the air, is useless for the purpose of a toy as it will make the finished work unstable. In Diagram 3 the movement is stretched out and the legs hardly touch the ground, consequently

15

this sketch will also be unsuitable for copying as a toy. Always consider when choosing your drawing that the bulk of the body has to be placed on firm sturdy legs. This will prevent the toy from falling over or collapsing in the joints.

2 and 3 Type of drawing not to be used for toymaking.

Having decided on Diagram 1, make an outline drawing of the illustration (marked by a dotted line in Diagram 4). As a beginner, never work on miniature toys, as these need a great deal of experience and patience. Therefore make your first profile toy at least 6″ to 7″ high (15 to 17 cm).

3 inches

base

4 Before making patterns, streamline the outline of the original drawing.

METHOD OF ENLARGING

For a profile toy, one cannot afford the refinements of the original
drawing. It is necessary to streamline the curves to make them
suitable for a pattern. First of all, the profile horse will stand on
two wide legs only. The shaping of the head, the saddle, and legs
is overlooked and brought into straight lines (Diagram 4 marked by
straight lines). It is also advisable to move the head back. If it is
left in its original position and adapted into the pattern, when
finally stuffed, the head, due to the weight of filling, will hang
forwards and sag downwards. After these alterations are completed,
the drawing is then ready for enlarging (Diagram 5). The easiest way
to enlarge is to measure the sketch as in Diagram 4, from the base to
the top of the head; in this case it reads 3″ (7·5 cm).

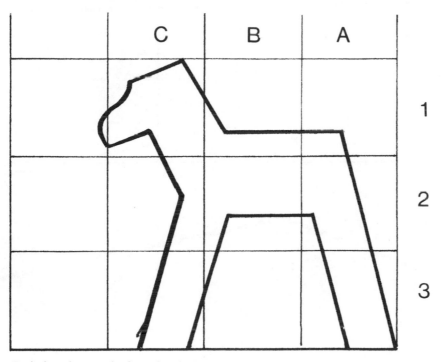

5 *A drawing ready for enlarging.*

Draw 1″ (2·5 cm) squares over the illustration. Decide to what
extent you wish to enlarge. My suggestion is to make the toy $6\frac{1}{2}$″
(16·5 cm) high from the base to the top of the head. This means an
enlargement of slightly more than 100 per cent. Then draw squares
each measuring $2\frac{1}{8}$″ (5·5 cm). Mark these squares with letters on
the top and figures down the side. Transfer from your original
Diagram 5 the lines in squares A/3 working to A/2 further on to
A/1 and so on, till the whole drawing is completed. Some workers

17

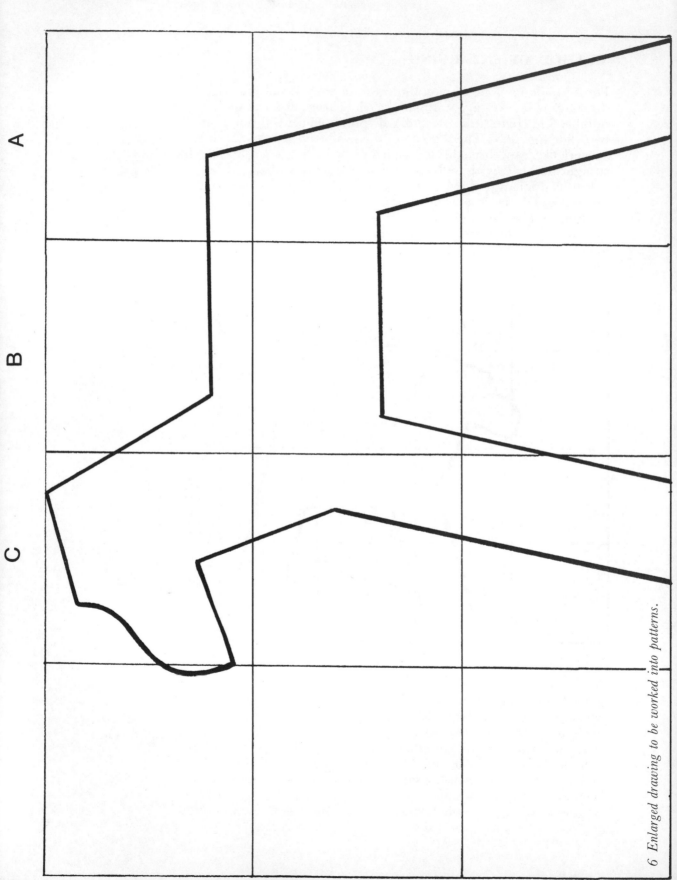

6 Enlarged drawing to be worked into patterns.

may find it easier to use more squares, i.e. $\frac{1}{2}''$ (1 cm) instead of 1″ (2·5 cm) for Diagram 5.

MAKING THE ELEMENTARY PATTERN

To work out the patterns from the drawing in Diagram 6, cut out in paper two pieces of the side view which will be marked body pattern. These will be joined together by gussets. The width of the gussets on a small toy standing some 6″ (15 cm) high should not be more than about $1\frac{1}{4}''$ (3·5 cm) wide, but they should be widened down the legs by another $\frac{1}{4}''$ (0·5 cm) to end at the feet, measuring $1\frac{1}{2}''$ (4 cm). This will make the toy, when finished, stand firmly on the ground. The length of the gussets is taken from one of the body pieces. Measure from the base of the front leg, up the front leg, continue up the front of the neck, round the head, following the back and ending at the base of the back leg (Diagram 7, line A). This is called the outer body gusset. To give depth to the toy, in other words three dimensions, an under body gusset is required. This has to be the same width as the outer body gusset and also widened out at the base of the legs. The length of the under body gusset is taken from the body pattern by measuring

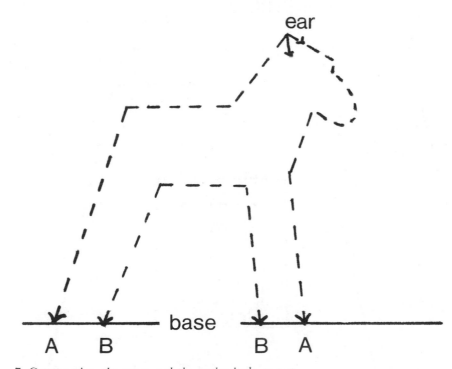

7 Constructing the outer and the under body gusset.
  A Measuring the outer body gusset.
  B Measuring the under body gusset.

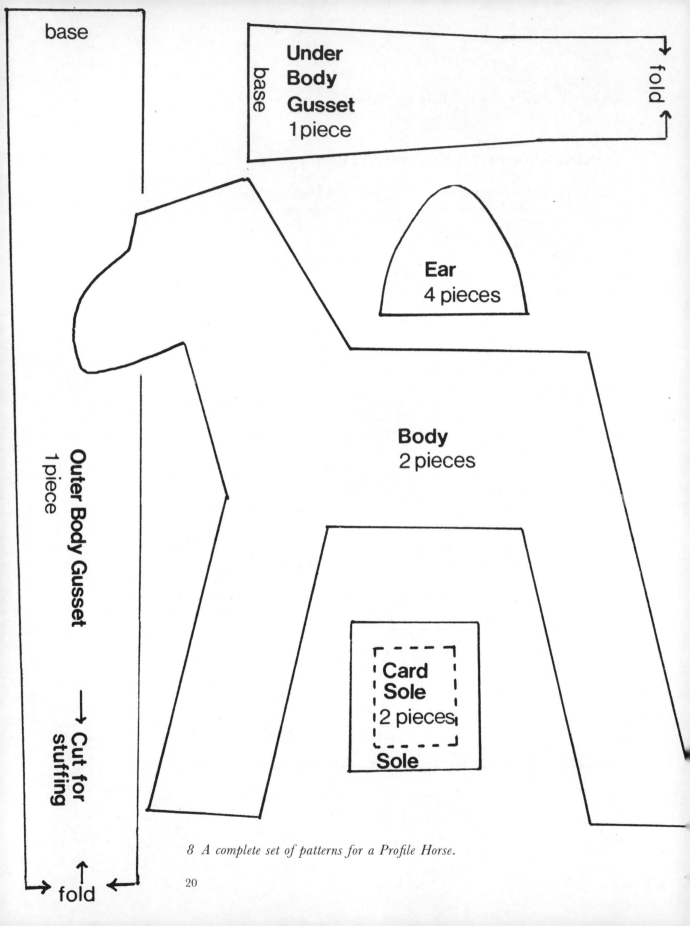

base

Under Body Gusset
1 piece

base

fold

Ear
4 pieces

Body
2 pieces

Outer Body Gusset
1 piece

→ **Cut for stuffing**

Card Sole
2 pieces

Sole

8 A complete set of patterns for a Profile Horse.

20

fold

along the inner line of the front leg, along the body and ending at the inner back leg (Diagram 7, line B). Draw the worked-out gussets on paper.

At this stage it is a help to cut the patterns in tissue paper and pin them together before committing yourself to a design which may well be wrong in proportions. By doing this, you will immediately realise that the feet have no soles. This, of course, is wrong because you must bear in mind that the stuffing has to be closed in, in order not to fall out.

Cut out two soles for the feet, each rectangular in shape, one side equal to the width of the leg and the other side—the width of the gusset. Your set of basic patterns for a profile horse is now finished and it consists of two body pieces, two gussets—one under body and one outer body gusset—and two soles. The ear pattern is worked out during finishing.

For the purpose of a set of patterns to be used in the future, as in Diagram 8, discard one body piece and one sole, since they are identical in shape, and copy the patterns from paper onto a thin card. Leaving them on paper makes the marking on fabric difficult and liable to cause mistakes. It is not necessary to buy special card, left-over cereal boxes are very good for making patterns. Mark each piece of pattern "Profile Horse", pierce a hole in each of them and string together.

MATERIALS

The most attractive feature about profile toys is that one can make them in any scrap of material, providing bright and gay colours are used. It is, however, worth while remembering that fabrics with large patterns will be unsuitable, as the design will be lost on a small toy. For a first attempt in toymaking avoid using fur fabrics. These will be too difficult to handle at this stage of experience. Cotton flock is, of course, the best for stuffing, but if it is unobtainable locally, any stuffing will do except plastic shavings and cotton wool. Eyes can be made by sewing on a pair of black buttons $\frac{1}{2}''$ (1 cm) in diameter each, or by cutting out felt discs of the same size. The finishing decorations are left entirely to the imagination of the student. Ric-rac, lampshade braids, ribbons and wool, may be used to enhance the charm of the toy.

CUTTING OUT

Lay the patterns on the material. If the fabric you have chosen has a right and a wrong side, lay the patterns on the wrong side and mark round, making the second body piece with the pattern turned over (Diagram 8A). There is one important thing to remember, never cut the body on a bias, because during the process of stuffing, it will pull out of shape. Cut out. The total number of pieces should be ten in all. If the gussets are made in two pieces each, due to the shortage of material, this will increase the number of pieces to twelve. Add on $\frac{1}{4}''$ (0·5 cm) to each of the "cuts" on the gussets, otherwise the overall length will be shortened by $\frac{1}{2}''$ (1 cm) and it will not fit round the body.

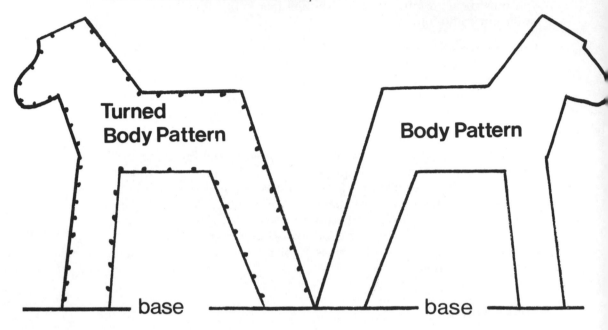

8a For making the body patterns on material, turn over the pattern.

Turnings of $\frac{1}{4}''$ (0·5 cm) are included in the patterns and no extra should be added on.

SEWING

All sewing should be done on the wrong side of the fabric. The only sewing done on the right side is when the opening for the stuffing is sewn up with a ladder stitch, and when ears and tail are attached.

To give the toy a professional finish, a domestic sewing machine is by far the best method of sewing the seams. Machine stitches are firm and do not give under pressure of stuffing. In the case where a machine is not available, good results can be obtained by using a firm backstitch.

Start machining by joining together the two halves of each of the gussets, if they are made in two pieces. Then pin the outer body gusset round the body. Sew on the wrong side, by working from the base of the back leg, going round and ending at the base of the front leg. Match the second side of the body piece to the outer body gusset, working on the wrong side of material, and pin into place and sew round.

Work on the under body gusset by pinning it to one part of the body and sewing into place. Repeat the same on the other half. Fit in the soles and machine round. Always remove pins immediately after a seam has been completed. The "skin" is now ready and is inside out. Inspect the work for any gaps in the sewing and correct if necessary. Cut a slit in the outer body gusset as marked on Diagram 8 and turn the toy right side out. Be careful not to tear the fabric round the opening. Turn slowly, by pulling the head through first, then the front leg, finally the back leg and the rest of the body. The "skin" is now right side out and ready for stuffing.

STUFFING

The proper technique of stuffing is essential to toymaking. It is wise to realise this as early as possible. To rush on with stuffing, a very natural thing to do, will ultimately spoil the toy. The finished product will be lumpy, bulging in places, and not firm enough to stand on its legs. Remember, good, even, patient stuffing is most important to the making of a good toy. Never hurry and always use only small amounts of flock at a time.

Rest the "skin" against the left hand and drive in the filling with the stuffing stick held in the right hand. It is the left hand which controls the shape. Of course, the process is reversed for left-handed people. What, in fact, happens during stuffing, is that one hand acts as a continuation of the stuffing stick, while the other hand is used for shaping and controlling.

Before stuffing, to make the feet stand firmly on the ground, insert into each foot a rectangle cut out in thin card. The measurement for the card is $\frac{1}{4}''$ (0·5 cm) smaller all round than the actual pattern for the sole. This is marked by dotted line on Diagram 8.

Start working by stuffing the head. Once the head is filled, continue stuffing the front leg, making sure that the leg is really firm. Fill the whole front part of the body holding the toy at the "waist". Still holding at the "waist", start stuffing the back leg and the back of the toy. Move your hand away, and fill the middle part of the toy, holding it approximately at neck level. The joints, where the legs meet the body, should be particularly well packed.

Practise the correct stuffing method on profile toys and it will help you greatly with the more advanced work.

Stuffing technique

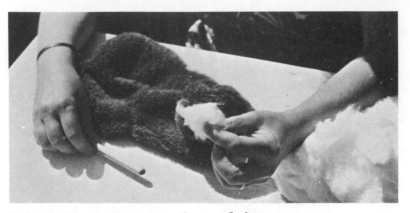

Plate 2a Use small amounts of cotton flock.

b Rest the head against cupped left hand to achieve the shape of a domed head.

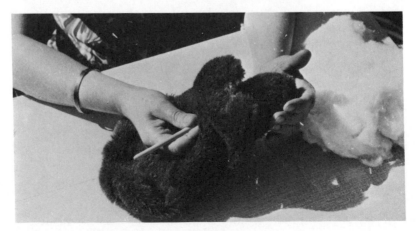

c Continue filling the head to shape.

d Shape the nose by holding it with left hand while filling with cotton flock.

e With small amounts of cotton flock fill the front feet.

f Finish stuffing the front part of the toy.

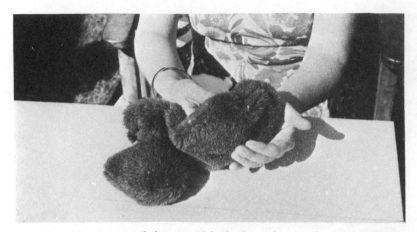

g Rest the back part of the toy with the haunches against the left hand, and stuff.

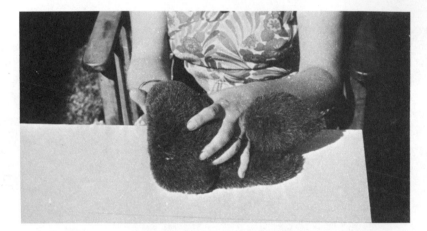

h Continue stuffing the haunches.

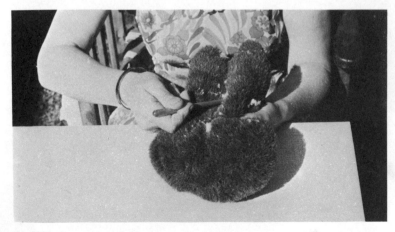

i Fill the centre of the toy.

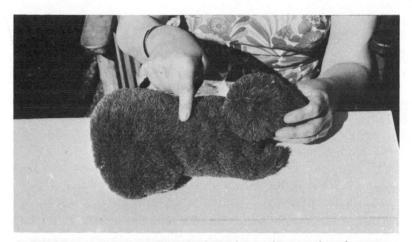

j Shape the toy, accentuating the haunches and narrowing the nose.

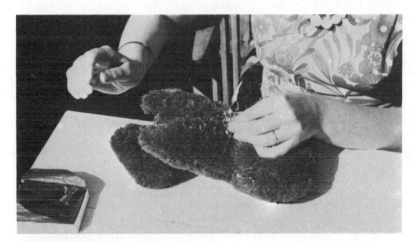

k Pin the stuffing opening.

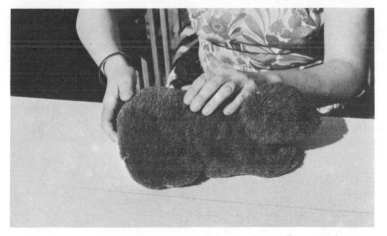

l Pat the toy into shape before sewing up the stuffing opening.

FINISHING

The most enjoyable part of toymaking is the finishing. You will feel that in your hands the toy begins to live. It suddenly has eyes to see with, a nose to give it character and ears to add to the general expression of alertness or pensive sadness.

The positioning of the features (eyes, nose, and ears) is left entirely to the student and the way he envisages the toy.

Start finishing by closing the opening for stuffing. Use a neat ladder stitch. Then cut out two triangles for the ears, in the same material as the body. Pin these to the head. For guidance, the position is marked on Diagram 7. Pin on the eyes. It is a good idea at this stage to leave the toy, with the pinned eyes and ears, and not look at it for a while. As a matter of fact it is a good moment to take a break for a cup of tea or coffee. When you return to your work, you will immediately realise whether a mistake was made in the positioning of the features. Sometimes too much "looking" prevents one from "seeing". You may find that the size of the ears needs to be enlarged or cut down. Alter this to your requirement; also correct, if necessary, the placing of the eyes. Once satisfied with the expression, mark the correct places for ears and eyes with a pencil or chalk.

Remember to make a card pattern from the cut-out ear, allowing $\frac{1}{4}''$ (0·5 cm) round for sewing. Add this pattern to the other set of profile horse patterns.

Cut four ears in material, arrange in pairs and machine round, leaving the base of the triangle open. Turn each ear right side out and finish off the raw edges of the base by hand.

Sew on eyes. Using strong buttonhole thread doubled and a thin, long darning needle, start working from the opposite side of the head to the eye. Insert the needle in the place where the ear is going to be, through the head, coming out at the eye position. Pull the thread through the loop on the button and push the needle back through the same hole back to the ear, coming out about $\frac{1}{4}''$ (0·5 cm) from the position of entry. Pull on the thread, so that the eye is well embedded in the head, almost forming an eye-socket. Tie a knot in the thread and finish off by sewing a few stitches before cutting off the thread (Diagram 9). Sew on the ears.

Now look at your assortment of braids and ribbons and experiment as much as you like. Don't be afraid of using unorthodox trimmings, providing the ultimate result is good.

Have fun playing around, this is the essence of finishing. Let your inventiveness and imagination take over.

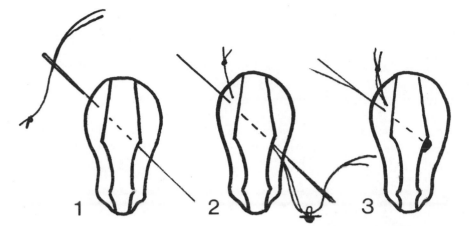

9 *Method of inserting eyes:*
1 *Start working from the opposite side of the head to the eye. Insert the needle in place where the ear is going to be, through the head emerging at the eye position.*
2 *Pull the thread through the loop on the bottom of glass eye and push the needle back through the same hole back to the position of entry.*
3 *Pull on the thread so that the eye is well embedded and forms an eyesocket.*
4 *Dotted line shows the passage of the thread inside the head.*

2 Designing an advanced toy

Once familiar with the method of making a profile toy, the next step is to develop this system into designing more complicated toys. The basis on which the patterns are built is a good side view of an animal one intends to make. This rule applies to profile as well as the advanced toys (Diagram 10). Having decided on, and having enlarged this drawing into a workable size (method of enlarging— see page 17), do not streamline the shape of the body as on the profile toys. On the contrary, emphasize the characteristic lines to make the finished product look as near the real thing as possible (Diagram 13).

10 A clear side-view drawing of a horse copied from a book.

Working with soft materials, only by using gussets, a designer can attain a three dimensional object. In profile toys, the gusset was a strip of fabric going round the body piece and legs. Progressing to a more sophisticated toy, this gusset is split into:

1   under front leg
1   under back leg
1   under body gusset
1   head gusset.

First of all, let us realise the importance of gussets and darts. To help a designer to sculpt a toy in material, he needs as his tools gussets which produce bulk and darts which control this bulk. By adjusting darts and gussets one can finally achieve the required shape. But one must add, that this "adjusting" often leads to mistakes, even amongst experienced designers. One can only correct these errors by completing the toy and then altering either the width of the gusset or the depth of the dart. It is important, however, to note that when making patterns one MUST continuously study the original proportions from a drawing which should be in front of the worker at all times. It is also useful to have an idea of the bone structure (Diagram 11).

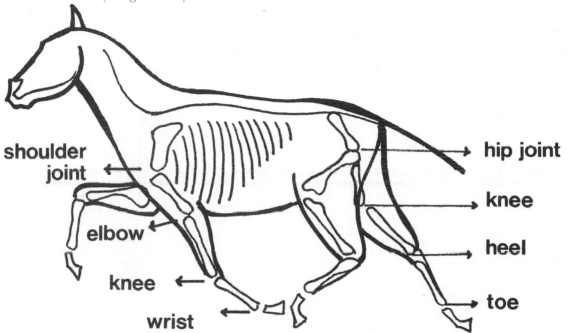

shoulder joint

elbow

knee

wrist

hip joint

knee

heel

toe

11 To understand the build of a horse, or any animal for that matter, a rough outline of the skeleton.

There are certain rules which must be obeyed:
1. Always set your under front and under back leg to the under body gusset on a dart as shown in Diagram 12 and 13a.

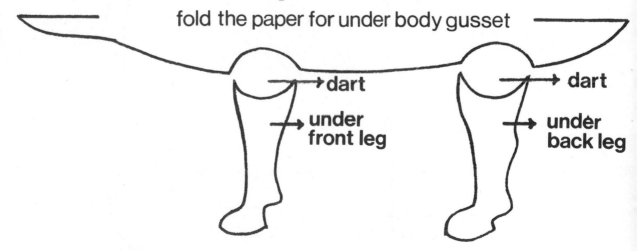

fold the paper for under body gusset

dart

under front leg

dart

under back leg

12 The method of designing an under body gusset with the front and back legs set in on a dart.

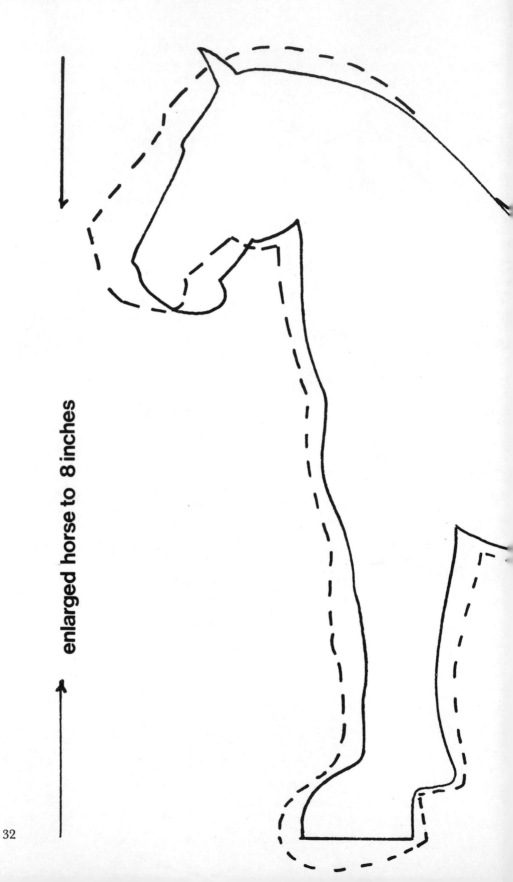

enlarged horse to 8 inches

13 *Necessary alterations to the basic drawing before working out a set of patterns.*

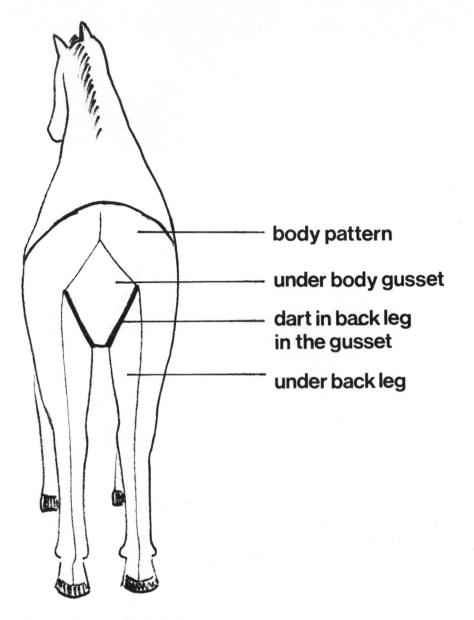

body pattern

under body gusset

dart in back leg
in the gusset

under back leg

*13a Back view of a finished toy
      horse with the legs set on a dart.*

2. The under body gusset controls the width of the toy. In its
   widest part it should measure three-quarters of the body
   pattern. This measurement is taken from the body pattern
   between the spine and stomach line (Diagram 14).
3. The head gusset gives character to the toy. To do this, it is
   inserted between the sides of the head on the body pattern and
   shaped to suit the animal in question (Diagram 15).

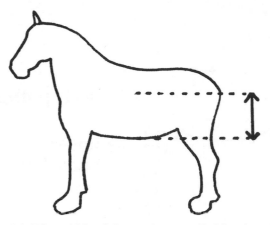

14 The width of the toy is controlled by the width of the under body gusset. The width of the under body gusset (marked by dotted lines in diagram) is three-quarters of body pattern.

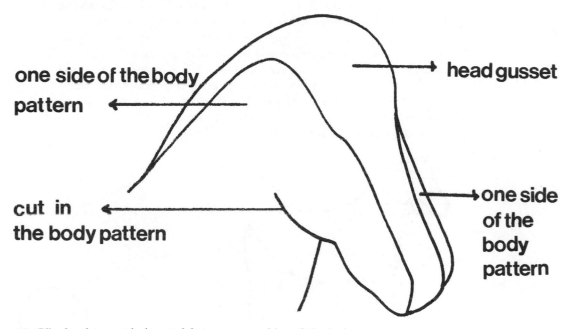

one side of the body pattern

head gusset

cut in the body pattern

one side of the body pattern

15 The head gusset is inserted between two sides of the body pattern.

Looking at the three rules let us take each of them in turn and explain.

1. To make the toy stand firmly on the ground and to prevent the legs from splaying out, always set them on a dart. The dart will help to pull the legs in as shown in Diagram 13a. Therefore, to make an under leg pattern of the front or the back leg, draw round the legs on the body pattern but, at the top, finish off by drawing a downward curved line i.e. half of the dart, Diagram 16.

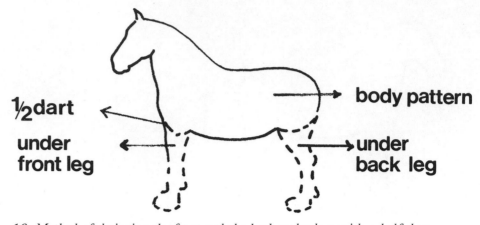

16 Method of designing the front and the back under legs with a half dart at the top.

2. The length of the under body gusset is related to the shape of the toy, and a careful study of the proportions is essential. On cuddly toys, such as a puppy dog, a nice fat rabbit or a Teddy Bear, to underline the rounded figure, the gusset will start at the haunches and will end above the front leg. On toys with wide strong necks such as a horse, or a giraffe, this gusset will be brought forward to end at the throat, thus adding bulk to the neck. The final conclusions are left to the designer, his experience and trials (Diagrams 17 and 17a).

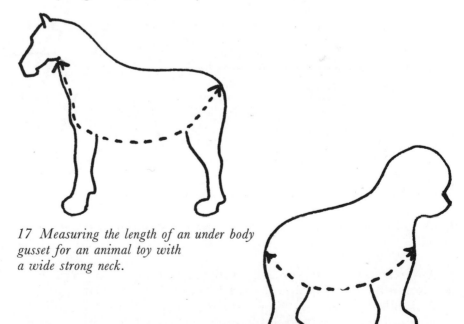

17 Measuring the length of an under body gusset for an animal toy with a wide strong neck.

17a Measuring the length of an under body gusset for a cuddly toy.

3. As a rule in shaping the head gusset one must be guided by the character of the toy. To make a large-headed animal, like a panda, the gusset will start at the base of the head, curve out generously alongside the top of the head to be narrowed down across the bridge of the nose, to end at the muzzle. On the other hand, on animals with narrow heads like a terrier dog or a horse, it is often necessary to keep the gusset narrow, to match the shape of the head without exaggerated curves and to run it beyond the muzzle to end at the throat (Diagram 18). In its widest point the head gusset should be two-thirds of the width of the head, measured between the top of the head and the throat. The two distinct shapes of gussets are featured in Diagram 19. Only by making several soft toys, will you get the "feel" of the right shape of head gusset, and will know immediately what type to use.

18 Measuring the length of the head gusset for a cuddly toy, marked A, and for an animal with a narrow head as shown in B.

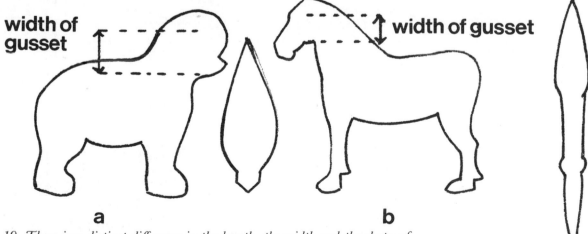

19 There is a distinct difference in the length, the width and the shape of the head gusset as used for a cuddly toy or a toy with a narrow head.

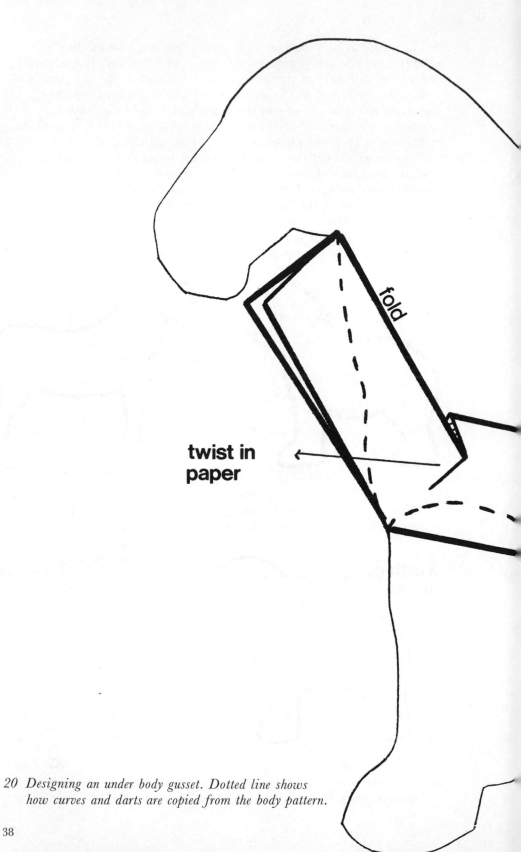

20 *Designing an under body gusset. Dotted line shows*
   how curves and darts are copied from the body pattern.

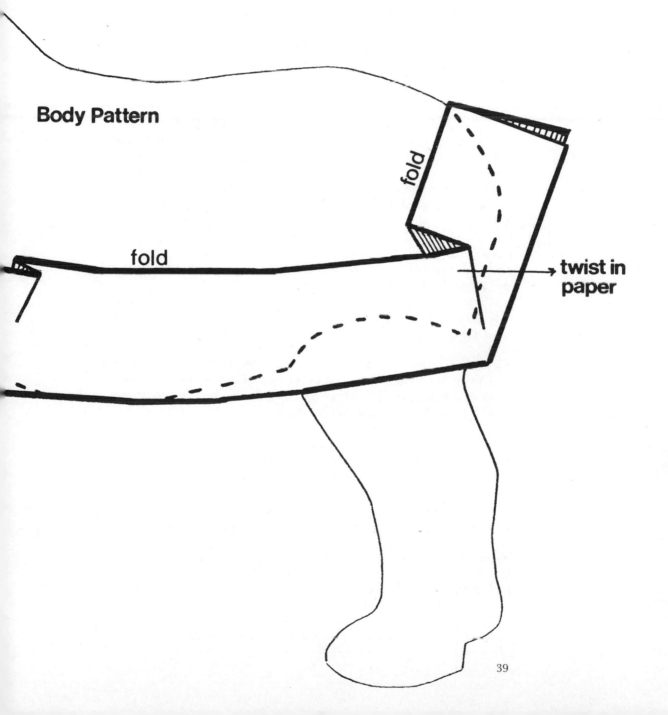

Body Pattern

fold

fold

twist in
paper

APPLICATION OF THE THEORY TO PRACTICE

To apply the theory to actual practice, let us follow step by step the working out of a set of patterns for a horse.

Choose a good illustration of a horse as in Diagram 10. Bearing in mind that it is impossible to work out a pattern from such a small drawing, enlarge to a size convenient for toymaking. This should be at least 8" (20 cm) high from the base of the legs to the top of the head. Since the height in Diagram 10 is 2" (5 cm), it has to be enlarged four times to be ready for splitting into patterns. Draw $\frac{1}{4}$" (0·5 cm) squares over the drawing and translate every line in each square on to 1" (2 cm) squares by employing the same method as used for a profile horse (page 17).

Looking at the enlarged picture on Diagram 13, the first thing which strikes one is the thinness of the legs. You must therefore widen the legs by $\frac{1}{4}$" (0·5 cm) on each side, thus allowing for turnings in sewing, and making the width of the legs at least $1\frac{1}{4}$" (3 cm). On standing toys it is essential to have firm solid legs, so err on the large side. Also curve the base of the front and the back leg. Further, add at least $\frac{1}{4}$" (0·5 cm) round the saddle, tapering the line towards the head. This will help to keep to the original shape after stuffing, as one loses about $\frac{1}{4}$" (0·5 cm) on each side of the body for the sewing up of the stuffing opening. Widen the neck underneath to flow gently into the widened front leg and move the head back, as shown on Diagram 13 by the dotted line. Now, the side view of the body, known as the body pattern, is ready to be used for making gussets.

First of all, copy the front and the back leg from the body pattern and finish off by a downward curve at the top of the legs to be used as a half dart. The other half will be marked on the under body gusset. Cut out and put aside.

Then measure the distance from the top of the haunches, following the outline of the stomach, to the throat, as in Diagram 17; this measures 12" (31 cm). The three-quarter width of the body pattern in our case is $2\frac{1}{2}$" (6·5 cm). Therefore take a piece of tissue or tracing paper 12" (31 cm) long and $2\frac{1}{2}$" (6·5 cm) wide and fold in half lengthwise. This is the basis for an under body gusset.

Start working out the under body gusset by laying the end of the paper gusset on the highest point of the haunches, with the fold facing the head. Trace from the body pattern the curve running from the haunches to the under leg, Diagram 20. Twist the paper gusset and mark on it the other half of the dart to match the downward curve at the top of the back leg. Continue tracing the curved line of the stomach. Twist the paper gusset again to match the half dart on the under front leg and copy it on to the under body gusset.

Go on working in this way, tracing the outward line of the muscle over the front leg. End by tapering the gusset to finish at the throat. Cut along drawn lines and unfold the paper. This is the finished under body gusset.

To work out the head gusset, measure the distance from the back of the neck, round the head to the throat. This measures $9\frac{1}{4}''$ (23·5 cm). The width of the gusset should be two-thirds of the width of the head, taken from the body pattern and illustrated in Diagram 19, which is $1\frac{1}{4}''$ (3 cm).

Take a piece of tissue or tracing paper $9\frac{1}{4}''$ (23·5 cm) long and $1\frac{1}{4}''$ (3 cm) wide and fold it in half lengthwise. Lay the paper on the table with the fold facing you. Start shaping, by placing the back of the neck of the body pattern at one end of the folded gusset, as indicated in Diagram 21, position 1. Draw following the neck line. Move the head forward and copy the shape of the forehead bulge (Diagram 21, position 2). Continue sliding the head on the folded paper, copying the shape of the head and at the same time narrowing the gusset across the bridge of the nose as in Diagram 21, positions 3, 4, 5. Taper the gusset to end at the throat. Cut along drawn line and unfold. This is the finished head gusset.

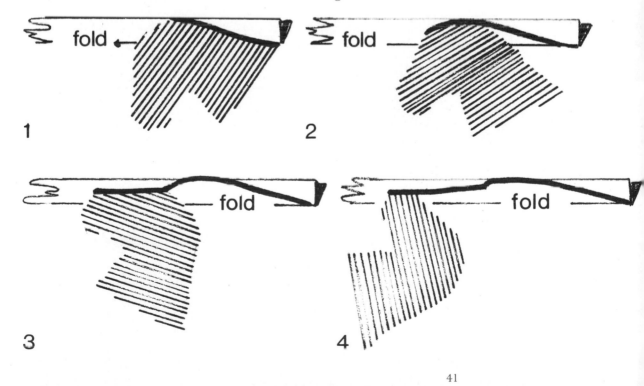

fold

1

fold

2

fold

3

fold

4

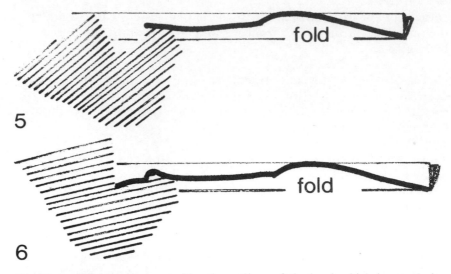

21 Designing a head gusset. Use the outlines of the head which is attached to the body pattern.

To stress the "cheek", cut a slit, starting at the throat and ending almost a third into the side view of the head. This slit, when the head is stuffed, will add character to the shape and will finally produce the necessary effect of a real horse's head.

For the soles, cut out oval discs, wider in the front, matching the curve at the bottom of the legs.

The ear pattern is worked out during the process of finishing and then added to the set of patterns for future reference.

A set of finished patterns for a standing horse is featured in Diagram 22.

Copy the patterns on to a thin card (see page 21) and cut out.

MATERIALS

The best results can be obtained by making the horse in felt. However, if one wants it to be a washable toy, any nylon fabric or brushed cotton can be used. (See pages 9 to 11 dealing with materials in general.)

The instructions for marking the patterns on material and cutting out are given on page 21 for the profile horse. After cutting out the patterns in fabric, there should be fourteen pieces in all. Turnings of $\frac{1}{4}''$ (0·5 cm) are included in the patterns and no extra should be added on.

SEWING

General instructions are to be found on page 22. Should nylon fabric or brushed cotton be used, and the worker is a beginner in toymaking, it is most helpful to have the pieces tacked together before machining. Felt does not need tacking. Pinning the parts together will be sufficient to prevent them from moving out of shape during machining.

First machine the "cheek" cut in the head parts. Then pin the head gusset to one side of the head and neck and machine. Remove pins and repeat the same work on the other side. Put the body aside.

Now take the under body gusset, and machine the two under front and two under back legs. Pin one side of the completed gusset to the body. Start sewing from the haunches, alongside the back leg, ending at the base of the back foot. Continue sewing from the front of the back leg up to stomach, alongside the stomach and end at the base of the front leg. Start machining from the front of the front leg, to the end of the gusset. Repeat the same on the other half of the body, but start sewing at least 1″ (2·5 cm) above the haunches, thus making the opening for stuffing. Sew in the soles with the wider curve facing forward. Make sure that there are no gaps in the sewing, correct these before turning work right side out.

While turning the "skin" be very careful not to stretch or damage the stuffing opening. The best way is to turn each of the back legs first and bring them completely through. Then bring through the front legs and finally the head.

GENERAL INFORMATION ON STUFFING

I cannot emphasise strongly enough that careful, patient stuffing, using only <u>small amounts</u> of flock at a time, is essential to the good shaping of the toy. It is also a good idea to pin the stuffing opening and to leave the toy to stand for some hours for the stuffing to settle. When picked up again, it is often necessary to drive more stuffing into places where the legs join the body.

STUFFING THE STANDING HORSE

As mentioned in the section on profile toys, page 23, stuff with very small amounts of flock at a time, packing it well into the feet and then the legs. Make sure that they are firm. Then stuff the head to shape, working in the "cheeks". Continue stuffing the neck and the front part of the body to meet the front legs. Holding the toy in the waist, stuff the haunches and the back part of the toy. Remove hand and fill the toy in the centre.

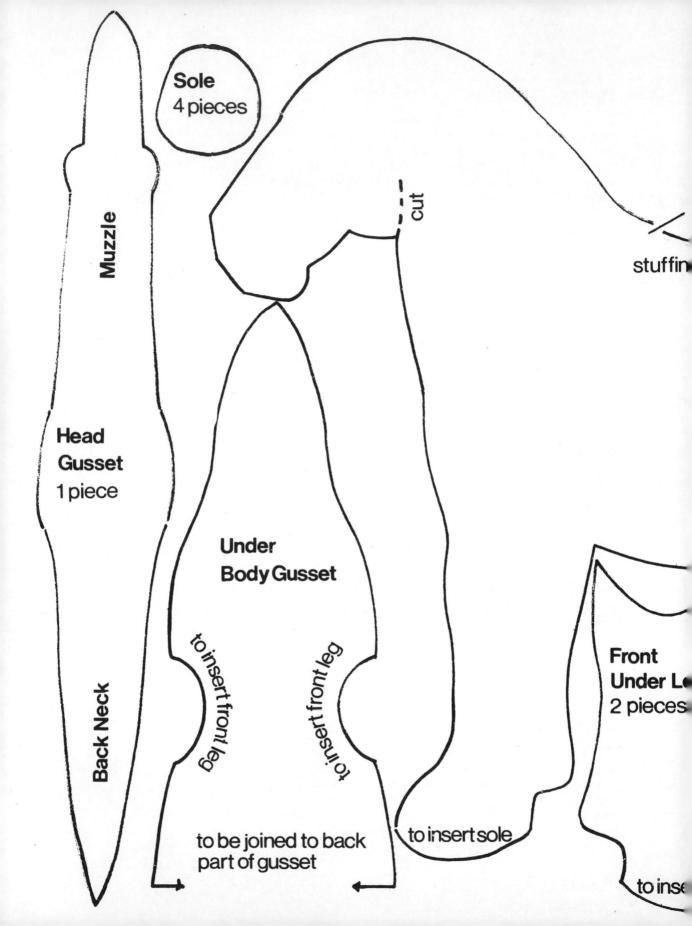

Sole 4 pieces

Muzzle

Head Gusset 1 piece

Back Neck

cut

stuffin

Under Body Gusset

to insert front leg

to insert front leg

to be joined to back part of gusset

to insert sole

Front Under L 2 pieces

to inse

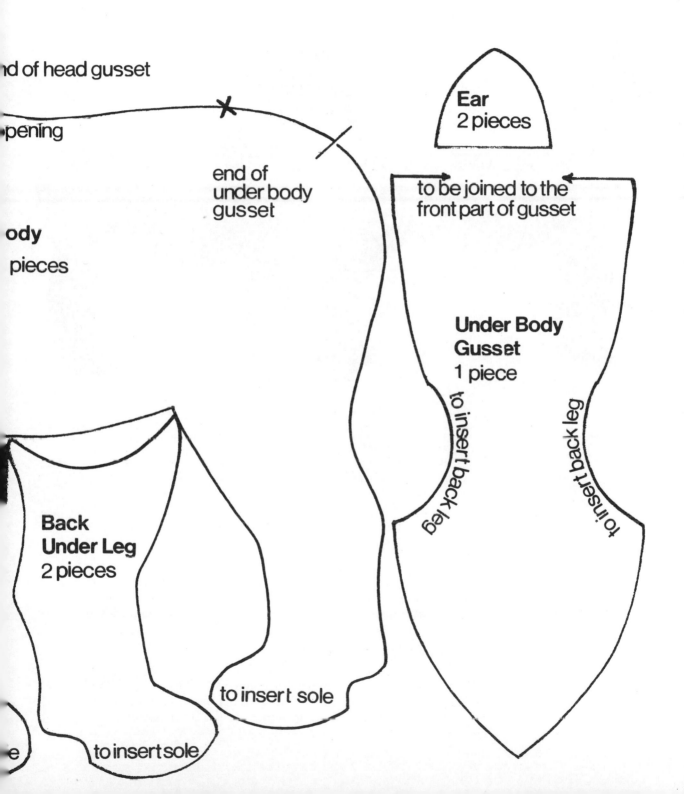

22 *A set of completed patterns for an advanced toy horse.*

nd of head gusset

pening

ody

pieces

end of
under body
gusset

**Ear
2 pieces**

to be joined to the
front part of gusset

**Under Body
Gusset**
1 piece

to insert back leg

to insert back leg

**Back
Under Leg
2 pieces**

to insert sole

to insert sole

CRITICISM OF THE MISTAKES IN THE ORIGINAL "FIRST OFF" PATTERNS

Only when the toy is filled can one realise the mistakes made in designing gussets and darts.

Plate 3 Two attempts at designing an advanced horse.

Shown here are the two first attempts at making a horse. The first, although it stands firmly on its legs, is too long in the body and the head resembles a dog rather than a horse. Realising the error, one has to change the under-body gusset by bringing the back legs a bit forward. With regards to the head and neck, it looks obvious that the head gusset will have to be worked out again to achieve the character of a horse.

The second horse, made of the altered patterns, is not good either. The body appears to be correct but the head is too small and not curved out sufficiently. The head gusset has to be redrawn, adding more curve and width to the back of the neck, with a complete reshaping of the nose and muzzle.

Finally the third set of patterns worked out well. The body is good and the head just as required, and these patterns were made into the final patterns for the standing horse, as seen in Diagram 22.

The first two examples are featured to show a student that the "play" with darts and gussets can only be fully appreciated when one sees the finished toy. Unfortunately toymaking requires more patience than painting or drawing, as one cannot rub out a wrong line or paint over it, one has to go through the complete process of cutting out, sewing and stuffing the toy before a mistake is discovered.

Plate 4 White circus horse made in felt with silky fringing for the mane and the tail. To add colour, pink is introduced on eyelids and the lining of the ears. Magenta bows on the tail and forehead complete his appearance.

FINISHING: GENERAL INFORMATION

The first step towards finishing is to close the stuffing opening with a neat ladder stitch. Next, one should place the eyes, ears and nose. But the proper positioning of these is derived from studying various illustrations and drawings on the subject. Thus looking and studying is a most necessary exercise for any toymaker, particularly if he or she wants to make their toys specially well.

Eyes are the important part of a toy, they add character and expression to the finished work. It is, therefore, interesting to note that one can divide animals living in their natural habitat into two groups—the hunted and the hunter. One will realise from books on animals that the hunted creatures have their eyes set well into the side of the head, almost in the "cheek" and their ears are usually slightly turned back to listen out for the footsteps of a pursuer. Rabbits are typical examples of these animals. The hunter, on the other hand, has a clear set of eyes looking sharply ahead of him and ears pointing forward towards its prey. Cats belong to this group.

This being a plain fact, it was also noticed and described in Margaret Hutching's book *Modern Soft Toy Making*.

In the world of toys there is yet another group of animals and these in their expression belong to the semi-human variety. Teddy Bear, panda and most of the cuddly nursery toys are in this category. They have almost human features and the positioning of eyes, ears and nose follows the pattern of a human face (Diagram 23).

23 Three different animal faces with eyes set according to their type.

EYELIDS AND EYELASHES: GENERAL INFORMATION

To apply a slight variation to the shape of the eyes one can add a pair of eyelids. These can be used either on glass or button eyes. To make the eyelids, cut out a felt disc slightly larger than the eye. Cut the disc in half and glue each half to the upper part of the eye. With small stab stitch sew round the edge of the felt. Working on the back of the eye, pull on the thread so that the lid lies flat against the eye. Sew the felt firmly on the back.

For a more exciting way of finishing an eye, use eyelashes. It is far simpler than it sounds. Glue to the bottom edge of the eyelid hairs cut from a brush or even a row of ready-made eyelashes. Stick the lid to the eye. Work in the same way as for the eyelid (Diagram 24).

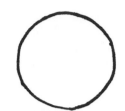

felt disc

**disc cut in half
stab stitched**

eyelid glued on

**pull on the thread
and finish off on the
back of the eye as
above**

**hairs glued to
the back of
the eyelid**

**finished eye with
eyelid and eyelashes**

24 Method of making felt eyes.

FINISHING THE STANDING HORSE

In the case of the standing horse, it is obvious that the eyes are set fairly high on the face, just below the domed forehead, and that they are placed closely to the head gusset. But to make quite sure, the best method is to cut out the ears first, and then pin the eyes and the ears to the head. Compare placing of the features with the illustration. When satisfied, remove the ears, mark the place for the eyes, remove the eyes and sew these on as shown in Diagram 9.

Once the eyes are in, sew on the ears and then finish the nose. With black Perle Sylko stitch the mouth and two large nostrils which are typical of a horse.

As to decorating the horse, there are as many ways as there are individual workers. One can make it into a farm animal with colourful trappings, or into a splendid circus horse or a pretty creature out of a fairy tale. The mane and tail can be made in wool or silk fringing and shiny plastic cloth or coloured felt, cut into strips, can be used for the hooves. The character of the toy and finishing details are the prerogative of the worker and there are no set rules which can be applied.

Plate 5 The same horse enlarged to represent a working horse. The body is light grey moquette with white cotton fringing and an orange saddle. A black harness in satin ribbon together with white lace gathered round the hooves add a touch of gaiety.

WIRING STANDING TOYS

The wire used for a frame is a galvanised or coppered wire 15 or 16 S.W.G. and the frame is built of two halves. Each half is constructed by measuring first from midway down the haunch to the end of the leg, back to the haunch, forward to the shoulder, down the front leg and back up to the shoulder, leaving about 2″ (5 cm) above the body section (Diagram 25).

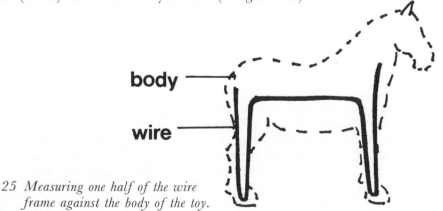

25 Measuring one half of the wire frame against the body of the toy.

Twist each leg-loop (Diagram 26 position B) and then join the two halves by twisting together the body sections and neck (Diagram 26 position C). Turn in the back leg ends and loop back the bare ends of wire at the neck. Tape the feet and bare ends of wire at neck and back legs with adhesive tape.

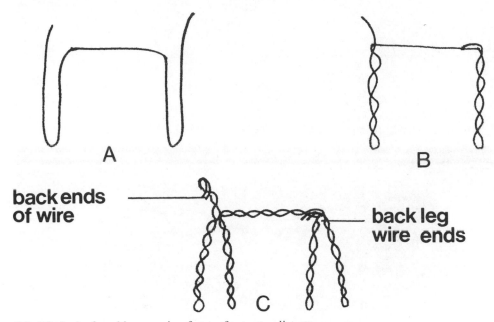

26 Method of making a wire frame for a standing toy.
   A Half of the basic wire frame.
   B Twist each leg loop.
   C Join the two halves by twisting together the body sections and neck.
      Tape the feet and bare ends of wire at neck and back legs.

Start stuffing with small amounts of flock, packing it well in to the feet to about ½" (1 cm) from the base. Stuff the head, working to about half way down the neck. Now insert the wire frame, spreading the legs of the frame to fit the legs in the "skin". Continue stuffing the legs, using only very small amounts of stuffing material at a time and filling tightly round the wire, keeping the wire in the centre. When the stuffing of the legs reaches the body, finish the neck and the rest of the body.

Making an animal standing about 5" to 7" (13 cm to 18 cm) high, it is not necessary to use a wire frame. Good firm stuffing technique will prevent the legs from folding under the body or spreading outwards. However, if you should wish to make a toy larger than 7" (18 cm) high, it is important to have it wired. The wear and tear a toy endures during its life will weaken the stuffing, particularly at the joints, and what originally was intended to be a standing toy, will in the end become an unsteady floppy animal.

3 Designing a sitting cuddly toy

Plate 6 A most appealing puppy. Creamy fur fabric is used for the body with large blue eyes and a shiny black satin nose.

The first essential in designing patterns is a good side view drawing as in Diagram 27. Enlarge this on paper to minimum height of 8″ (20 cm). Use the enlarging method as described on page 17.

27 Side view drawing for a sitting animal.

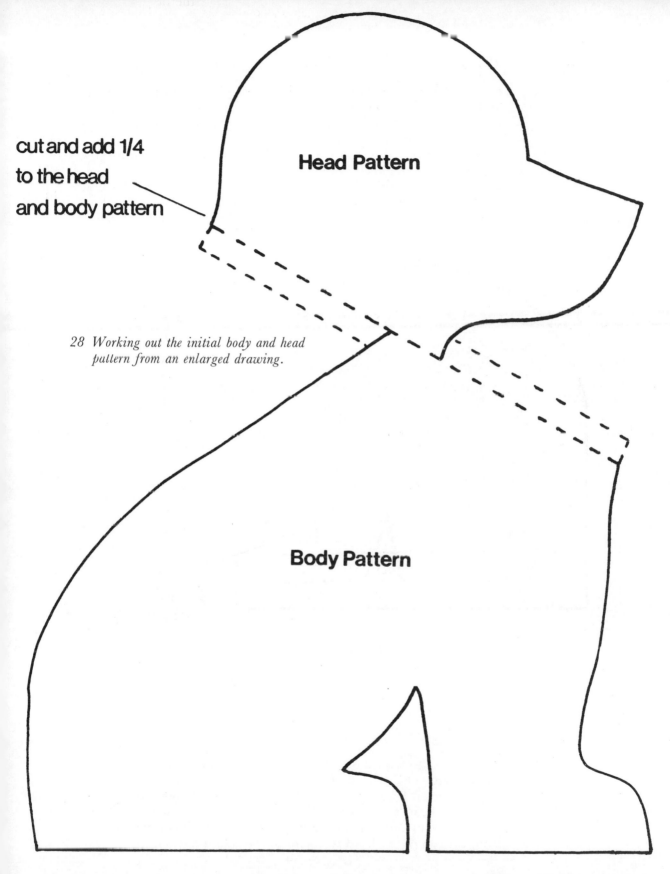

cut and add 1/4
to the head
and body pattern

Head Pattern

*28 Working out the initial body and head
pattern from an enlarged drawing.*

Body Pattern

Cut the head off as shown in Diagram 28. Take the head portion and extend the paper along the cut by sticking on an extra piece. On this extend the pattern by $\frac{1}{4}''$ (0·5 cm) where it was cut. See Diagram 29. To obtain a nice round shape of the head it is necessary to put a dart in the neck. This should be one-fifth of the new height of the head in depth and about $\frac{3}{8}''$ (1 cm) in width. Place the dart 1″ (2·5 cm) from the throat (Diagram 29). Because the dart when sewn is going to draw the fabric in $\frac{3}{4}''$ (2 cm), this must be replaced by adding $\frac{3}{8}''$ (1 cm) at the throat and the back of the neck (Diagram 29). Round off to these new points.

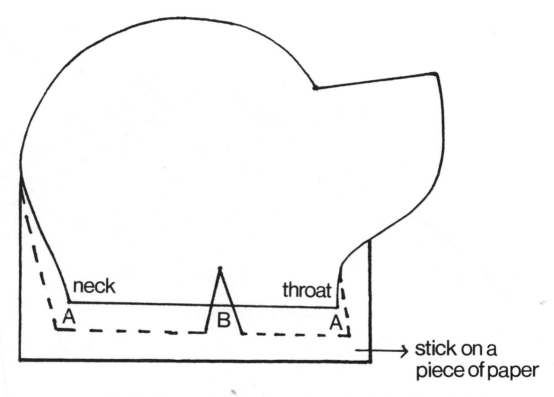

29 *Working out the head pattern after cutting the head from the body.*
  1 Stick a piece of paper at the neck-throat line.
  2 Add on $\frac{1}{4}''$ (0·5 cm) along this cut line A to A.
  3 Work out the dart B. One fifth of the height of the head in depth
    and $\frac{3}{8}''$ (1 cm) wide.
  4 Add on at the throat and neck to compensate for the dart.

Now proceed to work out the head gusset, bearing in mind the round shape of the head. The length is measured from a third of the way down from the nose, along the top of the nose, over the top of the head to end half way down the back of the head. The width, in its widest part, is half the width of the head measured from the top of the head to the neck (Diagram 30).

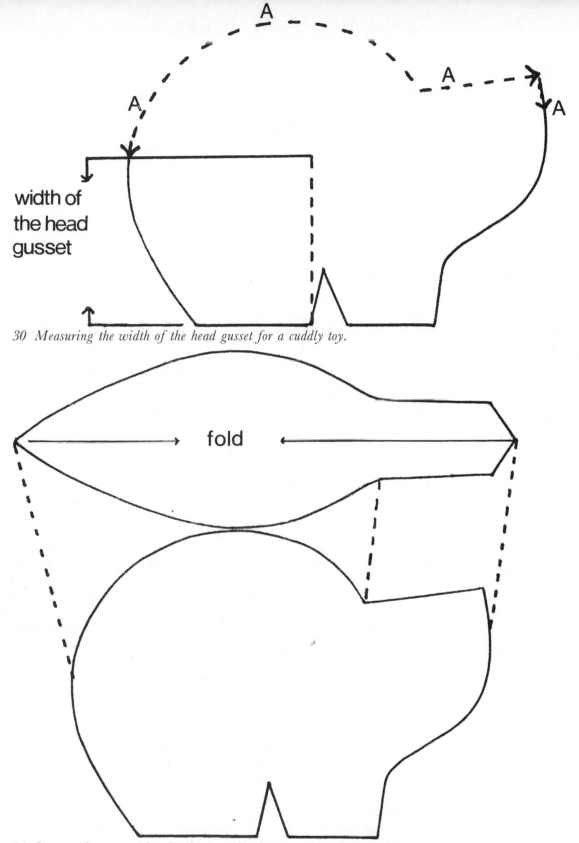

width of
the head
gusset

30 Measuring the width of the head gusset for a cuddly toy.

fold

31 Constructing a complete head gusset for the same type of toy.

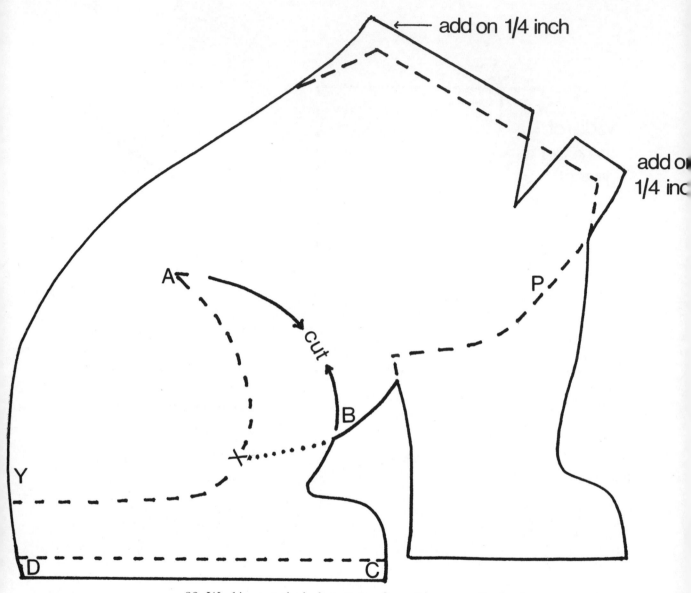

add on 1/4 inch

add on 1/4 inch

32 *Working out the body pattern after cutting away the head.*
  1 *Stick a piece of paper at the neck-throat line.*
  2 *Add on* $\frac{1}{4}''$ *(0·5 cm) along the cut, at the neck-throat line.*
  3 *Mark the dart in the neck. Add on* $\frac{1}{4}''$ *(0·5 cm) at the neck and throat to compensate for the dart.*
  4 *Mark the inner front leg by a dotted line and point P which is three-quarters down the dotted line.*
  5 *Drop the base of the back leg by* $\frac{1}{4}''$ *(0·5 cm), D-C.*
  6 *Mark the "cut" for the haunches. Copy by a dotted line the shape of the inner back leg from A to X to Y inside of the back leg.*
  7 *Continue the stomach line in a dotted line to the inner curve of the back leg, point X.*

Head continued: Take a piece of tissue or tracing paper the length and width as worked out from the head pattern; fold in half. Working out the shape of the head gusset, start from the back head, add a generous curve along the top of the head and narrow the gusset considerably to about a third of its width, finishing off, round the nose, a third of the way down towards the chin (Diagram 31).

With the head patterns completed concentrate on working out the body pattern, the under body gusset and the inner legs.

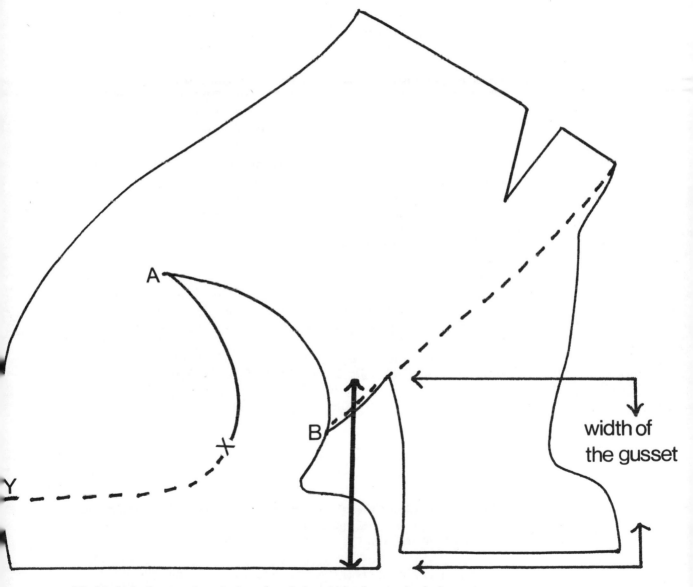

33 Method of measuring the length and the width of an under body gusset for a sitting animal toy. The length is marked by a dotted line.

Draw a dart at the neck $\frac{3}{8}''$ (1 cm) wide and $1''$ (2·5 cm) long, starting about $\frac{1}{2}''$ (1 cm) from the throat. This is to give the toy fullness at the shoulders. Because this dart when sewn is going to draw the fabric in $\frac{3}{4}''$ (2 cm) this must be replaced by adding $\frac{3}{8}''$ (1 cm) at the throat and at the back. Round off to these points as with the head. Mark a line from A to B curved for the back haunches and cut along this line (Diagram 32). This will help to emphasise the sitting position and the bulk of the back body. Also drop the base of the back leg by $\frac{1}{4}''$ (0·5 cm) (Diagram 32).

To make the inner part of the front leg pattern, the theory is the same as on the standing animal. Draw round the front leg and at the top finish off by a deep downward curve which is half of a dart. Mark this curve by a dotted line on the body pattern and point P which is one third along from the front, as in Diagram 32. This is going to be used in constructing an under body gusset. Mark also the inner back leg line from A to Y as in Diagram 32. Note that point X is the natural continuation of the stomach line.

In order to work out the under body gusset, measure the distance from the throat, across the top of the front leg, along the stomach line to point B. Slide the paper to bring point B over point X and continue following the curve from X to Y (Diagram 33). The width, in its widest part, is one third of the body, taken from the base of the back leg to the neck (Diagram 33).

Take a piece of tissue or tracing paper, the length and width as worked out from the body pattern, fold in half lengthwise and lay it at the throat with the fold facing upwards (Diagram 34). Copy the curve of the throat down to point P. Now match the remaining three-quarters of the dotted curve with the curve going upwards on the gusset. Continue copying down to point B, again slide point B to correspond with point X and finish off by tapering the gusset to end at point Y. Cut along this drawn line and unfold. This is the under body gusset and is featured in Diagram 34.

Work out two oval shapes for the soles, one smaller fitting into the front foot and one larger corresponding to the shape of the back foot. Always widen the sole patterns at the front of the foot.

Having worked out the original patterns in paper, check them over carefully and when satisfied that they are correct, copy on to a thin card and cut out.

The ear and tail patterns are designed during the process of finishing, as these are the only parts which vary to make different types of dogs.

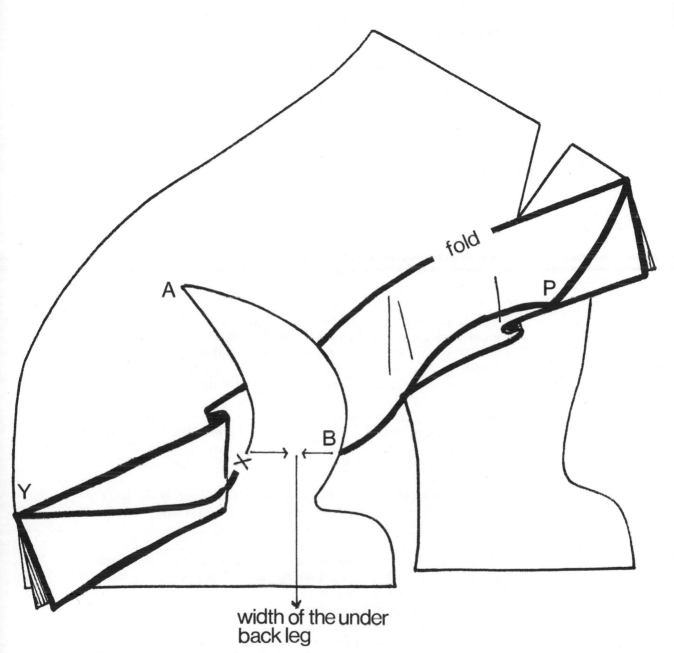

width of the under
back leg

34 *Working out the under body gusset.*
  1 Lay folded tracing paper at the throat. Fold facing upwards. Copy
  the line to point P on the inner front leg. Mark the remaining
  three-quarters of the dart in an upward curve on the under body gusset.
  2 Trace the outline of the stomach.
  3 Leave out the width of the inner back leg. Slide the paper gusset so
  that point B matches point X.
  4 Continue copying from point X to Y so that Y finishes at the fold
  of the paper.

MAKING UP

To make these patterns into a toy, follow instructions for marking patterns on material and cutting out as given on page 21. Using fur fabric, be extremely careful to reverse the patterns in order to have a right and a left side of the head and body patterns (Diagram 8A, page 22).

Sew the darts in the head patterns. Then sew the head gusset to one side of the head starting at the nose and going round the curve of the head to the end of the gusset, leaving the pointed end of the gusset to be sewn later on. Repeat the same on the other side of the head. Bring the pointed end of the gusset to one third down the chin and machine. Work in the same way on the other side but continue sewing to the end, namely to the throat. Leave the back of the head open from the end of the gusset to the neck. Put head aside.

Start working on the body by sewing the dart in the neck. Sew the inner back leg along the curve from A to B to C. Take the front portion of the "cut" on the body pattern and sew from A to X, matching point B on the body pattern to point X on the inner back leg. Repeat the same on the other side. Pick up the under body gusset, sew on the inner front legs. Pin the gusset to one side of the body, starting at the throat and down the front of the front leg. Machine along this line. Remove pins. Machine the back of the front leg and continue along the short stomach line, and down underneath from point X to Y. Repeat on the other side.

Sew the two halves of the body starting at the base of the back legs at Y and ending half way up the back. Insert soles into the front and back feet.

Pick up the head and match the centre of the head at the throat to the centre of the body. Machine round the neck. Close the back of the head bringing the sewing to about 1″ (2·5 cm) below the neck. Leave this gap open for stuffing.

Stuffing has been discussed in full on page 23. Finishing is described on page 28.

The method of making safety glass eyes is featured in Diagram 35 and the inserting of these eyes is described in detail on page 29.

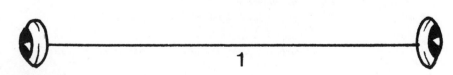

1

35 *Method of making a safety glass eye.*
  1 Glass eyes are sold in pairs attached to each end of wire.
  2 Cut them off ¾″ (2 cm) from the eye.
  3 Push the spike through a felt disc, to form an eye background.
  4 Turn the wire back to form a loop.

It is a known fact that a healthy animal has a shiny nose. To achieve this in a soft toy, use a disc cut out in black satin. The size of this disc depends entirely on the size of the head. For this particular sitting puppy, the nose disc measures 1¼″ (3 cm) in diameter.

To work the disc into a nose, thread black cotton about ⅛″ (3 mm) from the edge, using a small stab stitch. Pull on the cotton and the disc will become a black satin ball. Shiny side up, flatten the disc and with the raw edges in, pin to the nose on the head. Start by pinning across the bridge of the nose. Using the third pin insert it in to the lower part of the disc and on the seam which joins together the two sections of the head. Leave sides loose. Stretch the sides with a darning needle and turn the surplus fabric into two pleats thus forming nostrils.

Sew neatly round with a small stab stitch (Diagram 36).

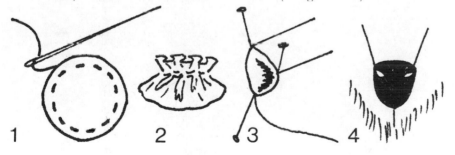

36 *Making a satin nose.*
  1 Cut a disc and gather it round the circumference at about ⅛″ (3 mm) from the edge.
  2 Pull on the thread and make the disc into a black satin ball. Shiny side of the material outwards, flatten it out and pin into place, raw edge outwards.
  3 Start working by pinning the lower part of the nose, then across the bridge, leaving the sides loose.
  4 With the aid of a long pin or needle, stretch the sides. Turn the surplus fabric back into two pleats thus forming nostrils.
  5 Neatly sew round.

4 Adaptation of patterns

Plate 7 Finished horse and reindeer. The same basic pattern is used for both these toys (reindeer was designed for *Homes and Gardens*).

The advantage of designing good patterns is that these can be adapted to make different toys. As an example, let us take the set of patterns for the standing horse. This can be altered into a stag.

Since each animal has its own special characteristics in body proportions, position and shape of the head and legs, it is always advisable to study the animal one wants to make before adapting the patterns.

37 *Adaptation of the basic body pattern for a horse and re-drawing it into a basic body pattern for a stag.*

A well worked-out sideview of a stag as based on the horse pattern is then split into under front and back leg, the under body gusset and the head gusset. All these to be designed using the same principle as applied to the horse.

The antlers or horns are made in felt and stuffed <u>very</u> hard with small amounts of cotton flock and then sewn on to the head, Diagram 37a.

I have used the basic pattern of a horse, the sideview of the body, which I have re-drawn into a stag. By looking carefully at the picture of a stag, it becomes obvious that the head and neck are different and the body rests on high, thin legs. One of the features of a stag is that his defence is his excellent hearing, eyesight, his speed and antlers.

So in the first place, one has to lift the body to elongate the legs. The sweep of the neck which is carried upwards instead of forwards as in the horse, becomes almost a natural line, drawing from the top of the front leg to the throat, Diagram 37.

37a A head of a stag. Note the placing of the antlers, the ears and the eyes.

As for the sitting puppy dog, this pattern can be easily made into a cat. Again by studying the shape of the cat, one will notice at a glance that the head is different. It is much smaller and flatter with an almost heart-shaped face, and the back of the animal is hunched up as in Diagrams 38 and 38a.

38 *Adapting the basic patterns for a sitting dog into patterns for a sitting cat.*

38a *Characteristic features of a cat's face. Note the position of the ears, the eyes and the nose.*

Plate 8 Cuddly white kitten sunbathing on a window sill is made in white nylon fur fabric. The only colour relief comes with the pink ears and nose, blue eyes and a large pink bow.

By drawing a correct profile of a cat, based on the dog pattern, this is then split into patterns in the same way as the patterns for the dog, namely—the under front and back leg, under body gusset and a head gusset.

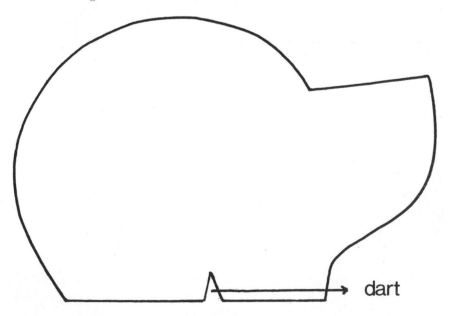

dart

To achieve this typical heart-shaped face, cut a dart into the side
of the cheek and another one at the mouth, Diagram 38b. Use
your darts for shaping because this is their role in designing
patterns.

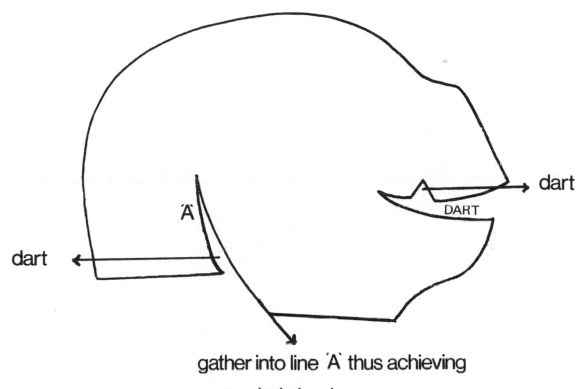

gather into line 'A' thus achieving

a rounded cheek

38b Shaping the head for a cat from head pattern of dog.
  1 Cut a dart in the side of the head, and gather the longer curve of the
    dart to achieve rounded cheeks.
  2 Open the mouth by inserting a curved dart.
  3 A small dart in the upper lip will add fullness to the face, which
    together with the dart in the side of the head will make the head
    heart-shaped.

Never destroy your patterns and always keep them neatly marked
and strung together for future use by punching a hole in the
middle of each piece and threading them on to a tape or string,
tying the ends.

5 Designing a doll

The essence of designing toys is the making of patterns. This was clearly explained in the chapter on soft animal toys and the same principle applies to dolls. Although designing may sound difficult and the instructions may seem lengthy, in practice if you follow them step by step working as you go, you will find that one process leads to the next quite easily, making the whole project into an exciting challenge.

What is, however, important before attempting making patterns for a doll, is a careful study of the proportions of the human body. There are several very good books which explain how a body is constructed and most of them can be obtained from a local Public Library.

There are two points to note, that the word proportions stands for the comparative relation of one thing to another. Secondly, the established unit of measuring this in a human body is the head.

By looking through the books it will be seen that all the drawings of a body are based on the rule that the total height is seven and a half times the head in an adult. But we are concerned with dolls which are basically a child's child, therefore our study must concentrate on a child's body.

It is noticeable when studying a human form that the younger the child the bigger the head in proportion to the total height. In practice this works out at approximately five to one heads for the total height of a child of five years and four and a half heads for a child of two.

To make a pattern use this measurement as a foundation. Remember, that one must never work on small patterns as these will be too difficult to handle in later stages such as sewing and stuffing. My advice is, make your first sample doll to stand 15″ (38 cm) from the top of the head to the bottom of the feet. Bearing this size in mind, take a large sheet of paper and mark a line which will be the central line of the body and 15″ (38 cm) long. At the top of this line draw a circle so that the top of the circle is at the top of the line. To simplify the drawing of a circle, use a glass or a cup. If the doll is to represent a five-year-old, for instance, the head circle will measure 3″ (7·5 cm) while for a child of two, it will be $3\frac{1}{2}$″ (9 cm), Diagram 39. The width of the body in its widest part i.e. shoulders, hips and thighs is about the width of the head, therefore mark this on one side of the central line as

Working out the proportions for a doll's body.

These are based on the proportions of a five-year-old, using the head as the measuring unit.

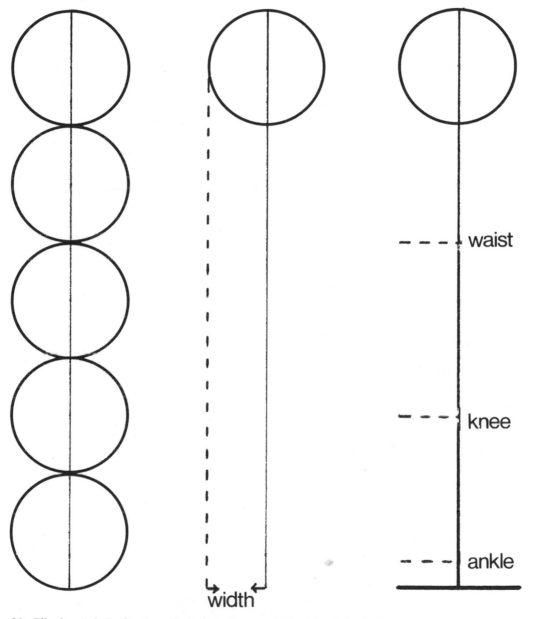

39 The head circle fits four times into the overall length of the body.
40 The width of the body in its widest part i.e. shoulders, hips and thighs, is about the width of the head. Marked by dotted line.
41 The waist is marked two heads down on the central line, measuring from the crown. The knee is marked one and a half heads down from the waist. The ankle is marked one and a quarter heads down from the knees.

in Diagram 40 (dotted line). The waist is two heads down on the central line measured from the crown, the knees one and a half heads down from the waist and the ankles one and a quarter heads from the knees. Mark as in Diagram 41. The arms with hands attached should finish half-way between the waist and the knees, Diagram 42.

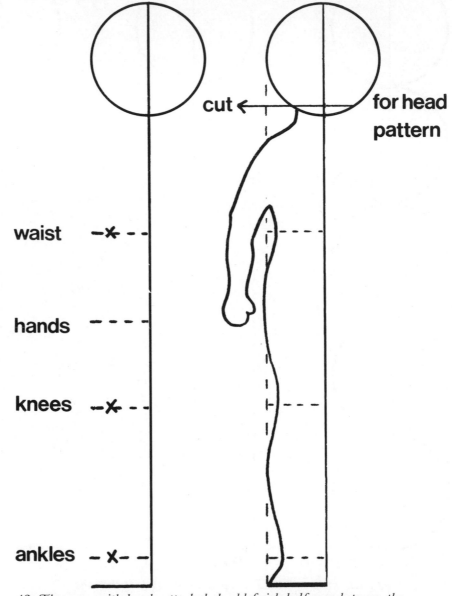

cut ←

for head pattern

waist

hands

knees

ankles

42 *The arms with hands attached should finish half-way between the waist and the knee. Mark with a cross a quarter of the waist, the knees and the ankle line.*

43 *For a rough outline of the body, draw a simple wave between the vertical dotted line and the quarter marks.*

A rough way of getting the outline of the body right is to mark a quarter of the waist, knee and ankle lines with a point, and then using these marks as in Diagram 42 draw a simple wave between the vertical dotted line and the quarter marks as shown in Diagram 43. Continue by drawing the shoulders and arms. Fold in half along the central line and cut out. This is the basic drawing to be split into the following patterns:

Head pattern consisting of one face and one back of the head pattern
Front body
Back body
Front and back arm
Front and back foot
Sole of the foot.

Cut off the head at the top of the neck, Diagram 43 and work on the face. An attractive feature of a child and consequently of a doll is its large head with rounded forehead and cheeks. To achieve this in a doll's face, copy the shape of the head on to a thin card and at the straight line of the "cut" extend downwards like the point of an egg. Now draw a $\frac{1}{4}''$ (0·5 cm) outside this line all the way round (dotted line), Diagram 44.

Working out a pattern for the face.

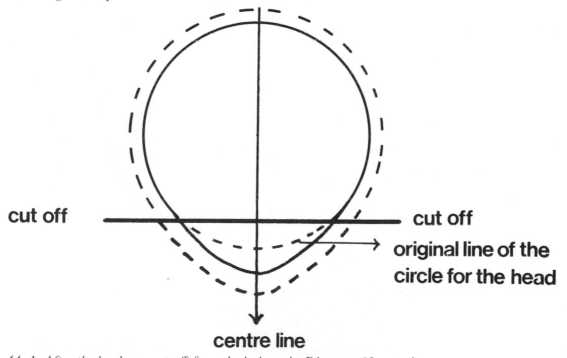

cut off — cut off

original line of the circle for the head

centre line

44 1 *After the head was cut off from the body as in Diagram 43, copy it on a thin card.*
    2 *Extend the straight line of the "cut" downwards like the point of an egg.*

71

3 Enlarge the whole pattern by drawing outside the face pattern a line ¼″ (0·5 cm) all the way round. Dotted line in diagram.

We know that the role of darts is to control and shape the bulk (page 30) and if we assume that the face is the "bulk" we have to shape it by inserting darts round it. These darts are not placed at random but are calculated to accentuate the forehead, the cheeks and the chin. They are ½″ (1·3 cm) deep and ¼″ (0·5 cm) wide. The first dart is placed ½″ (1·3 cm) from the central line of the face to be followed by two darts at 1½″ (3·8 cm) distance and a fourth dart 1¼″ (3·2 cm) away from the third. It will be noticed that the first three darts point towards the centre of the face, while the fourth dart is almost upright and is put there to emphasize the chin, Diagram 44a. On a larger doll with a larger head and face more darts will be necessary in the side of the face.

Shaping the face with the aid of darts.

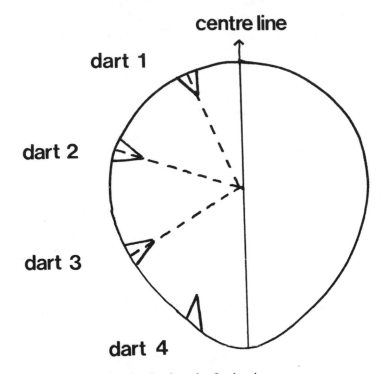

44a Dart 1 helps in shaping the forehead.
   Darts 2 and 3 shape the cheeks.
   Dart 4 emphasizes the chin position.

The back of the head is made in two parts to give the head a shape resembling a human head. The pattern is derived from the face pattern. Draw an outline of the half face without darts, and shape it as in Diagram 45 curving the back of the head and adding a

slight outward curve down the centre line. If a larger head is
required, make up a short gusset to go between the two halves
of the back head, starting at the face and ending $1\frac{1}{2}''$ (3·8 cm) down
the back of the head, Diagram 46.

Designing the pattern for the back of the head.

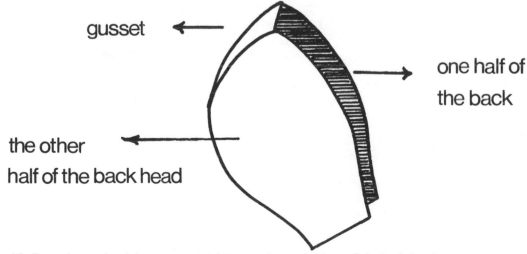

centre line

**outward curve
to fit round
the face**

**back of the
head curve**

**half pattern
of the face**

*45 Using half of the pattern of the face, re-draw it into a shape
corresponding to the side-view of the back of the head.*

gusset

**one half of
the back**

**the other
half of the back head**

46 For a larger head insert a gusset between the two halves of the back head.

The next stage is to adapt the drawing into front and back body patterns. Working on the front body pattern, cut off the arms and the feet and complete the neck line. Then move the legs sideways, leaving a slight gap between them and shaping this gap at the knees and the ankles, so that the legs are well formed, Diagram 47.

Working out the front body pattern.

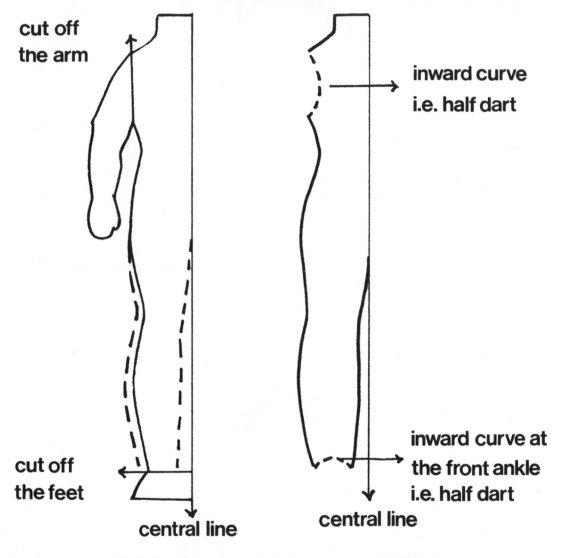

cut off the arm

inward curve i.e. half dart

cut off the feet

inward curve at the front ankle i.e. half dart

central line

central line

47 1 *Cut off the arms and the feet.*
    2 *Move the leg sideways leaving a slight gap between the leg and the centre line and shape this gap at the knee and the ankle.*

48 *Set the arms and front feet on a dart. To do this, draw an inward curve at the "cut" for the arms and the feet.*

Since the arms and feet are set into the front body on a dart, draw an inward curve at the arm cut and another at the ankle cut as in Diagram 48. Fold the front body section along the centre line and cut out following the drawn line. Flatten out the cut-out piece and this is the front body pattern.

The back body is worked out from the front body pattern by copying the pattern on to a thin card. But instead of drawing a half dart at the armpits and the ankles, this pattern has an outward curve at the arm cut and finishes in a straight line at the ankles as in Diagram 49.

Working out the back body pattern.

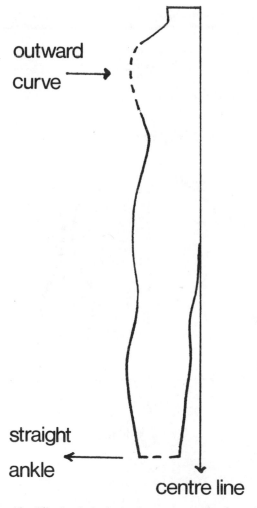

outward curve →

straight ankle ←

↓ centre line

49 *The back body is the same as the front body in shape.*
   1 Draw an outward curve at the arm cut.
   2 Draw a straight line at the ankle.

At this point a student may well wonder why the added curve in the back body pattern and why a straight line at the ankles. The explanation is simple, since the front arms are set on a dart to the front body to compensate this one must add extra material at the back so that the arms can bend towards the front of the body, otherwise they will be in line with the sides instead of sweeping forward. As to the ankles, the idea is to set the feet so that the finished doll will stand firmly on the ground. By allowing a dart in the front body pattern and a straight line at the back, the centre of gravity is brought forward over the feet.

To make the arm pattern, use the cut off arm as a basis. Draw round it and for the front arm finish it off at the top in an inward curve i.e. half dart, corresponding to the half dart in the front body pattern, Diagram 50.

For the back arm, finish it off by an outward curve to match the outward curve in the back body as shown in Diagram 51.

Designing patterns for the front and the back arm.

front body and front arm   back body and back arm

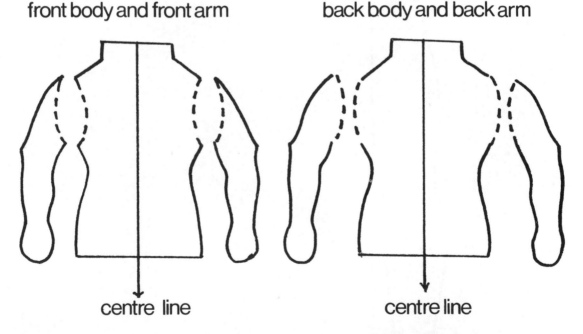

centre line   centre line

50 *To make the arm pattern, use the cut-off arm as a basis. Draw round it and for the front finish it off at the top in an inward curve to match the curve in the front body.*

51 *For the back arm, work as for the front arm but finish it off at the top in an outward curve to match the curve in the back body.*

Designing patterns for the front and the back feet.

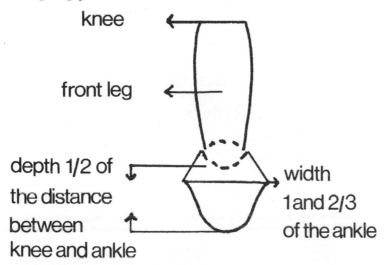

52 The front foot pattern is in depth half-way between the knee and the ankle and in width, $1\frac{2}{3}$ the width of the ankle. The curve at the top matches the curve at the front foot.

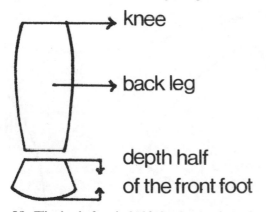

53 The back foot is half the depth of the front foot and is straight at the top matching the back leg.

To make the doll stand firmly, it is important that the feet are well designed. Each consists of two parts, the front and the back foot. The front foot pattern is rather like the top of a shoe cut straight down in line with the front of the shin. In depth, it is half way between the knee and the ankle and in width one and two thirds of the width of the ankle, Diagram 52. The back foot pattern, as in Diagram 53 is half the depth of the front foot pattern and is straight at the top matching the back leg and curved at the bottom. The sides extend on both parts of the foot patterns to add length to the sole. Sideview of the foot is seen clearly in Diagrams 54 and 54a.

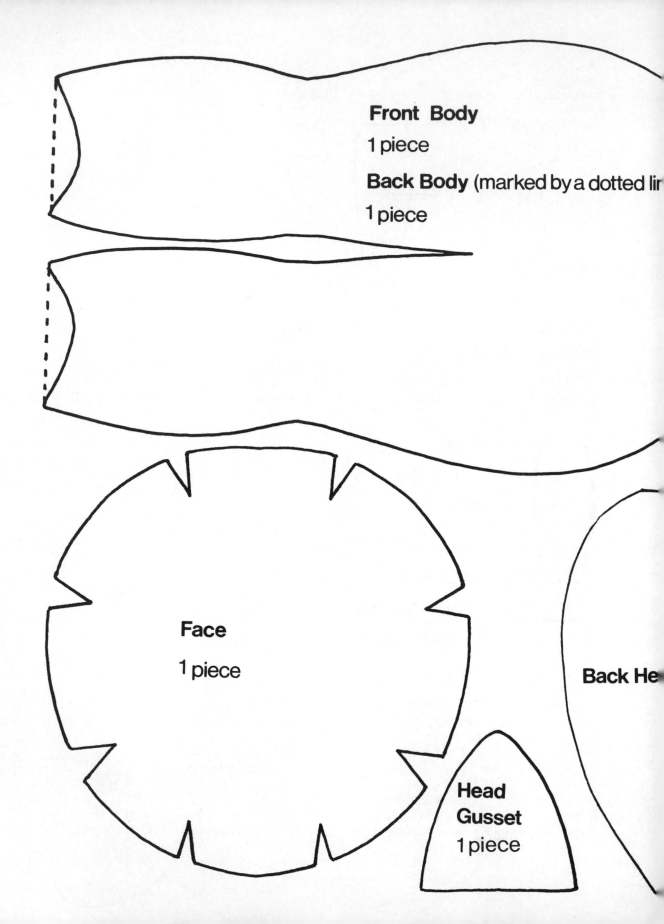

Front Body

1 piece

Back Body (marked by a dotted lir

1 piece

Face

1 piece

Back He

Head Gusset

1 piece

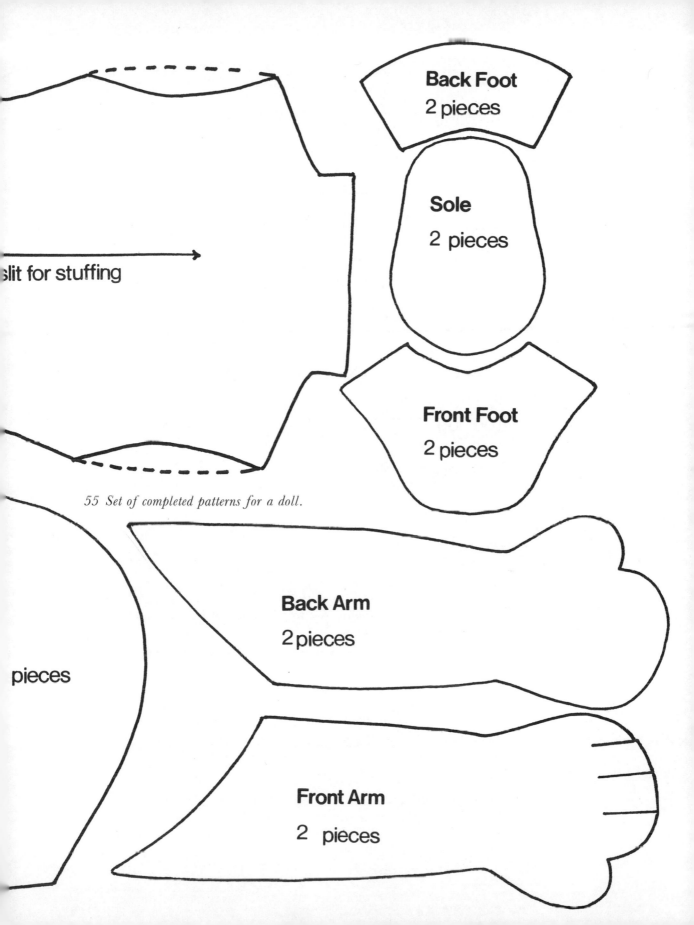

Back Foot
2 pieces

Sole
2 pieces

slit for stuffing

Front Foot
2 pieces

55 Set of completed patterns for a doll.

Back Arm
2 pieces

pieces

Front Arm
2 pieces

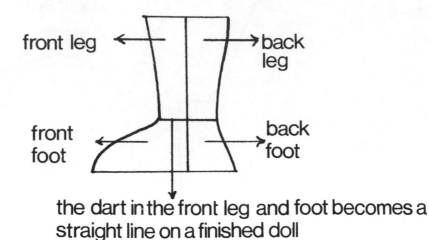

front leg ← → back leg

front foot ← → back foot

the dart in the front leg and foot becomes a straight line on a finished doll

54 Side view of the foot.

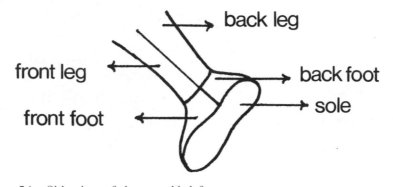

back leg

front leg ← → back foot

front foot → sole

54a Side view of the assembled foot.

The sole is an oval shape, wider in the front and matching the circumference of the front and the back foot less the seams between the two sections of the foot. A completed set of patterns for a doll is shown in Diagram 55.

VARIATION APPLIED TO THE DOLL PATTERN

Should one wish to make a floppy doll able to sit rather than stand, the basic patterns are the same, except the arms with attached hands are NOT cut off but moved outwards from the body, Diagram 56. The loose limbs are introduced by stuffing these lightly and machining along the lines as shown by thick lines in Diagram 56.

The same pattern can also be used for making dressed animals. Again the body pattern will remain the same but instead of a doll's head an animal's head will be sewn in and the hands and feet will be made in fur fabric.

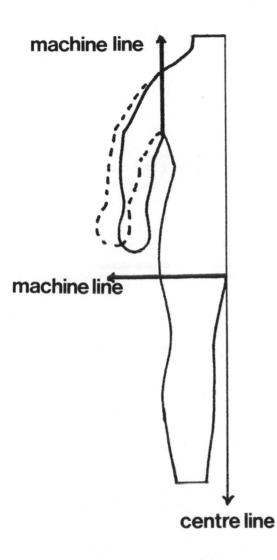

machine line

machine line

centre line

56 For a doll with floppy arms and legs, move the arms outwards.

By having worked out a good basic pattern for a doll, one can apply it to several different characters with great success.

MAKING UP THE DOLL

Once the patterns for the doll are made, cut them out in flesh-coloured calico or in felt, remembering that $\frac{1}{4}''$ (0·5 cm) for turnings is already allowed for in the pattern. All sewing is done on the wrong side of fabric.

Start by machining the darts round the face and sew on the face at the neck to the front body. Then machine the front arms and the front feet to the front body, sewing these on a dart. Put work aside.

Join the two halves of the back head and sew them at the neck to the back body. Machine the back arms and the back feet to the back body.

Pin the front body to the back body, starting at the centre of the face which corresponds to the centre of the back head. Working on one side of the body, continue pinning along the shoulder, the arm, round the hand, then down the side of the body ending at the base of the foot. Machine along this line. Remove pins, and machine from the bottom of the foot on the inside leg to the crutch. Work in the same way on the other half of the body. Insert the soles. Cut a slit about $2\frac{1}{2}''$ (6·5 cm) down the centre of the back body and turn the work right side out through this slit as marked in Diagram 55.

Into each foot insert a piece of cardboard, the shape of the sole but slightly smaller, and proceed to stuff. This cardboard sole will make a flat base to the foot.

Two important things to watch out when stuffing a doll are; first, the legs which have to be stuffed <u>very</u> hard with small amounts of cotton flock in order to make them strong and solid; and second, the face which is shaped by stuffing the darts to achieve the moulding of the cheeks and chin.

To make the fingers, stuff the hands lightly and then machine along the drawn lines as featured in Diagram 55. Close the stuffing opening with a neat ladder stitch.

FINISHING

Before making up the face it is important to realise the positioning of eyes, nose and mouth. Always bearing in mind that a doll represents a small child, the placing of features is based on a child's face.

The rule is, divide the face equally both ways and mark the horizontal line in four and the lower half of the vertical line in two, Diagram 57. Place the top of the eyes touching the horizontal line and just below it, leaving a fine forehead. The mouth is placed immediately below the fourth part of the face as shown in Diagram 57a. One of the mistakes most frequently made by my own students and also while I have been judging toy competitions is that, in most cases, the eyes are put too high on the face and often too close together, thus cutting into the forehead and missing the whole essence of a child's expression, Diagram 57b.

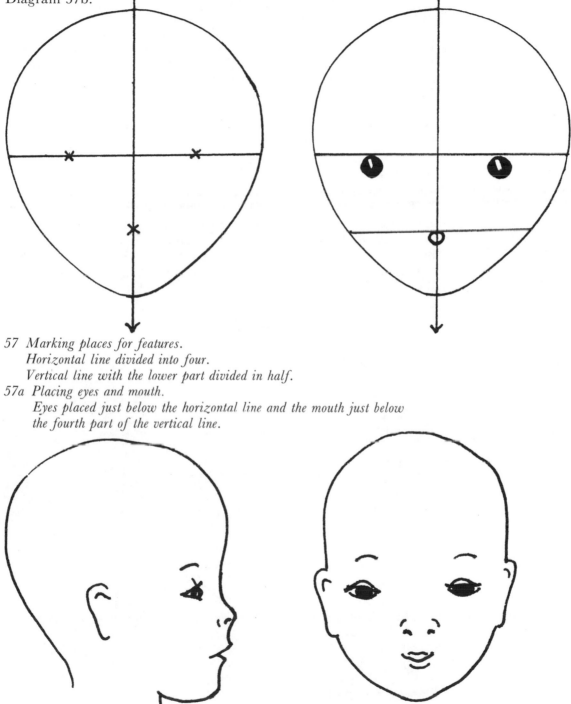

57 *Marking places for features.*
  Horizontal line divided into four.
  Vertical line with the lower part divided in half.

57a *Placing eyes and mouth.*
  Eyes placed just below the horizontal line and the mouth just below the fourth part of the vertical line.

57b *Impression of a child's face in profile and full view.*

The eyes can be made in felt, or by using small buttons or glass eyes mounted on felt discs to add depth to the face. It is important that the eyes, when set into the head (see page 28 and Diagram 9) are well pulled into the face, which will accentuate the eye-sockets and consequently will bring the forehead well forward. On animal toys, you worked (page 29) by inserting the needle in place where the ear was going to be; in a doll you should start at the base of the head, just above the back neck, and work from the opposite side of the head to the eye.

When the doll is completely stuffed, one can improve on the features by using a strong darning needle, and inserting it into the face scooping the stuffing further into the cheeks and chin to underline their existence.

As for hair styles, the choice lies entirely with the worker. The doll can have plaits, a fringe and short hair, a fringe and plaits—the variety is unlimited. The best way of making up a wig is, in the first place, to decide on the style. Should you want to make a doll with a centre parting and plaits, the system is this. Measure sideways across the head as in Diagram 58 adding on an

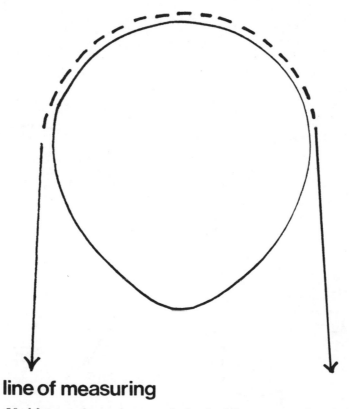

line of measuring

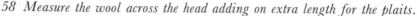

58 Measure the wool across the head adding on extra length for the plaits.

approximate length for the plaits. Using double knitting wool of this length, divide it in half and lay the wool very tightly with the centre of the wool resting on a flesh coloured tape. Make sure that there are no gaps and machine with two rows of stitching along the tape, Diagram 59. Pin the tape in the centre of the forehead, ending at the back of the neck. Sew firmly by hand into place, then plait the wool and finish off with gay ribbon bows, Diagram 60.

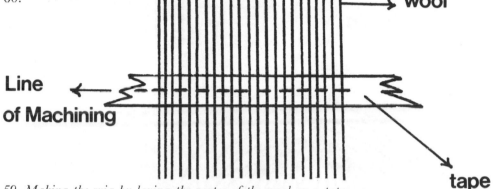

59 *Making the wig by laying the centre of the wool on a tape.*

60 *Tape sewn firmly into place*

Should you wish the doll to have a fringe, work in the same way as for the main wig but, of course, the length of the strands of wool will be shorter and sewn only on one side of the tape, Diagram 61. Pin the fringe to the face first, then sew into place, and on top of this sew on the main wig, Diagram 62.

61 Making a fringe.

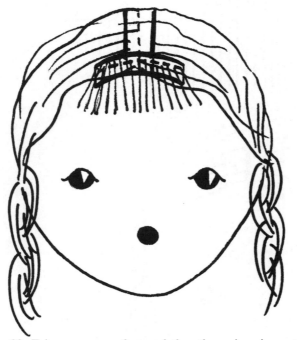

62 Fringe sewn on first and then the main wig on top.

MAKING CLOTHES

Clothes are an exciting problem for a doll maker. If you are a good needlewoman, you can have great fun making a large wardrobe with several changes of clothes. Some of my students made delightful underwear in linen, and the outer garments were knitted. Some made their dolls into Alice in Wonderland, with neat little boots, a blue dress and a pretty apron, and some into Victorian ladies. Again the choice is left entirely to the worker and her capabilities.

The principle in designing clothes is to base the dress pattern on the body pattern of the doll.

As for making underwear, such as pants and vests, take the body pattern, lay it on a piece of thin card and copy the body from the shoulders down to the knees. You must take into consideration that the doll you are going to dress, is now stuffed and therefore more rounded and not as flat as the pattern. Because of this, make the vest $\frac{1}{2}''$ (1·3 cm) wider on each side of the body, and flare it comfortably over the hips. Cut the neckline to approximately half way between the shoulder and the bottom of the armpit, Diagram 63.

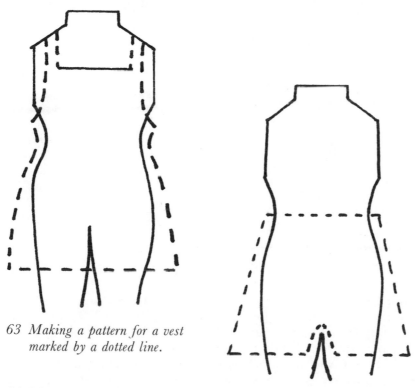

63 *Making a pattern for a vest marked by a dotted line.*

64 *Making a pattern for a pair of pants (dotted line).*

Pants are easy to make. Draw a straight line at the waist $\frac{3}{4}''$ (2 cm) wider on each side than the waist on the pattern. Draw another straight line $\frac{1}{2}''$ (1·3 cm) above the knees. Mark two points on the bottom line $1\frac{1}{4}''$ (3·25 cm) beyond the side of the legs and join the bottom marks to the ends of the waist line. Copy the gap between the legs, making it wider by $\frac{1}{10}''$ (0·25 cm) on each side. Cut out two pieces of material, sew them on the sides and in the crutch. Finish off at the bottom of each leg with lace or ric rac. At the top, either sew a long row of tape and leave a small slit in the side of the pants, so that the tape can be tied into a bow. Or, machining on the inside of the pants, a row of bias binding, thread thin elastic and then the pants can be pulled on and off, Diagram 64.

The dress is also based on the body pattern. The doll featured in this book has a summer dress, which was extremely easy to make and took a very short time.

Take a piece of striped cotton 24½″ (61·25 cm) long and 6½″ (16·5 cm) wide. First of all machine a hem on one long side of this strip of fabric, finishing it off on the right side with a row of ric rac.

Fold the strip in half vertically, and mark and cut two slits 6″ (15·25 cm) from the centre. Each slit is 3¼″ (8·25 cm) deep. Finish it off with bias binding in contrasting colour, picking the colour of the stripe in the fabric, Diagram 65.

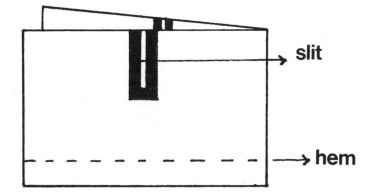

65 Cutting a slit for arms in a simple summer dress.

Measure the neckline, which is 8½″ (21·5 cm) and gather the raw edge of fabric into the neckline, finishing it off with 1″ (2·5 cm) bias binding folded in half, and in the same colour as the binding used for the arm slits. Sew up the back seam and either finish it with a button at the top or a bow made of bias binding used for the neck; in which case one would use a longer strip, allowing for tying the bow.

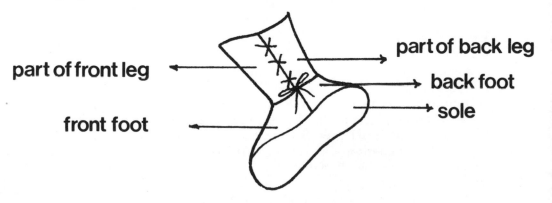

66 Making shoes or boots based on the leg and foot pattern.

The foot pattern is an excellent guidance for making up the shoes. But remember, if you want to make shoes, allow an extra $\frac{1}{4}''$ (0·6 cm) all round the sole. If using socks, allow more than $\frac{1}{4}''$ (0·6 cm). The patterns of the front and the back foot have to be enlarged at the base to fit round the larger sole.

If you want to make boots, then apart from using the foot patterns, you will have to use part of the pattern of the front and the back leg, also enlarged to fit the pattern of the foot, Diagram 66.

There is a lot of fun to be had in dressing dolls and they can be made to look most attractive in simple, as well as in elaborate garments, providing the colours and trimmings are gay. It is, however, a known fact that whatever doll you make for a child and in whatever clothes she is dressed, the little owner, sooner or later, will devise her own dress for her "baby". But, after all, this is the whole purpose of children having dolls and making them into characters they enjoy having around.

Part 2: Patterns

1 Pram toys

Having studied the first part of the book on designing and readapting patterns, it will be easy for a student to understand, to make up, and, if necessary, to alter patterns featured in this section.

The best way for a toymaker to realise how he can help in the development of a baby is emphasised by a quick look at the changes which have taken place over the last 40 years in the attitudes towards babies and children.

In the old days, little was known about the scientific care of babies, and even less of their intelligence, muscular reflexes and emotions. The arrival of a child was wrapped up in superstition and in warm, blind love. The story that what a mother saw during her pregnancy would determine the sex of the baby, or would influence its character, was only one of the old wives' tales.

Over the last 40 years, child psychology has become a real science. To obtain accurate knowledge of children's development, extensive work and research has been carried out by teachers, behaviourists and psychologists in clinics, schools and nurseries. The result is that today we know much more than ever before about a baby growing into a child, further into a teenager and finally into an adult. A child is allowed to be noisy, rebellious, destructive, untidy and at times difficult. We have come to understand that the process of growing up is a painful, tedious and difficult operation. It is, therefore, up to the adults to help and assist with this process.

Both professional bodies and parents have agreed that play is one of the most important activities in the development of a child. In play, the muscles grow stronger, intelligence gets sharpened and social behaviour is established. A child learns through play to experience, give vent to its imitative emotions, rid itself of the destructive impulses and find outlets for its dramatic dreams.

The reaction to playthings starts at a very early age, towards the end of the second month. Before then, toys are of no value at all, as the baby is only concerned with the problem of feeding and any object however charming and cuddly, does not register. So the buying or making toys for a newly-born baby is a sheer waste of time and money.

At about two and a half months old, the hours of sleep become slightly reduced, and some time is given to "observation" of the surroundings. This is the time when a baby will notice, and it will even try to grip a toy. Great help can be given to these first reactions by choosing the right kind of plaything. Above all, it has to be bright in colour and small in size. One must remember that at that tender age, the eye muscles are still weak, and a child encounters difficulty in focusing. A toy in pale colours will merge into the background of a cot or a pram, and will become completely meaningless. Bright red is a very good colour to use, as it will stand out and register, and even black is better than anything pale or white. Also if the object is placed too near the baby, it will have difficulty in focusing, and it will voice its disapproval with frustrated cries.

As from the third month, a baby starts to experiment with its senses and tries them out. It will touch a toy, look at it, shake it to see if it makes a noise, smell it, and even try to eat it, thus exercising all five senses. So a rattle or any noisy object, perhaps with a bell, will please it enormously, particularly when this toy is small enough to grip, and so to make the noise by itself. But it is important to remember that anything like a bell must not be capable of being detached and possibly swallowed. Attached pram toys are good at that age, as the baby moves its arms, and by so doing will start the bell tinkling.

From the fifth month onwards, a baby begins to rely on visual and physical sensations. It can distinguish between hard and soft, hot and cold, its movements of hands are getting more coordinated and the growing strength of muscles is seen in the first attempts at sitting up and the firm clutching of objects.

Suitable toys for this period, would be the very first soft toys, in good bright colours, and with arms and legs small enough for the baby to clutch. The addition of a squeaker is useless, because a baby with still weak grip will be unable to produce the force required to operate a squeaker, this will create deep disapproval and tears of failure.

At about nine months a baby can crawl. This indeed is a great event in its life. It brings more independence, more interest and consequently more fun. A toy like a ball would be particularly appreciated. It is a good object to chase round the room, and this is even more so if the ball makes a noise. Anything with a noise is great!

So let us consider a selection of soft toys for a child up to one-year-old.

RATTLES

Rattles have a very ancient history and there are a few on display in the British Museum in London, made of clay. These were found during the excavations of Ur, Asia Minor, and are about 5000 years old. The mushroom or flower rattles featured below are bright in colour and very quick and easy to make.

Plate 9 Have fun choosing colours and materials for these rattles. There is a Flower Rattle with green head, white stem and petals and a face framed in yellow ric-rac. The same set of patterns is used to make a gay red mushroom with white dots on the hat and markings of a face. Finally there is Baba Rattle in emerald green felt broken up by white braid, a white corduroy bonnet and white fluffy fur mittens. Blue eyes, a little red mouth and a bright magenta ribbon add extra colour.

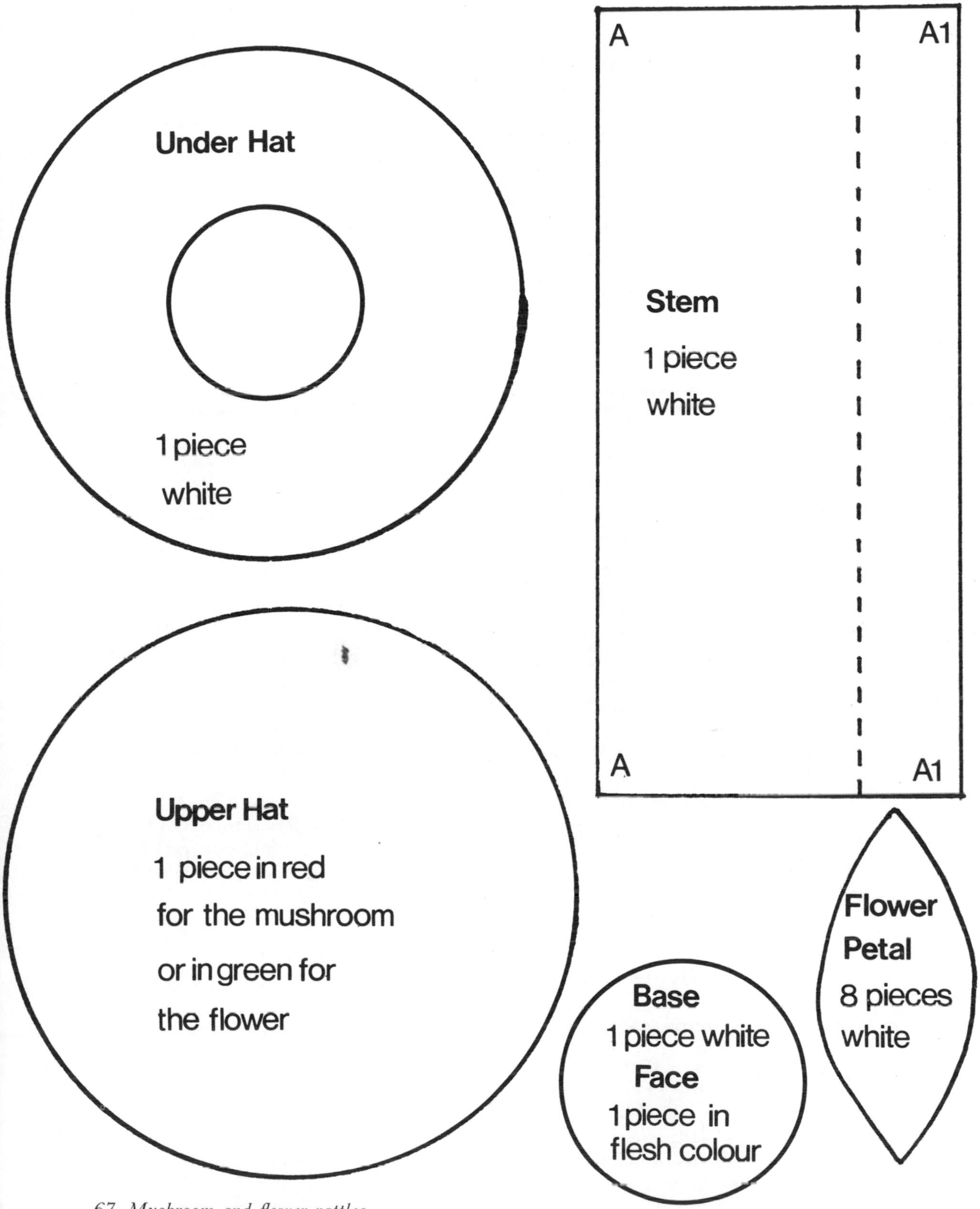

Under Hat

1 piece

white

Stem

1 piece

white

A

A1

A

A1

Upper Hat

1 piece in red
for the mushroom
or in green for
the flower

Base
1 piece white
Face
1 piece in
flesh colour

**Flower
Petal**
8 pieces
white

67 Mushroom and flower rattles.

93

The mushroom rattle

Obtain a tubular container which is used for the stem. An empty pill-container, acquired from most chemists would be suitable. Should your tubes differ in size from the patterns, you will have to re-adjust them. The piece marked 'stem' will have to be altered in height and width to fit round your tube allowing a bit extra for seams, and the hole in the under hat will have to fit the screw top of your container. A few small stones put into the tube will make the rattling noise.

Materials

4″ × 4″ (10 cm × 10 cm) red felt or corduroy
6″ × 5½″ (15 cm × 14 cm) white felt or corduroy
1¾″ × 1¾″ (4·5 cm × 4·5 cm) green felt or corduroy
Offcuts of white and black felt or of any non-fraying fabric to make the face.

Instructions for making

Take your container, insert a few stones, screw on the top and seal round it with adhesive tape. Cut the stem, the under and upper hat and the base from Diagram 67. Sew a strip of green felt or ric-rac ¾″ (2 cm) up the stem following the dotted line on the pattern. Close the side seam from A to A1. Fit the stem into the hole in the under hat and sew round it, still working on the wrong side of the fabric. Lay the under hat on the upper hat and sew round, gathering the upper hat as you go along. Turn the work right side out through the hole in the base and stuff the hat with cotton flock. Stuff lightly so that it keeps its shape yet does not become too hard or lumpy. Insert the container with the screw top just inside the hat. Sew round the base by hand to finish the toy. I have trimmed the mushroom hat with a few small discs in white and a strip in black felt to make it into a smiling face. These parts must be stuck on first and then sewn round with a neat stab stitch.

The flower rattle

Materials

4″ × 4″ (10 cm × 10 cm) green felt or corduroy
6″ × 8″ (15 cm × 20·5 cm) white felt or corduroy
1¾″ × 1¾″ (4·5 cm × 4·5 cm) flesh-coloured felt or silk
5½″ (14 cm) yellow ric-rac
Offcuts of black and blue and red felt or any non-fraying fabric for the face.

Instructions for making

For the flower rattle work in the same way as for the mushroom (Diagram 67), but before fitting the under to the upper hat, arrange the eight petals on the upper hat, working from the centre outwards and spreading them in a flower pattern. Pin these petals in place and sew round working from the centre to half way up each of the petals, returning to the centre and going on to the next petal.

Pin the under hat, with the stem attached, to the upper hat with the petal side inwards. You will have to be careful before sewing round it. The easiest way is to fold the petals into the centre and stick them together with adhesive tape. Sew round the hat and turn the work right side out. Remove the adhesive tape to release the petals and work as on the mushroom.

To finish, cut out a disc about the same size as the base in flesh-coloured felt. On this lay the features such as the eyes and the mouth and when satisfied with the expression, stick them on and then sew round each of them with a neat stab stitch for firmness.

The final touch is a row of ric-rac or a ribbon round the face.

The mushroom and the flower rattles are only two basic ideas for a rattle built round a tubular container, but the fun in inventing new ways is unlimited.

Teething rattle

Materials

$3\frac{1}{2}'' \times 7\frac{1}{2}''$ (9 cm × 19 cm) dark green felt for the front and back body
$8'' \times 1\frac{1}{2}''$ (20 cm × 4 cm) dark blue felt for the gusset
$3'' \times 7\frac{1}{2}''$ (7·5 cm × 19 cm) pink felt for the face
$6''$ (15 cm) white ribbon
$10\frac{1}{2}''$ (26 cm) lampshade trimming
3 ozs cotton flock
1 teething ring

Time for making about 2 hours.
This ring rattle is different from the other rattles in so far as it has a teething ring attached. The material used is felt, but it can be made in wool fabric. The body is dark green, with a gusset in dark blue, contrasting with a large pink face and white hair arranged in a "Beatle" cut.

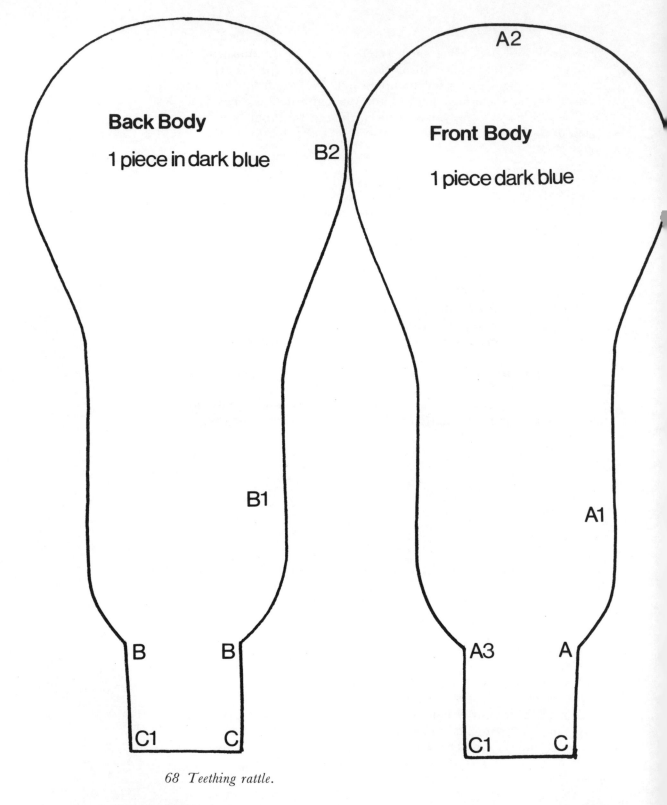

Back Body

1 piece in dark blue

B2

B1

B

B

C1

C

Front Body

1 piece dark blue

A2

A1

A3

A

C1

C

68 Teething rattle.

Instructions for making

When a "fold" is indicated on the pattern, it is advisable to cut the pattern in one cardboard piece, doubling it on the fold. This method will prevent any future mistakes, such as forgetting to mark the "fold" on the material. Trace, mark and cut out the patterns from Diagrams 68 and 69. There should be five pieces altogether. Lay these on the material, draw round and cut out. There should be two body pieces, one long gusset, one face and one crown.

Work on the wrong side of the fabric. Pin the gusset to the front body from A alongside A1 and ending at A2. Continue pinning round from A2 and finishing at A3. Sew in place.

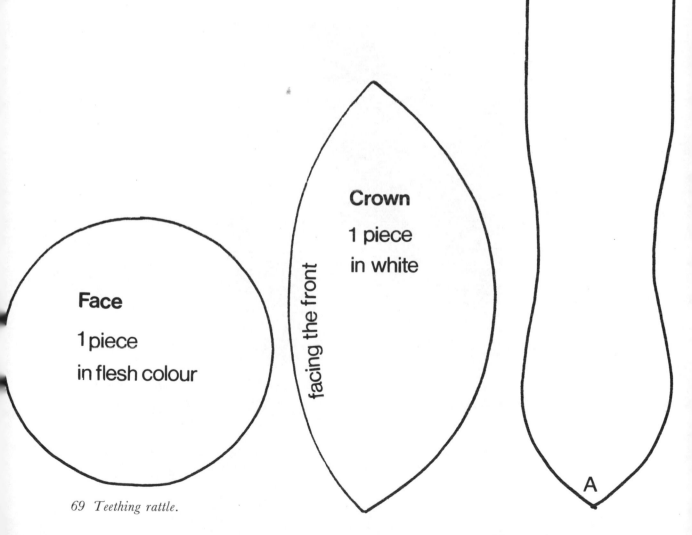

Gusset

1 piece

dark green

A2 fold A2

A

Face

1 piece

in flesh colour

Crown

1 piece

in white

facing the front

69 Teething rattle.

Plate 10 This rattle is also made in felt. The body is in bottle green and royal blue felt with a pink face, white cushion fringing for hair and white ribbon to match the whiteness of the teething ring.

Fit the back body round the gusset working in the same way as for the front body, but leaving an opening between B and B1. Sew the sides. Turn the work right side out.

Insert four small stones into a round tobacco tin, close the lid and run a line of adhesive tape round it to prevent it from opening, and put aside. The stuffing starts from the lower part of the body towards the face. Continue beyond the neck, then stop and insert the tin, making sure that it fits and is neither too low nor too high in relation to the face. When the tin is in the proper place, stuff round with small pieces of stuffing. Once the tin is well embedded in the head and the rattle feels firm but soft to the touch, close the B to B1 gap with a small ladder stitch.

To insert the teething ring, place it between the two parts of the body and let it hang loose. Turn in the raw edges on both pieces at C/C1 and sew them together with a firm backstitch. Run a row of backstitching along A/A3 going through the front and back parts.

Lay the face on the front body and sew round with a neat stab stitch. To make the nose cut out a disc, 1″ (2·5 cm) in diameter and with a small tacking stitch sew round, some $\frac{1}{8}$″ (3 mm) from the edge. Pull on the cotton, gathering the felt into a little ball. Secure, and still using the same needle and thread, sew it very firmly to the face. Arrange the eyes and the mouth on the face, glue into place, and then sew round using a small stab stitch.

When the face is finished, pin the crown on the gusset alongside the top of the head. Sew round and finish by sewing a row of lampshade trimming round the crown. A white bow under the chin will complete the ring rattle.

BaBa rattle

This rattle is made in felt, but you can use any bits of fabric to hand and it should take a worker about two hours to make. (See plate 9.)

The patterns for the rattle are built round a tin, which measures $3\frac{3}{8}$″ (8·5 cm) in diameter. Should your tin be smaller, you will have to pad round with cotton flock. On the other hand, if the tin is more than $3\frac{1}{2}$″ (9 cm) the patterns of the base will have to be enlarged and correspondingly the bottom edges of the four body panels.

Materials

12″ × 5″ (30·5 cm × 12·5 cm) green felt
$6\frac{1}{2}$″ × 5″ (16·5 cm × 12·5 cm) white felt
9″ × $\frac{1}{2}$″ (23 cm × 1 cm) white lace
9″ × $\frac{1}{2}$″ (23 cm × 1 cm) ribbon
$\frac{1}{2}$ yard (46 cm) ric-rac
4 ozs cotton flock for stuffing

Instructions for making

Place three to four small stones in the tin, close the lid and secure it with a band of adhesive tape.

Trace, mark, and cut out the patterns from Diagram 70. There should be six pieces in all. Lay these on the appropriate materials and cut out. There should be four pieces in green felt, five pieces in white felt and one piece in flesh-coloured felt for the face.

Working on the wrong side of the fabric, join and sew the four body panels to each other, starting at A to B, leaving an opening from A to B1 between one of the side panels and the back panel. Fit the felt base into the body with the raw edges facing out, pin and sew round.

To make the head, still working on the wrong side, sew the gusset round the face from C to C1 and from C1 to C2 in the head. Tuck the head, still wrong side out, inside the body, matching D on the front panel of the body to D on the face. Pin round and sew, leaving an open gap from C2 on the head to B1 on the body. Stuff firmly but lightly. This rattle should not feel hard or heavy.

Start stuffing from the base, and if necessary round the tin, working towards the head. Holding at the neck, stuff the head, then remove your hand and fill the neck. Close the opening from C2 to B1 with a firm ladder stitch, and while sewing add bits of stuffing to shape the body.

The next step is to make the face. Using small felt features, experiment with them on the face, and when the correct position is found, glue them in place and then sew round each with a stab stitch. Gathered lace or nylon frilling round the face will give a bonnet effect. Trim the body with ric-rac, arranging it into a motif of your own design.

Using white wool or fur fabric for the hands, cut two discs from the pattern. With tacking stitch, sew round the disc, about $\frac{1}{8}''$ (3 mm) from the edge. Pull on the thread, gathering the fur into a pom-pom. Secure in the centre with a few stitches and still using the same needle and cotton, stitch these to the rattle. The position for the hands, should be about 1" (2·5 cm) down from the neck and on the seams of the front and the side panels.

A ribbon in a contrasting colour, tied round the neck in a bow will complete the toy.

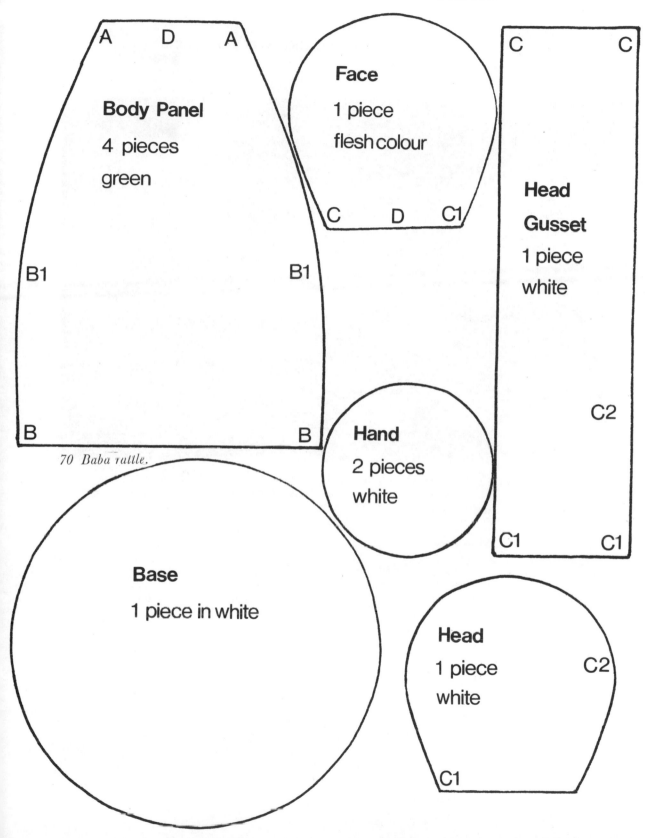

Body Panel

4 pieces

green

A   D   A

B1   B1

B   B

70 Baba rattle.

Face

1 piece

flesh colour

C   D   C1

Head

Gusset

1 piece

white

C   C

C2

C1   C1

Hand

2 pieces

white

Base

1 piece in white

Head

1 piece

white

C2

C1

PRAM CHICKS AND DUCKS WITH BELLS

Large white chicken

Plate 11 Nesting mother chicken supervises her young. She is made in white nylon fur with royal blue ric-rac round the body and a red felt comb and a yellow beak.

Materials

12″ × 8½″ (30·5 cm × 21·5 cm) fur fabric
14″ (35·5 cm) ric-rac
Offcuts of gingham for the under wings and coloured felt for the beak and comb
2 tiny black buttons for eyes
2 ozs cotton flock for stuffing

Time to make should not exceed 2 hours.

Instructions for making

Trace, mark and cut out the patterns from Diagram 71. There should be seven pieces of patterns. Lay these on the wrong side of fabric, mark round and cut out. There should be seven pieces in white fur fabric, three in red felt and two in gingham. When using fur fabric sew on the wrong side.

Machine the under wing (gingham) to the upper wing (fur fabric) from A to A1 ending at A2. Then turn out each wing right side out through the opening between A and A2. Insert the wings into "cuts" marked on the upper body pattern, matching A to A2 on the wings to A and A2 on the upper body. Make sure that the pile on the wings faces the pile on the upper body and sew into place, and put work aside.

Sew on the two parts of the beak, one to the upper and one to the under head from B to B1 ending at B2. Fit in and then sew the comb into the "cut" marked in the upper head, sewing from C to C1 marked on the comb and on the upper head.

Pick up the upper body, lay the under head matching the hole in the upper body to the head, and with the pile on the head facing the pile on the upper body, pin into place round the hole, making sure that the beak points forward. Sew round this pinned circle and remove pins. Pull the under head through the hole, flatten it out and fit and pin the upper head with the pile on the upper and the under head facing inwards. Match the two halves of the beak and pin into place. If necessary gather the upper head to fit into the under head. Sew round. Sew up dart on upper body to make tail.

Take the two halves of the under body and machine from D to D1 and from D2 to D3 leaving an opening between D1 and D2.

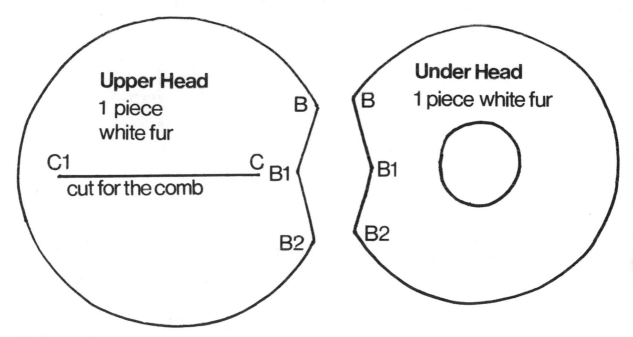

71 Large white chick (continued overleaf).

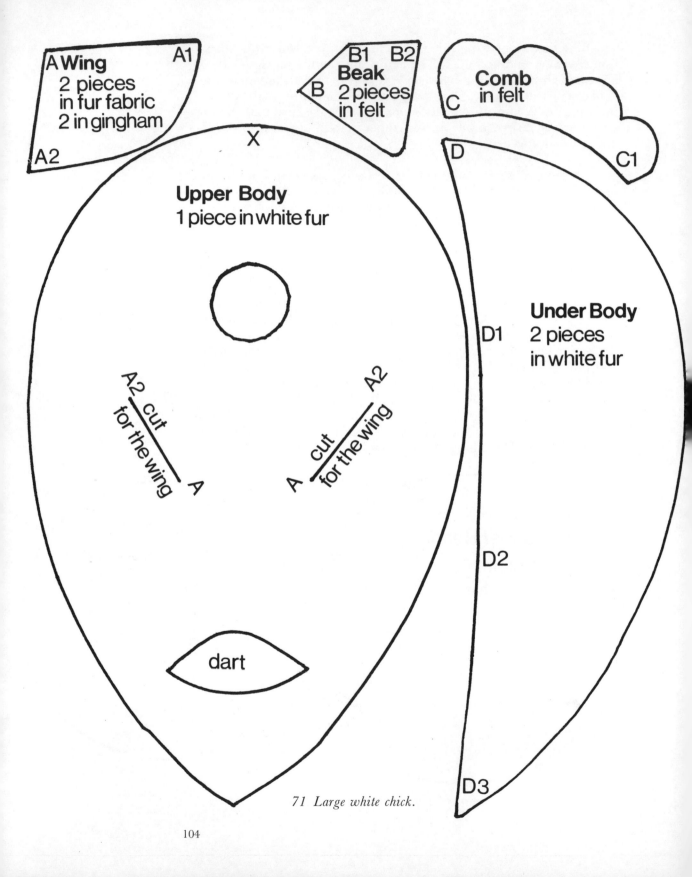

A **Wing**
2 pieces
in fur fabric
2 in gingham
A1
A2

B1 B2
Beak
B 2 pieces
in felt

Comb
in felt
C
C1

X

Upper Body
1 piece in white fur

D

D1

Under Body
2 pieces
in white fur

A2 cut for the wing A

A cut for the wing A2

D2

dart

D3

71 Large white chick.

Match the centre of the upper body marked X to point D on the under body and pin round. With the pile of the fabric facing in, machine round.

Turn the work right side out and stuff lightly with cotton flock. Start filling the beak with small amounts of stuffing, then continue filling the head and the rest of the body. The finished chicken should be stuffed to shape but should feel light and soft. Close the stuffing opening with a ladder stitch. Remove any pile lodged in the seams and brush well particularly along the seams. Insert eyes as described on page 29 but work from the neck at the opposite side to the eye and then continue as instructed in paragraph six on page 28.

Finish off sewing by hand a row of ric-rac and tying a bow just above the tail. The finishing, of course, can be varied according to the ideas of the worker but since the basic toy is made in white fur fabric, bright and colourful decorations are essential.

This chicken can be attached to the pram by a ribbon or elastic and adding a bell under the beak and one at the tail, it will make a nice and noisy gift for a child spending long hours in the pram.

The same chicken can have two small chicks or ducks and the whole set can be fixed to the pram.

Small chicks or ducks

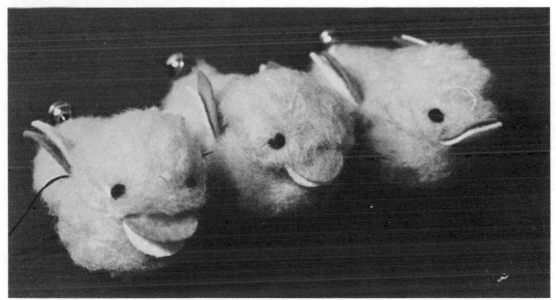

Plate 12 These little cuddly ducks in yellow fur with tiny blue eyes and orange and white beaks and wings can be used for pram toys. Suspended on an elastic thread with little bells on the tail, they will amuse many babies.

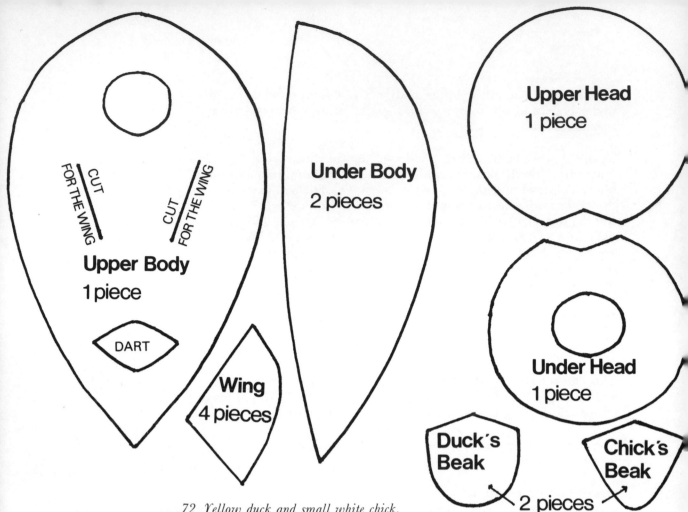

On the patterns (within the illustration):

Upper Body
1 piece

CUT FOR THE WING

CUT FOR THE WING

DART

Under Body
2 pieces

Wing
4 pieces

Upper Head
1 piece

Under Head
1 piece

Duck's Beak

Chick's Beak

2 pieces

72 Yellow duck and small white chick.

Materials

$5\frac{1}{4}'' \times 6\frac{3}{4}''$ (13·5 cm × 17 cm) fur fabric
Offcuts of coloured felt for the wings and beaks.
$1\frac{1}{2}$ ozs cotton flock for each toy.

Instructions for making

The work involved is identical to the instructions given for the large white chicken. The only difference is that the little chick has no comb therefore there is no "cut" marked on the upper head pattern and there is no pattern for the comb. Also with regard to the wings and the beak on these very small toys, the best way to treat them is to make them in felt using bright and contrasting colours i.e. for the duck—orange upper wing and top beak and white under wing and under beak. Machine them into place without sewing them in pairs and turn right side out. The beak is put in the head seam when sewing the upper to the under head.

The eyes are made in dark blue felt discs and stuck on. The pattern is shown in Diagram 72.

JUMPING CLOWN

Materials

$4\frac{1}{2}'' \times 36''$ (11·5 cm × 91·5 cm) glazed cotton for body and sleeves
$9'' \times 9''$ (23 cm × 23 cm) flesh-coloured felt for head and nose
$9'' \times 9''$ (23 cm × 23 cm) magenta coloured felt for the hat
$6'' \times 8''$ (15 cm × 20 cm) white fur fabric
$\frac{3}{4}$ of a yard of $\frac{1}{2}''$ wide pink ribbon (68 cm × 1 cm)
$\frac{1}{2}$ yard of magenta coloured ribbon $\frac{1}{2}''$ wide (46 cm × 1 cm)
$\frac{1}{2}$ yard cotton fringing used for lampshade trimmings (46 cm)
5 small bells
$1\frac{1}{4}$ yard elastic thread (1 m 23 cm)
4 ozs cotton flock for stuffing

Time of making about 2 hours.

Instructions for making

Trace, mark and cut out the patterns from Diagrams 73 and 74.
There should be ten pieces of patterns including eye, nose and
mouth. Lay the patterns on the wrong side of materials, mark
round and cut out. There should be six pieces in glazed cotton,
four pieces in flesh-coloured felt and six pieces in fur fabric, a
mouth in red and eyes in black or dark blue felt.

Sew on the wrong side of materials.

Start sewing by joining two body pieces along the line B to B1
this being the front body of the clown. Sew on the feet, gathering
the body to fit the top of the feet from A to A. Take the remaining
two parts of the body, used for the back and sew on the feet and
then join them from B1 to half way up the back. Put work aside
and start working on the sleeves and hands.

Sew the hands to the sleeves along the line C/C gathering the hand
to make it fit. Fold the sleeve in half and sew starting from point
C1 passing point C going along the curve of the hand to C2,
continuing round to finish at C1 on the other side of the sleeve.
Stuff the hands lightly and then pin the sleeves to the front and
the back body between D and D1 making sure that point D on the
sleeve corresponds to D on the body and D1 matches C1 and sew.

Pin the back to the front body, starting at B2 and going to D and
then from D1 round the curve of the leg to A. Continue pinning
to A1, pass point A on the inside of the leg and finish at B1.
Machine along the pinned line and repeat the same on the other
half of the toy.

Plate 13 A Jumping Clown is hung on an elastic thread with bells on his hat, hands and feet. He is dressed in bright blue-and-white spotted glazed costume, a bright pink hat with white cotton fringing framing his cheerful face.

108

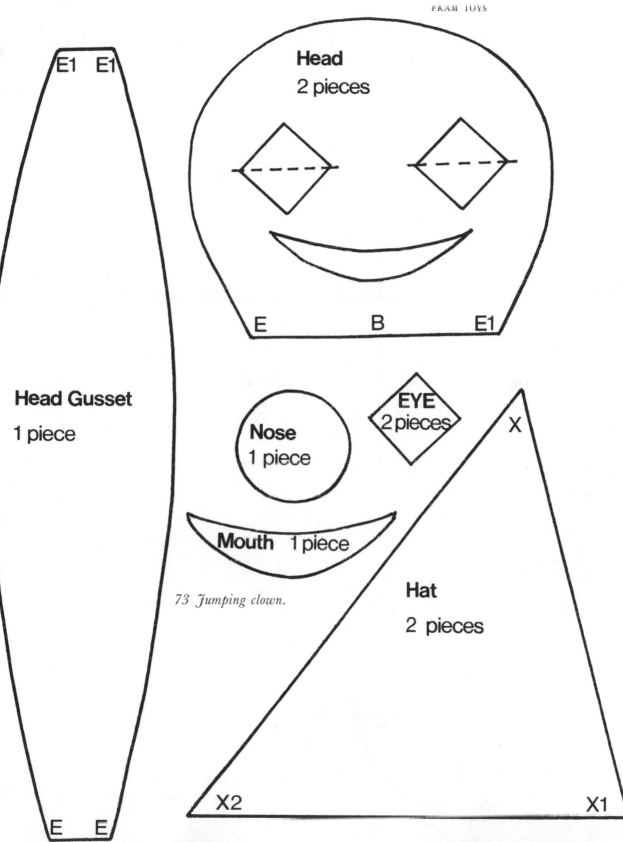

Head
2 pieces

E   B   E1

E1   E1

Head Gusset

1 piece

Nose
1 piece

EYE
2 pieces

X

Mouth 1 piece

73 Jumping clown.

Hat
2 pieces

E   E

X2

X1

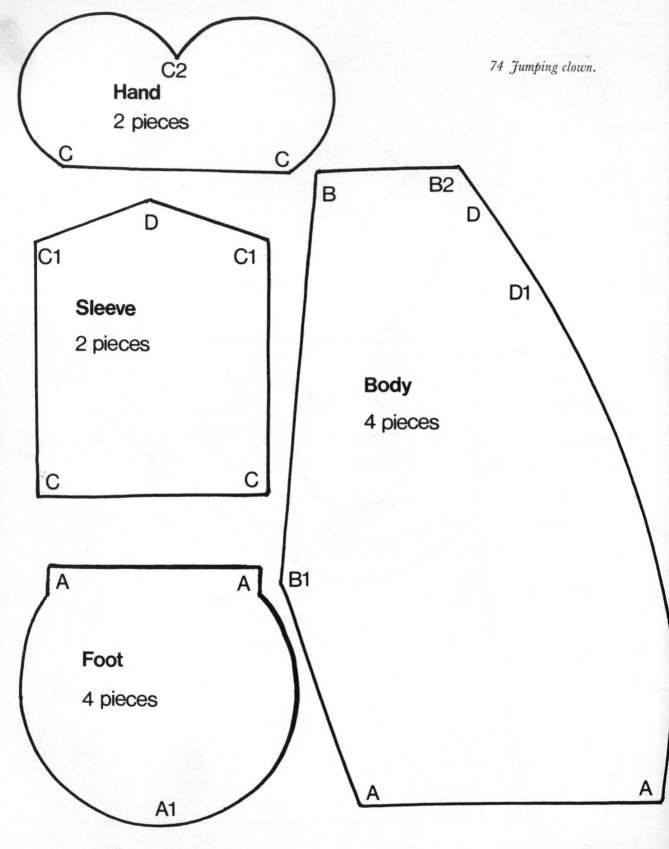

Hand

2 pieces

C2

C

C

Sleeve

2 pieces

D

C1

C1

C

C

B

B2

D

D1

Body

4 pieces

B1

A

A

Foot

4 pieces

A

A

A1

A

A

Make the head by sewing the head gusset to the two halves of the head, starting at E and sewing round the curve of the head ending at E1. Repeat the same on the other half of the head.

To fit the head to the body, cut an inch (2·5 cm) slit in the back of the head and match point B on the front head to B on the front body. Pin along the neck and machine.

Turn the clown right side out and stuff the body starting with the feet and working towards the body. Stuff the head firmly but lightly. The finished toy should feel light but should be stuffed to shape.

Hand sew the opening on the back running from the head and finishing half way up the back. Use a neat ladder stitch.

With a good adhesive stick on two dark blue squares in place of eyes with a white felt line going across the centre of the square as shown on the head pattern in Diagram 73 by a dotted line. The nose is made of a felt disc. Thread cotton round this disc, pull on the cotton to make the nose into a small felt ball. Flatten this and sew into place. Cut out the shape for the mouth in red felt and stick on.

Arrange lampshade trimmings round the face and the back of the head to give an appearance of hair and sew firmly round.

Cut two triangles for the hat in magenta felt. Sew them together leaving the bottom open from X to X2. Fit on and sew firmly to the head.

To finish the toy use five small bells obtainable from most department stores in the section which sells dog leads and cats' bells. Sew one to each foot and one to each hand leaving the fifth one for the hat.

Tie ribbons round the ankles and a ribbon round the neck finishing with a bow. Take a strong elastic thread and sew it by starting from the hat, then sewing it to the hand, the foot and again to the foot and the hand on the other side, ending at the hat. Leave enough elastic thread to make a loop above the hat. A gay bow at the top of the elastic loop will finish off the toy.

2 The first soft toys

A cuddly doll, a Teddy Bear or a Panda are ideal soft toys for a baby about five months old. The arms and legs on these toys are small enough for the child to grip and the toy can be hugged and loved quite safely.

Plate 14 Two cuddly toys made by using and adapting the same pattern. Cuddles, the doll, is dressed in red-and-white striped cotton with a white fur hat, hands and feet which make her particularly desirable. The Teddy Bear in silky royal blue nylon fur with pink palms, and soles and large surprised eyes makes a good companion to Cuddles.

CUDDLES

The same patterns with slight alterations can be re-adapted into a Teddy Bear a Panda or a rabbit.

Materials

8″ × 36″ (20 cm × 91 cm) gingham
5″ × 26″ (13 cm × 66 cm) white fur fabric
3″ × 3″ (7·5 cm × 7·5 cm) pink felt
1 yard × ½″ wide (91 cm × 1 cm) ribbon
6 ozs of cotton flock
Offcuts of dark blue and red felt for making up the features.

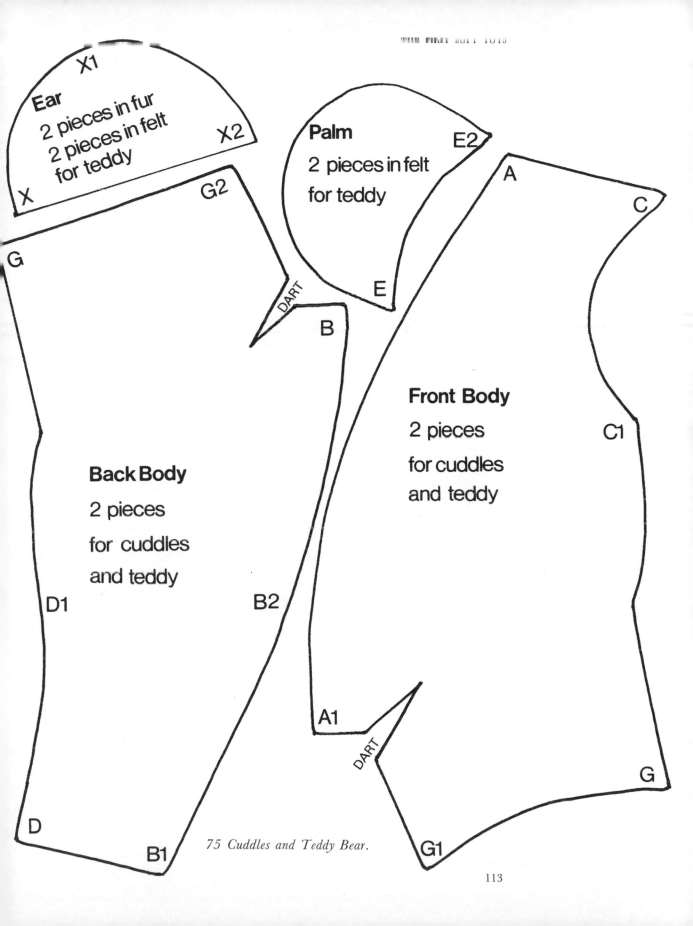

Ear

2 pieces in fur
2 pieces in felt
for teddy

X1

X2

X

G2

G

Palm

2 pieces in felt
for teddy

E2

E

A

C

DART

B

Back Body

2 pieces

for cuddles

and teddy

Front Body

2 pieces

for cuddles

and teddy

C1

D1

B2

A1

DART

G

D

B1

G1

75 Cuddles and Teddy Bear.

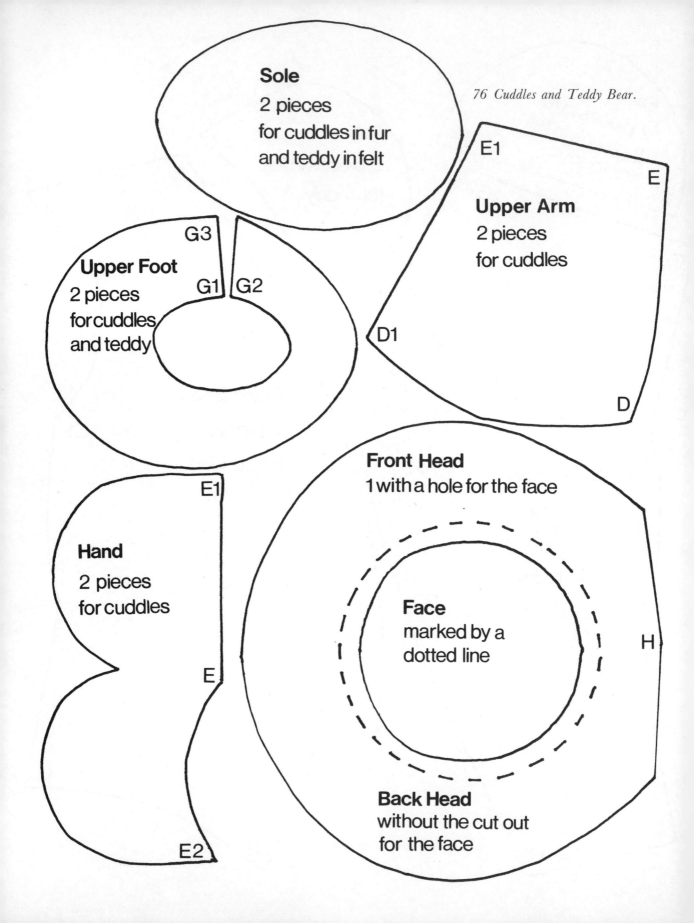

Sole
2 pieces
for cuddles in fur
and teddy in felt

76 Cuddles and Teddy Bear.

E1

E

Upper Arm
2 pieces
for cuddles

G3

Upper Foot
2 pieces
for cuddles
and teddy

G1 G2

D1

D

E1

Hand
2 pieces
for cuddles

E

E2

Front Head
1 with a hole for the face

Face
marked by a
dotted line

H

Back Head
without the cut out
for the face

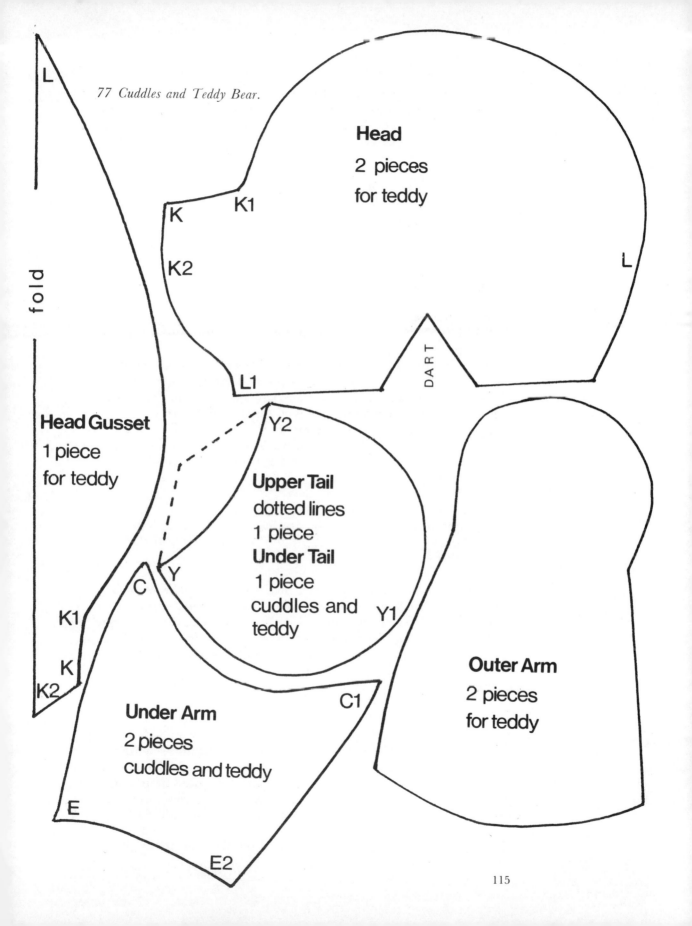

77 Cuddles and Teddy Bear.

L

Head
2 pieces
for teddy

L

K

K1

K2

fold

L1

DART

Head Gusset
1 piece
for teddy

Y2

Upper Tail
dotted lines
1 piece
Under Tail
1 piece
cuddles and
teddy

Y1

C

Y

K1

K

K2

Outer Arm
2 pieces
for teddy

C1

Under Arm
2 pieces
cuddles and teddy

E

E2

When buying the white fur fabric for this toy, one has to cut to waste, and so it becomes a much more economical proposition to make both the Teddy Bear and Cuddles. The time for making this type of toy should be approximately three hours.

Instructions for making

Trace, mark and cut out the patterns from Diagrams 75, 76 and 77. Lay out and mark round the patterns on the wrong side of the fabric. Cut out. There should be ten pieces in white fur fabric, eight pieces in gingham and one piece in pink felt. Sew on the wrong side of fabric.

Proceed to work by closing the darts in the front and the back bodies. Join the two front body pieces along A to A1 and the two back bodies from B to B2. Sew the two under arms to the two front bodies from C to C1 and the two back arms to the two back bodies from D to D1. Lay the front body on to the back body and pin along the arms, starting at point D/C on the bodies to point E/E on the arms. Sew along this line. Open and flatten the arms and pin the hands, with the fur facing inwards, matching E on the hand to E on the arm. Work outwards towards E1 on the hand and E1 on the arm continuing to E2 on both the arms and the hand. Sew the hands on to both arms.

Pin and sew the back to the front body starting from the wrist at E2, going round the hand to the armhole and down the side of the body, ending at G on the front and back leg. Repeat the same on the other half of the toy.

Fit in the upper foot by flattening the legs at the ankles from G to G1 and to G2. Pin the upper foot matching G1 and G2 on the legs to G1 and G2 on the upper feet. If necessary gather the legs to fit into the upper feet and machine along this line. Close the legs with the feet attached, sewing from G3, passing point G1/G2 and ending at A1. Pin the soles into the feet with the wider part of the soles facing forwards. Close the back of the body by machining from B to B2.

Pin the pink felt face into the front head and sew round. Lay the front on to the back head with fur facing inwards and sew round, leaving the neck open. Cut a 2″ (5 cm) long slit in the back head. Turn the head right side out and push into the body, matching point H on the head to point A on the front body. Sew round the neck. Inspect the seams and then turn the toy right side out.

Stuff lightly but to shape, working from the feet into the body.

Holding in the waist fill the head and the arms and then complete the middle part of the body. Close the stuffing opening with a ladder stitch.

Experiment with the position and expression of the eyes and mouth. Once satisfied glue in place and sew round with a neat stab stitch. Instead of felt eyes this toy has long felt lashes in dark blue. The lock of hair is made of a triangular piece of yellow felt $1'' \times 1\frac{1}{2}''$ (2·5 cm × 4 cm). Cut a few slits parallel to the long arm of the triangle, and turn it into a tiny cone. Sew in the centre of the forehead. Machine and stuff the tail lightly and sew at the back of the toy. Trim with a bow under the chin and a little bow on each of the shoes.

TEDDY BEAR

Essentially Teddy Bear is made from the same patterns as Cuddles.

Materials

7″ × 48″ (18 cm × 1 m 22 cm) dark blue fur fabric
4″ × 5″ (10 cm × 12·5 cm) pink felt
9″ (23 cm) nylon frill
2 jet button $\frac{1}{2}''$ in diameter (1 cm)
8 ozs of cotton flock

Instructions for making

Work in the same way as for Cuddles. The only difference between this toy and the doll lies in the shape of the head and the work entailed on the arms and hands.

Start sewing by closing the darts in the front and the back bodies. Join the two front body pieces. Sew throughout on the wrong side of materials. Machine pink, felt palms to the under arms and then sew the arms to the front bodies, and the outer arms to the back bodies.

Pin and sew the back body to the front body starting at C on the front body and D on the back body, going round the arm, round the hand and finishing at the armhole. Continue from the armhole down the side of the body ending at G on the front and the back leg. Repeat the same on the other half.

Pin the upper feet and work exactly as for Cuddles.

Insert the soles.

Machine the back bodies from B to B2 and put work aside.

To assemble the head, start by closing the darts in each half of the head. Pin the head gusset to one half of the head from K to K1 and ending at L. Machine along this line and remove pins. Work in the same way on the other half of the head.

Sew the gusset from K to K2 on one side of the head. On the other side of the head, bring the sewing beyond point K2 and end at L1.

Sew the ears starting from X, sewing along the curve, passing X1 and ending at X2.

Also sew the under to the upper tail working from Y to Y1 and ending at Y2. Turn work right side out and stuff. Close the stuffing opening with a ladder stitch and remove any pile caught in the seams while sewing. Brush well. Experiment with the features by pinning the eyes, nose and ears to the head. Once satisfied, insert the eyes as described on page 28. Neaten the raw edge on each of the ears, sewing from X to X2, and then sewing them firmly on to the head.

As for the nose, you can either work it as described on page 61 and shown in Diagram 36 or sew on a black jet button instead.

Stuff the tail lightly and pin it to the back of the toy. Sew firmly into place. Finish off with a ribbon in contrasting colour round the ankles and a row of nylon frilling and a ribbon round the neck.

THE BALL

A colourful felt ball with a rattling noise is always a most welcome toy for a baby about nine months old. At that age a child goes through the crawling period, when it can crawl after a ball, throw it across the room and crawl after it again.

For the ball in this book, I have used dark and light magenta felt panels with white and green for decoration, cotton flock for stuffing and a small tin containing a few stones. Whatever material you intend to use, make sure that it is bright in colour with red and white predominating.

Materials

$7\frac{1}{2}'' \times 6''$ (19 cm × 15 cm) dark magenta felt
$5'' \times 6''$ (12·5 cm × 15 cm) light magenta felt
$3'' \times 6''$ (7·5 cm × 15 cm) white felt
3 ozs cotton flock
Small offcuts of green felt.

Plate 15 This ball is a nice toy and its attraction lies entirely in the arrangement of colours. Any bright pieces of felt left over from making other toys can be used.

Instructions for making

This toy should take about one and a half hours to make.

Following Diagram 78 cut six panels and sew them together with the raw edges facing inwards. Start sewing from A to B leaving a gap from A to B1 between the fifth and the sixth panels. Turn work right side out and make sure that there are no unwanted openings in the seams.

Take a small metal container, such as used for tablets, films or tobacco, insert three or four small stones, close the lid and secure with adhesive tape to prevent it from opening.

Fill the ball with cotton flock, working through the gap and shaping the curves on the panels as you go along. When the ball is about half stuffed, fit in the tin in the centre and continue stuffing round till the ball feels firm but soft to the touch. Close the gap with a ladder stitch, and as you are sewing keep filling with flock against the seams of the fifth and the sixth panels.

Cut out one large and one small star in a contrasting colour and stick these in a motif over the points where the panels meet.

These motifs are a matter of choice and you may well find a better way of finishing the ball and introducing a more interesting arrangement.

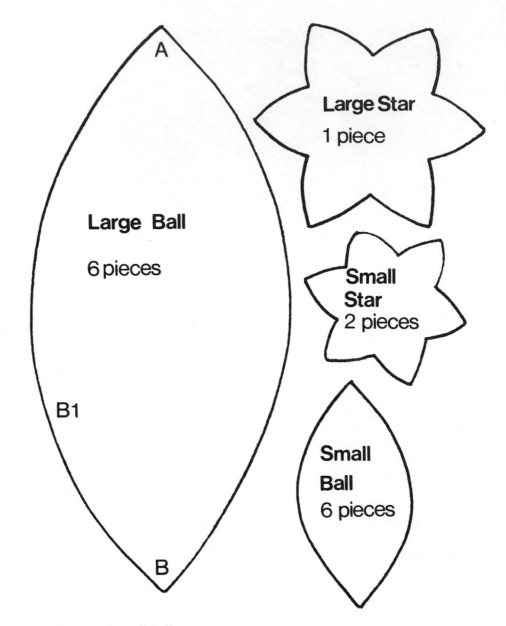

78 Large and small balls.

Small ball

The small ball is made in the same way as the large one, but without the rattle. A string of these little balls, about five in all, made in very bright, contrasting colours, and hung on an elastic thread, make a nice pram toy.

Bells, like those used for cats' collars, fixed between each of these balls are an added attraction.

3 Toys for 1- to 3-year-olds

At about the time of the first birthday, the crawling changes into early attempts at walking. This is the first big advance in a baby's life. From then on it will develop more rapidly, and from walking it will gradually learn to run and then to skip and jump.

An animal toy on wheels with a solid handle is most suitable for this trying period. Also a firm wooden trolley or any kind of toy designed to help the child in keeping its balance is useful.

The child will also begin to talk, and it will be noticed that the muscles will become more coordinated with the result that a two-year-old will be fascinated by manipulative games. It will try to show off his prowess by building houses and garages in constructional bricks and it will have a go at dressing and undressing—but all these efforts will be still very clumsy. Typical of that age group is that a mother will be asked suddenly to provide clothes such as a vest, a dress or a coat for a soft toy because it "feels cold".

At bedtime, a soft cuddly toy, large enough to be noticed and colourful to attract becomes a comforter and a confessor. After the great experiences of the day it is nice for a baby to cuddle up to this "friend" and go off into a peaceful sleep.

These first "friends" in due course become life long associates, and, I am sure, many of us still have, or at least remember our own with deep affection.

SCAMP

A cheerful puppy dog heads the list of the first "friends". Time for making this toy should not exceed four hours.

Materials

48″ × 7″ (1 m 20 cm × 18 cm) in dark fur fabric
5″ × 3″ (13 cm × 8 cm) in white fur fabric
3″ × 4″ (8 cm × 10 cm) pink felt
1¼″ × 1¼″ (3 cm × 3 cm) black satin for the nose disc
½″ (1 cm) in diameter glass eyes or black button
1 lb cotton flock

Instructions for making

The body gusset is a separate piece marked in Diagram 80 by a dotted line. Trace, mark and cut out the patterns in thin card from

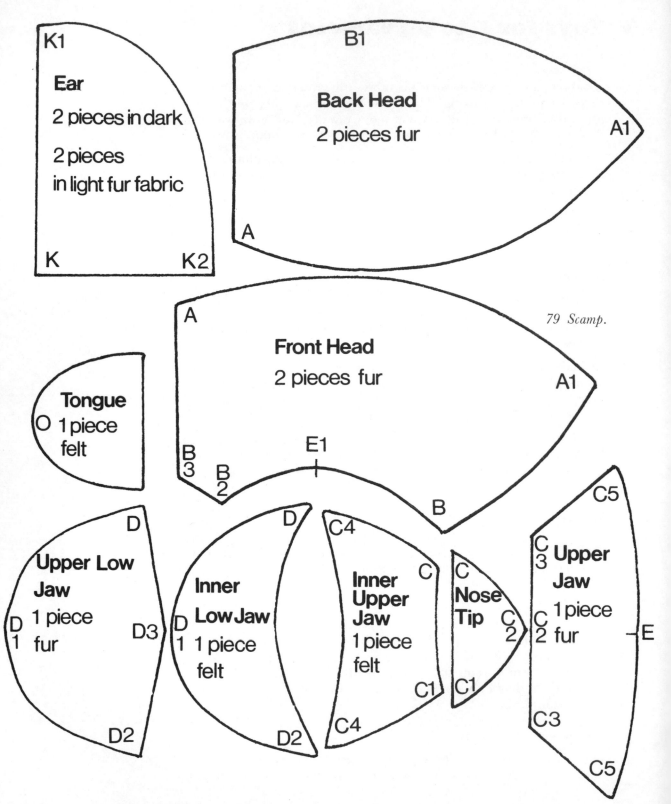

K1

Ear

2 pieces in dark

2 pieces
in light fur fabric

K   K2

B1

Back Head

2 pieces fur

A1

A

79 Scamp.

A

Front Head

2 pieces fur

A1

Tongue
O 1 piece
felt

B
3   B
2   B
2

E1

B

D

Upper Low Jaw

D
1   1 piece
fur   D3

D2

D

Inner Low Jaw

D
1   1 piece
felt

D2

C4

D

Inner Upper Jaw
1 piece
felt

C
C1

C4

C

Nose Tip

C
2

C1

C5

C
3   **Upper Jaw**
1 piece
C
2   fur   E

C3

C5

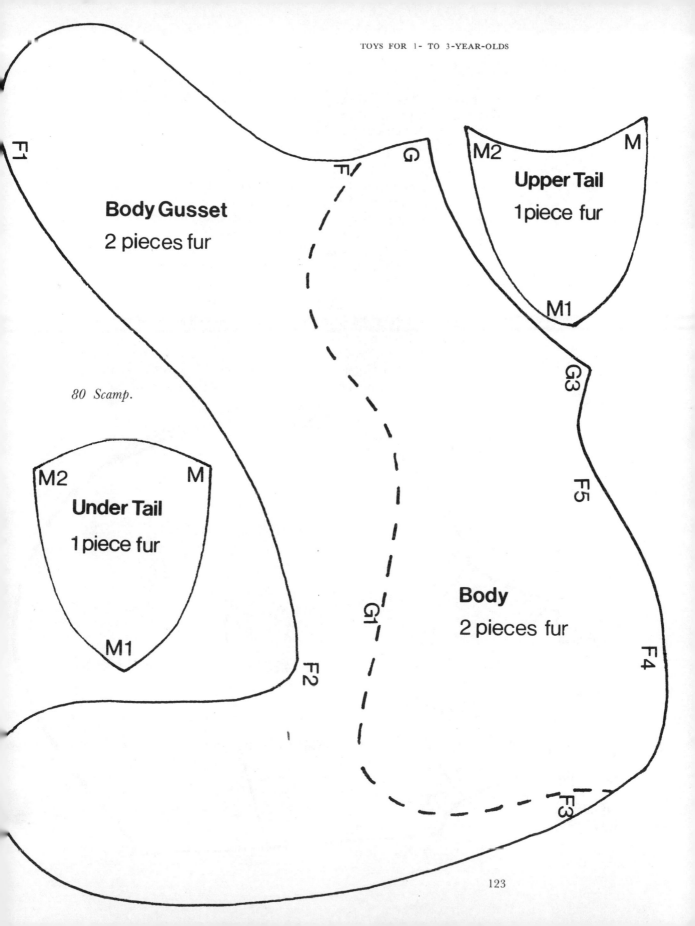

F1

Body Gusset

2 pieces fur

F

G

Upper Tail

1 piece fur

M2

M

M1

G3

F5

80 Scamp.

M2

M

Under Tail

1 piece fur

M1

Body

2 pieces fur

G1

F2

F4

F3

Diagrams 79, 80. Lay them on the wrong side of the fur fabric and mark round. Cut out. Be sure that the body and the head patterns are reversed. When cut out there should be seventeen pieces in fur fabric, three pieces in pink felt and one round satin disc for the nose.

Sew on the wrong side of the fabric. Turnings of $\frac{1}{4}''$ (0·5 cm) allowed in the patterns. Start working on the head by machining the back to the front head from A to A1. Repeat on the other two sections of the head. Then pin the two halves of the head from B1 passing point A1 and ending at B. Machine along this line and remove pins. Machine from B2 to B3 on the front section of the head.

Put the head aside and assemble the muzzle (Diagram 81). Start by pinning the tip of the nose to the inner upper jaw from C to C1 and machine. Then pin this piece to the upper jaw, matching C2 on the tip of the nose to C2 on the upper jaw and point C/C to C3 ending at C4 on the inner upper jaw corresponding to C5 on the upper jaw. Machine along this line and repeat the same on the other side.

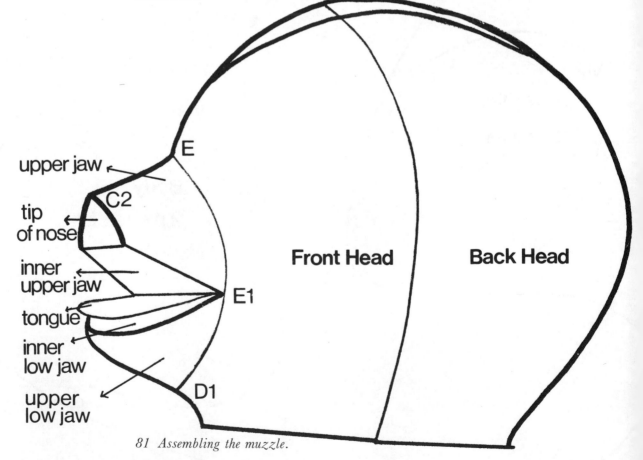

81 Assembling the muzzle.

124

Plate 16 A playful puppy in curly fur fabric is a good friend for any child to have. This puppy is made in light brown mohair fur fabric with touches of white on the tail and on the ears. The shiny black satin nose matches his shiny black eyes and an open pink felt mouth with the tongue showing typifies the pose of a puppy at play.

Sew the inner to the upper low jaw starting at D going on to point D1 and finishing at D2.

With the two parts of the muzzle assembled, namely the upper and lower jaw, sew them together along the line D/C4 to D2/C4 on the inner jaws catching the tongue in the seam as you go along. Make sure that O on the tongue faces towards point D1 on the lower jaw.

Fit the completed muzzle into the hole in the front part of the head. Pin and match point E on the upper jaw to B on the front head and point D/C4 on the inner jaws to E1 on the side of the head. D3 on the low jaw corresponds to B2 on the front head. Continue pinning to point E1 on the other side of the head which matches point marked D2/C4 on the inner jaws, finishing at E on the upper jaw and B on the front head. Machine round.

With the head now completed, put it aside and work on the body. Arrange the body parts and the body gusset into pairs with the pile of the fabric facing inward.

Start sewing from F on the body and F on the body gusset round the front leg to F1, then to F2 and round the back leg ending at F3. Repeat on the other half of the body.

Take the two halves of the completed body and pin from G to F on the body, then further on along the body gusset to G1, continuing to F3 and finishing at F4. Machine and remove pins.

Fix the head inside the body with the pile of the fabric on both pieces facing in. Match B3 on the head to G on the body and sew along the neck line ending at G3 on both halves of the body. Since the head is larger than the neck line, gather it to fit into the neck.

Close the back of the head from B1 to F5, leaving an opening between F4 and F5 for stuffing.

Make sure that there are no openings in the sewing. Turn work right side out. Before stuffing the toy, go over the seams with a darning needle and dislodge any pile caught in the seams.

Holding the work in the waist, proceed to stuff the feet with small amounts of filling. Work towards the head. When the shoulder is reached, leave the stuffing of the body and concentrate on the head. Start with the muzzle, first the upper jaw working from the tip of the nose, and then the low jaw. Do not stuff hard, and when stuffing the muzzle with your other hand try to keep it closed. By filling the muzzle too hard, it will stretch apart and the whole expression of the head will be lost.

Continue stuffing the head, shaping it well as you go along. Fill the whole of the front body. Still holding the puppy in the waist fill the back legs and the back body. Remove your hand and stuff the centre of the body well. Pin the stuffing opening and leave the toy to stand for several hours. It is possible that the stuffing will "settle" and a bit more can be added in the centre of the body before sewing up the opening with a ladder stitch.

It is important to remember that the feel of the toy should be light and soft, so do not stuff too hard.

Before finishing, machine the ears and the tail. Work on the ears

by sewing the inner to the upper ear from K to K1 ending at K2.
Machine the tail from M to M1 to M2. Remove any pile caught in
the seams and by hand neaten the base of the ears from K to K2,
by turning the raw edges in and sewing with small stitches. Stuff
the tail lightly.

Make and sew on the black satin nose as described on page 61.
Pin the eyes and the ears to the head. When a suitable position is
found, mark the places and then insert the eyes as described on
page 60. Sew the ears into place.

Pin the tail to the body and sew securely by turning the raw edges
inwards. A ball (see page 120) can be added to stress the playfulness
of this puppy dog.

LITTLE BUNNY COTTONTAIL

This happy little rabbit first appeared in a spring issue of the
magazine *The Lady*. He is an attractive and cheerful companion
and easy to make, taking some four to five hours to complete.

*Plate 17 Bunny Cottontail in honey-and-white nylon fur, gazes with his large
blue eyes at the world!*

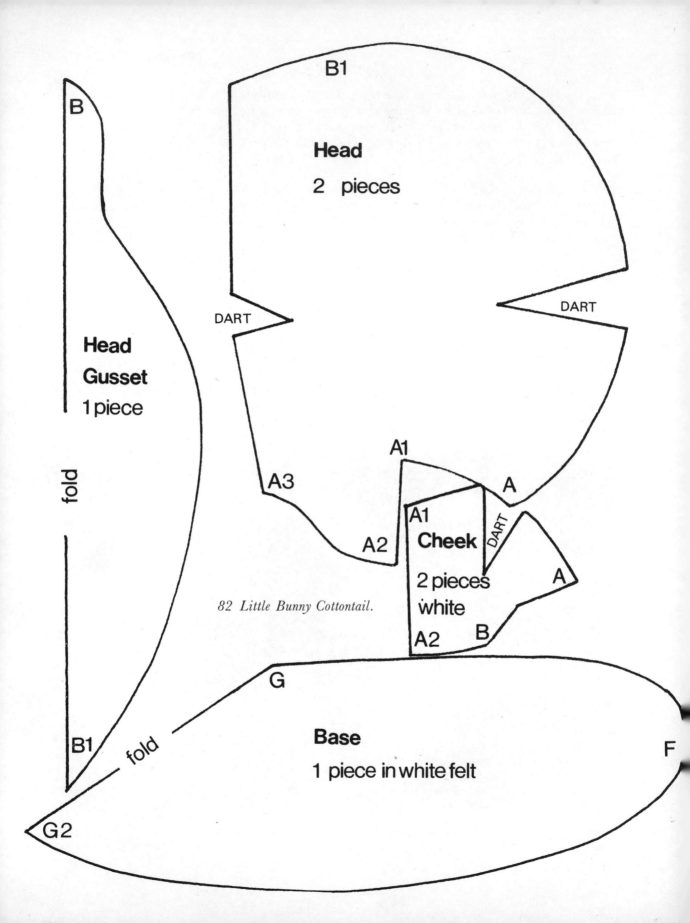

Head

2 pieces

B1

B

Head

Gusset

1 piece

fold

DART

DART

A3

A1

A2

A1

A

Cheek

2 pieces

white

DART

A

A2

B

82 Little Bunny Cottontail.

G

B1

fold

Base

1 piece in white felt

F

G2

This monkey is dressed in a checked gingham party frock. Pink felt was used for the body, face and ears and black fur fabric for the head.

Little Bunny Cottontail made from yellow and white fur fabric. His nose is a shiny black button and the whiskers are lengths of black embroidery silk.

From left to right—Scamp, Prunella, cuddly white kitten, Cookie and a sitting puppy dog.

Baby Lamb made from white nylon fur fabric. His big droopy ears are lined with pink felt, and the nose is embroidered with pink embroidery silk.

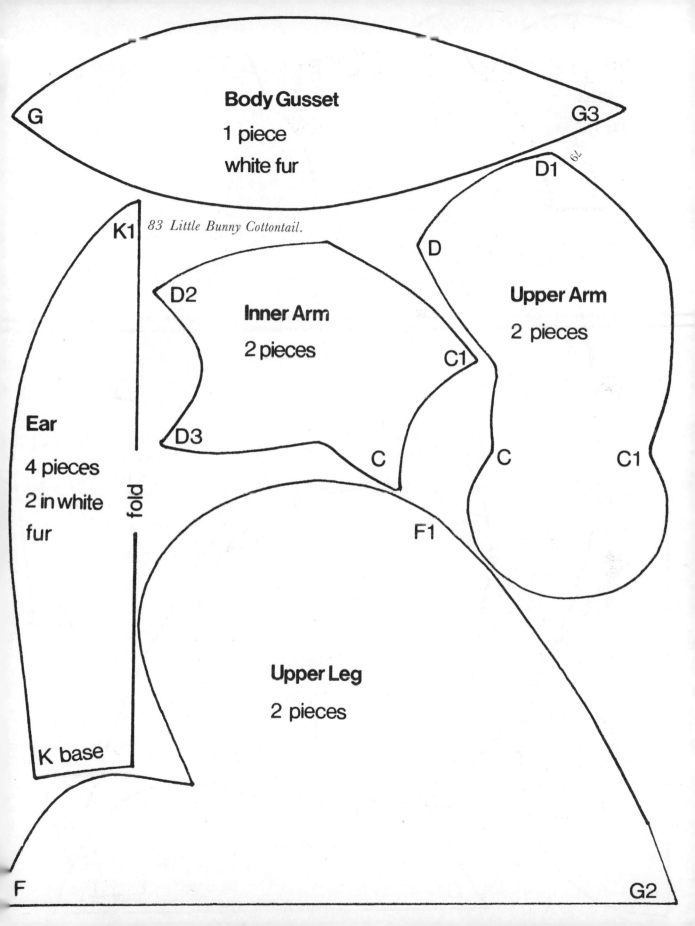

Body Gusset

1 piece

white fur

G

G3

D1

79

K1

83 Little Bunny Cottontail.

D2

Inner Arm

2 pieces

D

D1

Upper Arm

2 pieces

C1

D3

C

C1

C

C1

Ear

4 pieces

2 in white

fur

fold

F1

K base

Upper Leg

2 pieces

F

G2

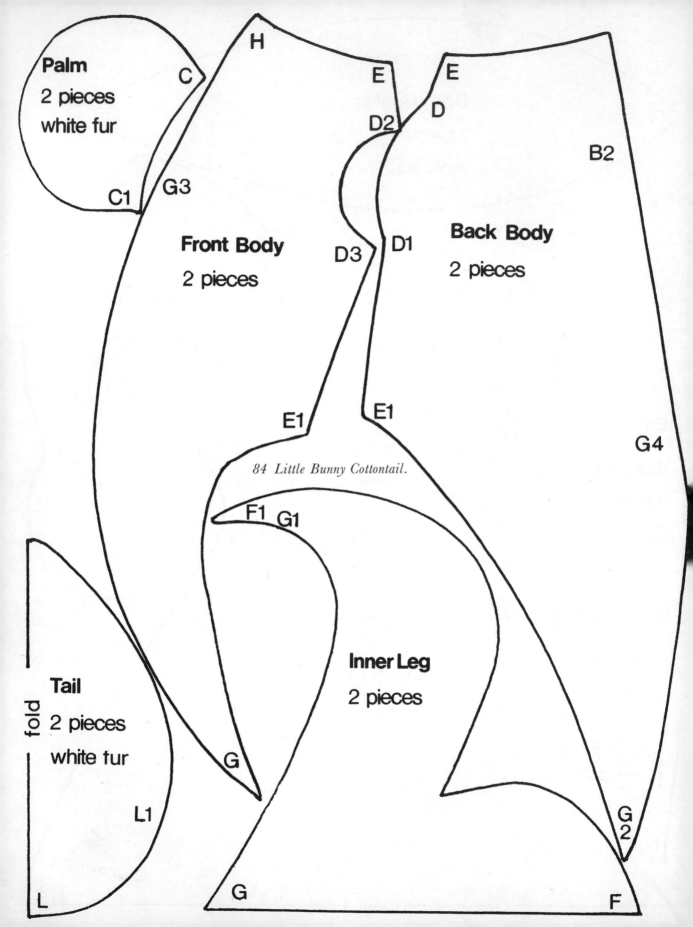

Palm
2 pieces
white fur

C

C1

G3

H

E

E

D2

D

B2

Front Body
2 pieces

D3

D1

Back Body
2 pieces

E1

E1

84 Little Bunny Cottontail.

G4

F1

G1

fold

Tail
2 pieces
white fur

Inner Leg
2 pieces

G

L1

G2
2

L

G

F

Materials

9″ × 48″ (23 cm × 1 m 22 cm) beige-coloured fur fabric
7½″ × 6½″ (19 cm × 16 cm) white fur fabric
9″ × 9″ (23 cm × 23 cm) white felt
1 lb cotton flock for stuffing
1 pair of glass eyes ½″ (1 cm) in diameter
1 black shiny button for the nose ½″ (1 cm) in diameter
2 daisies

Instructions for making

Treat the tracing and copying out of patterns as described on page 21. The head gusset, the ear and the tail are drawn in the diagrams with a "fold". Use this line of the fold as the centre line of the pattern, and for the purpose of working out the toy, cut these patterns in full size. (Diagrams 82, 83 and 84.).

There should be fourteen pieces of patterns. Lay these on the wrong side of materials making sure that the two parts of the head, the front and back body, the inner and the upper arm and the inner and the upper leg have a left and right side. Cut out. There should be seventeen pieces in beige fur fabric, nine in white fur fabric and one piece for the base of the toy in white felt.

Sew throughout on the wrong side of materials. Turnings of ¼″ (0·5 cm) are allowed in the patterns.

Start assembling the head. Stitch the darts in each of the two head pieces and in each of the white cheek pieces. Pin the cheeks to each part of the head, gathering them to fit from A to A1 and finishing at A2. Sew into place and remove pins. The pattern for the cheeks is larger than its corresponding place on the head. This was specially designed so to achieve a puckish expression in the finished toy.

Sew together the two head parts from B to A3 then pick up the head gusset and join it to one of the assembled head pieces by sewing from B to B1. Work in the same way on the other side of the head and when finished put head aside.

Assemble the body by joining first the white palms to the inner arms from C to C1. Pin and sew the arms to the body pieces with the upper arms fitting from D to D1 to the back bodies, and the inner arms from D2 to D3 to the front bodies.

Sew the front to the back bodies starting at E and sewing to point D2/D, working round the arms matching C1 on the inner arm to point C1 on the upper arm, ending at point D3/D1. Continue sewing down the side finishing at E1.

Fit the legs to each half of the body, by first sewing the inner to the upper leg from F to F1. Then pin each completed leg to the appropriate half body. Start at G on the inner leg and G on the front body, continue to the side seam, to point E1/E1 which matches G1 on the inner leg and finish at G2 on the upper leg and the back body. Sew into place and remove pins.

Pick up the body gusset and pin it to one of the front body pieces from G to G3. Sew and repeat the same on the other half of the body ending at the neck, point H. Close the back body sewing from G2 to G4.

Attach the head to the body matching A3 on the head to H on the body and working outwards round the neck. Close the back of the head from B1 ending at B2 on the back body. Leave the gap between G4 and B2 open for turning the work right side out and for stuffing.

Insert the white felt base. From point F on the leg which corresponds to point F on the base work outwards to G2 at the back and to G on the front body. Sew into place.

Inspect work for any openings in the sewing and repair these before turning work right side out. As soon as the work is turned, use a darning needle or a bradawl and remove any pile caught in seams while sewing. Put work aside.

Sew the ears, arranging them in pairs from K to K1 and ending at K on the other side, leaving the base open. Also sew the under to the upper tail leaving a gap between L and L1. Turn the ears and the tail right side out and remove any pile caught in the seams.

Stuff with small amounts of cotton flock driving it well into the toes and working towards the legs. Make sure that the toy can sit firmly on its back legs. Continue filling the body up to the waist. Then lightly stuff the arms starting with the palms and finishing the rest of the arms as far as the armpits. Fill the head working from the tip of the nose and stuffing the cheeks well so that they show prominently on the head. Finish the rest of the head stuffing to shape and making the head nicely round and soft to the touch. Finish stuffing the rest of the body. This toy must feel soft to the touch and this can only be achieved by using small quantities of stuffing at a time. Close the stuffing opening with a neat ladder stitch.

Finishing touches are a matter of personal choice but there are certain rules which have to be observed and these apply to fixing the features.

To achieve an appealing expression on a toy always use large eyes, either buttons or glass, and fit them low on the face on the level with the bridge of the nose and fairly well apart.

Pin the eyes and the ears to the head, and when a correct position is found, mark these places. Insert the eyes whether they are made of glass or are buttons, as described on page 28, Diagram 9.

Neaten the base of the ears by turning the raw edges in and sewing with a small stab stitch. Firmly sew them into place on the head with the white inner ear facing forward.

For whiskers use embroidery silk Perle 5. Start working from the centre of the tip of the nose making two large loops in the form of number eight. Secure each loop of the "eight" with a stitch into the side of the cheek so that it can't be pulled out. Cut whiskers to shape.

For the nose sew on a small black shiny button to cover up the stitching of the whiskers.

The scut, after being stuffed lightly, is sewn to the back body turning the raw edge inwards. Leave the tip of the scut free.

As to other details on finishing such as a bunch of flowers, a gay ribbon or even a little waistcoat—these are left to the imagination of the worker.

BABY LAMB

There are many stories and nursery rhymes describing various frolics of little lambs. It is therefore a popular character with children and a good and easy toy to make, requiring some four hours of work.

The idea of the design was to create a toy unsteady on its legs and somewhat clumsy in appearance. However, if the worker feels that a more solid toy would suit his purpose then a wire frame will have to be fitted in. How to work and place the frame in a toy is fully described on page 50 and in Diagram 26.

Materials

$9'' \times 48''$ (23 cm × 1 m 22 cm) white fur fabric
$5\frac{1}{2}'' \times 4\frac{1}{2}''$ (14 cm × 11 cm) pink felt
1 lb cotton flock
1 pair of glass eyes or black buttons $\frac{3}{8}''$ (1 cm) in diameter

133

Plate 18 Lambs either in white or in black make a good toy. The white lamb made in nylon fur has a pink nose, pink linings to its ears and pink shadows in place of hooves. With large blue eyes it looks on the black curly companion.

Instructions for making

Follow the instructions regarding patterns as given on page 21. There should be ten pieces of patterns including the standing tail. If a hanging tail is used this will increase the total amount of patterns to eleven pieces, since the hanging tail is made in two parts with an under tail marked on the pattern by a dotted line. (Diagrams 85, 86 and 87.)

Lay patterns on the wrong side of the fur fabric, mark round and cut out. Make sure that the body, neck, head and front and back upper legs have a right and a left side. Cut out. There should be twenty-four pieces in white fur fabric and two pieces in pink felt for the inner ear.

Sew throughout the work on the wrong side of the fabric and turning of $\frac{1}{4}''$ (0·5 cm) are allowed in the patterns.

First of all sew the legs to the bodies and to the front and back upper legs from A to A1. Attach each part of the neck to each body piece from A2 to A3. Machine the small darts in the head parts and pin each head to each section of the neck from B to B1. Machine and remove pins.

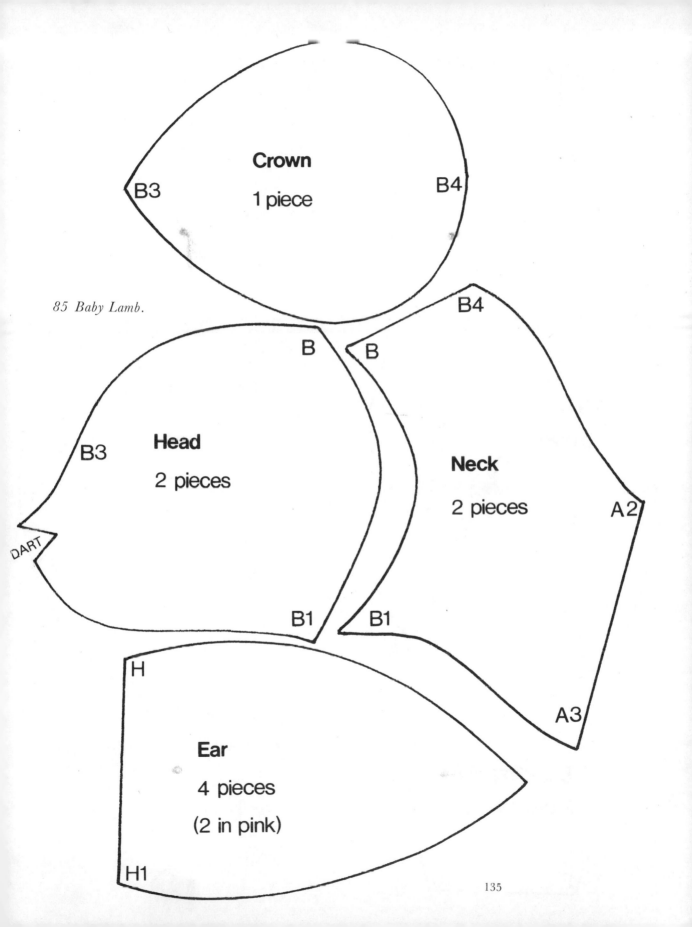

Crown

1 piece

B3

B4

85 Baby Lamb.

B

B

B4

Head

2 pieces

B3

DART

Neck

2 pieces

A2

B1

B1

A3

H

Ear

4 pieces

(2 in pink)

H1

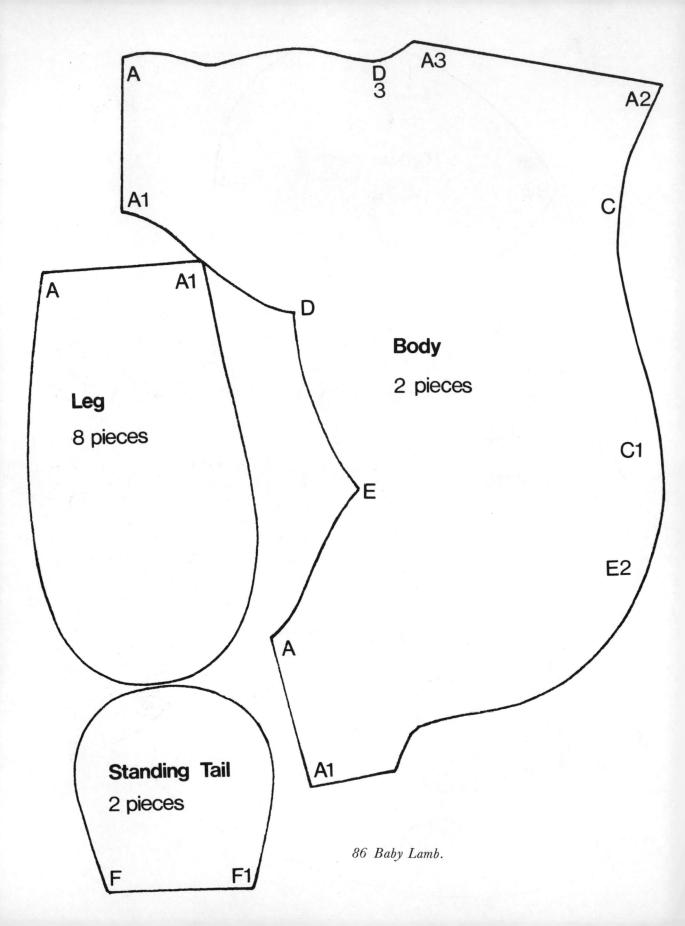

A

D
3

A3

A2

A1

C

A1

D

Body

2 pieces

A

Leg

8 pieces

C1

E

E2

A

A1

Standing Tail

2 pieces

F   F1

86 Baby Lamb.

The elephant and the camel in unusual familiarity. Grey moquette was used for the elephant and sandy-coloured felt for the camel with brown fur fabric for neck and hump.

From left to right—Bunny Cottontail, Teddy Bear, Sunny Bear, Panda and Cuddles.

A family snapshot line-up of Mr. and Mrs. Duck, Donalda and small chicks.

Monkey, Clown and Horse getting pushed out of the picture somewhat by the author's dog, Susie.

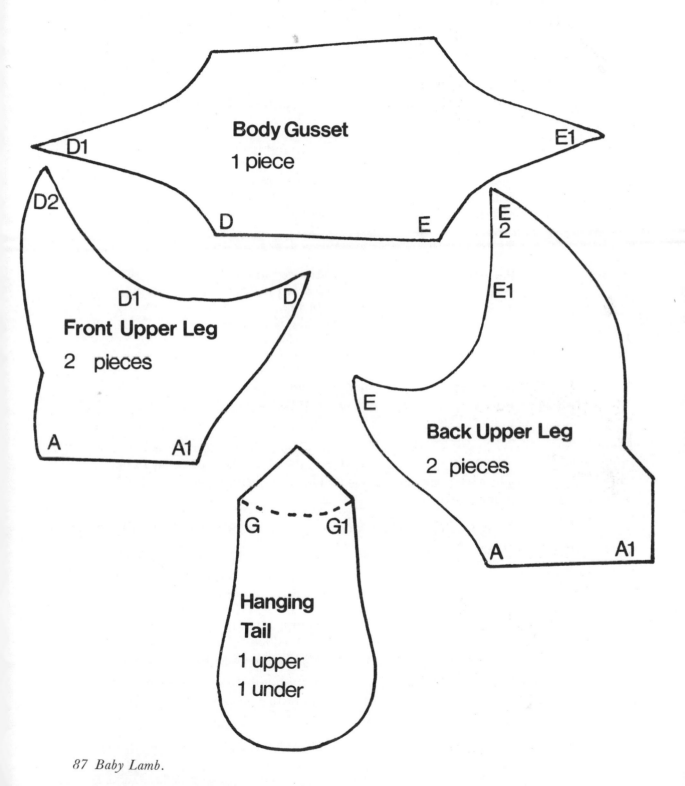

Body Gusset

1 piece

D1

E1

D2

D

E

D1

D

E
2

E1

Front Upper Leg

2 pieces

E

Back Upper Leg

2 pieces

A

A1

G

G1

A

A1

**Hanging
Tail**

1 upper

1 under

87 Baby Lamb.

The head will have to be gathered into the neck as it is larger than its corresponding place on the neck. The purpose of this is to get full cheeks on a finished toy.

Pick up two halves of the now completed body with a neck and head attached, and pin from B3 to A3 and from B4, passing point A2 and ending at C on the body. Machine along these lines and remove pins.

Work on the body gusset and front and back upper legs.

Machine both front and back upper legs to the body gusset from D to D1 and continue machining on the front upper legs to the end, marked D2. Work in the same way on the back upper legs, sewing them to the body gusset from E to E1 and then continuing on the back upper legs to finish at E2.

Pin the body gusset with legs attached to one half of the body. Start pinning at the neck at A3 down the body to the top of the upper leg point D2/D3. Carry further on from D3 to A and down and round the front leg to D on the body gusset and D marked on the body, then along the line of the body to E and E on the body gusset, down the leading edge of the leg and up passing point A1 and round to reach E2 on the back upper leg and E2 on the body. Machine along this pinned line and remove pins. Repeat the same work on the other half of the body but continue sewing beyond point E2 ending at C1 on the body.

Insert the crown into the head by pinning it first and then sewing from B3 to B4, going round to end at B3. The crown has to be gathered to fit into the head. This will give the finished toy a domed head.

Look carefully at the seams to make sure that there are no gaps, repair these if necessary and turn the "skin" right side out through the opening between C and C1. First turn the legs inwards to reach the upper front and back leg and then turn the head. Pull each leg through and finally the head.

Machine the tail. If a standing tail is used, leave the base between F and F1 for turning the tail right side out. On the hanging tail leave an opening between G and G1.

Arrange the ears into pairs with a pink inner ear and white upper ear. Machine leaving the bottom of the ear open between H and H1. Turn right side out.

Remove from the seams any pile of fur caught in the sewing, and brush the seams well.

Proceed to stuff. It cannot be stressed strongly enough that by using only small amounts of stuffing at a time, the finished toy will be firm but neither hard nor lumpy.

Begin by stuffing the legs, driving the flock well into the bottom part of the legs and working towards the haunches. Leave the legs and holding the toy in the waist fill the head working out the cheeks and the domed head. Stuff the neck and the front part of the toy. Still holding in the waist, fill the back, remove hand and stuff the centre of the toy. Pin the stuffing opening and leave the baby lamb to stand for several hours for the stuffing to "settle". If required add more flock and then close the stuffing opening with a neat ladder stitch.

Finishing starts with pinning the eyes and ears and working the features as described on page 28, Diagram 9.

Sew on the ears as described on page 28 and the tail as described on page 118.

The nose on this lamb is worked in pink embroidery silk and the shape is shown in Diagram 88.

88 The shape of nose for little lamb.

THE SUNNY BEAR

There can be very few children who do not possess a Teddy Bear. It is the Teddy who has survived the fashions, trends and the changes of the last 100 years. The classical shape of a Teddy cannot be altered, he has to be cuddly and round. The only adaptation in shape I have allowed myself to introduce is the smiling mouth, which does not detract from the toy's appeal.

The best material to use for a Teddy is a nylon fur fabric, as it is washable and endures any amount of "loving", though it can be made in baize. As for colour, any one will do from warm brown to white. I have used a golden yellow baize for my Sunny Bear with white trimmings in felt.

The approximate height of the toy when finished is 12″ (30 cm) in the sitting position and approximately 16″ (40 cm) when standing. The total time of making should be about three and a half to four hours.

Plate 19 The same set of patterns is used to make this honey-coloured Sunny Bear and the Panda. White felt paws, soles and inner ears together with large brown eyes and an open pink felt mouth add colour relief to the completely honey-coloured body.

Materials

$\frac{1}{4}$ yard × 54″ (23 cm × 1 m 37 cm) yellow fur fabric
6″ × 5″ (15 cm × 13 cm) white felt
12 ozs cotton flock
1 pair of brown eyes or buttons $\frac{1}{2}$″ (13 mm) in diameter.

Instructions for making

The instructions how to treat patterns and how to cut out materials were given for previous toys on page 21.

When cut out, there should be sixteen separate pieces of patterns in thin card and twenty-one pieces in fur fabric with eight pieces in white felt. Before cutting out, however, you must make certain that the patterns are so arranged that you have the right and left side of the body parts, the head and the sets of arms and legs. If you go wrong at this stage, it will result in re-cutting an extra set and would waste material. (Diagrams 89, 90, 91 and 92.).

Sew throughout the work on the wrong side of fabric; turnings of $\frac{1}{4}$″ (0·5 cm) are allowed in the patterns.

Start working on the head. Close the darts on the right and the left side of the head and then fit in the head gusset starting at A on the head matching A on the head gusset and going round the curve of the head to B. Machine this in place and similarly fix the other side of the head. Close the head at the neck from A2 to A3.

To assemble the pieces for the muzzle, start with the tip of the nose and join it to the white felt piece for the inner upper jaw from C to C1, marked on both pieces. This, being now one piece, fits to the upper jaw starting at D and going round to D1, and from D to D2 with the pile of the fabric facing in. Sew. The low jaw consists of two parts, one in white felt and one in fur fabric. Join these two together with the pile on the inside, beginning at D3, continuing to D4 and finishing at D5. Now pin the two white felt inner jaws along the line D1/D2 to D3/D5 and machine.

Fit this into the head, pinning the fur part of the muzzle with the pile still facing in, along the curve of the hole from A1 matching D2/D5 and going over the points A/A down to A1 on the other side of the head. Machine. Work in the same way for the low jaw, fitting the fur piece of the muzzle to the head with the pile facing in and starting at A1 matching D5, going to A2 which corresponds to D6 on the low jaw, and finishing on the other side of the head with point A1 on the head falling on point D3 on the low jaw. Sew into place.

141

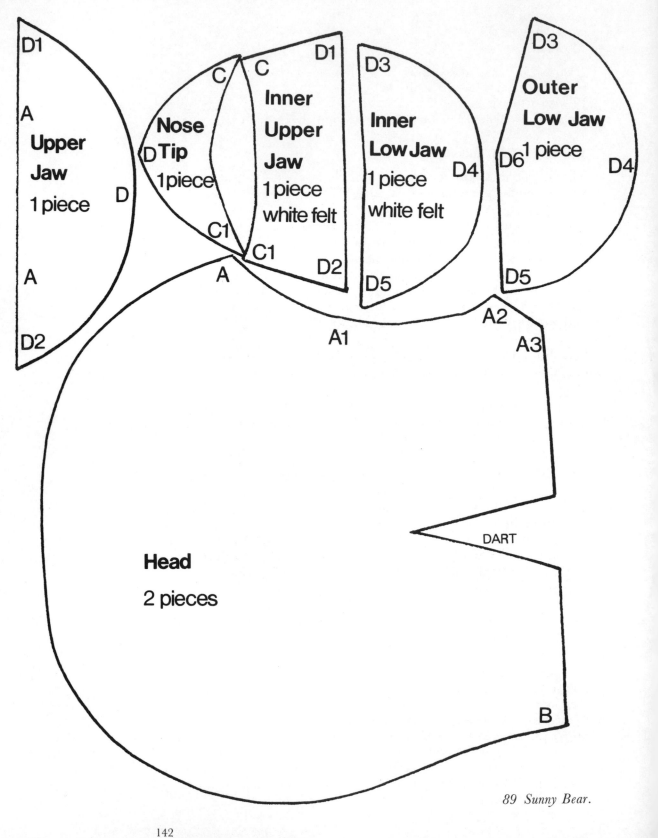

D1

A

Upper Jaw

1 piece

A

D2

D

D

Nose Tip

1 piece

C

C

C1

C1

A

A1

Inner Upper Jaw

1 piece white felt

D1

D2

D3

Inner Low Jaw

1 piece white felt

D4

D5

D3

Outer Low Jaw

1 piece

D6

D4

D5

A2

A3

DART

Head

2 pieces

B

89 Sunny Bear.

142

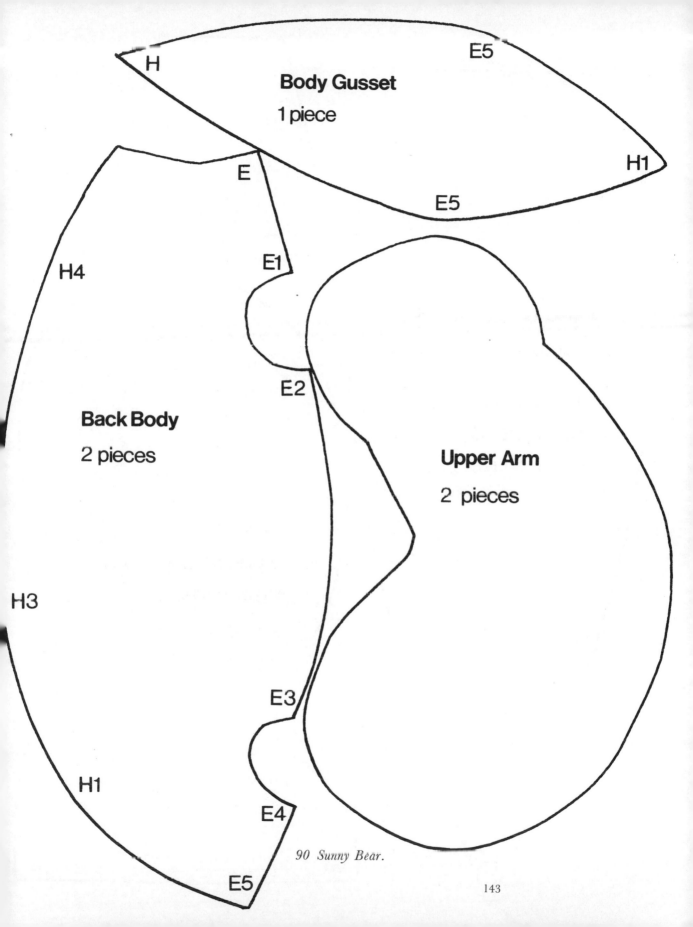

Body Gusset

1 piece

H

E5

H1

E5

E5

E

H4

E1

E2

Back Body

2 pieces

Upper Arm

2 pieces

H3

H1

E3

E4

90 Sunny Bear.

E5

143

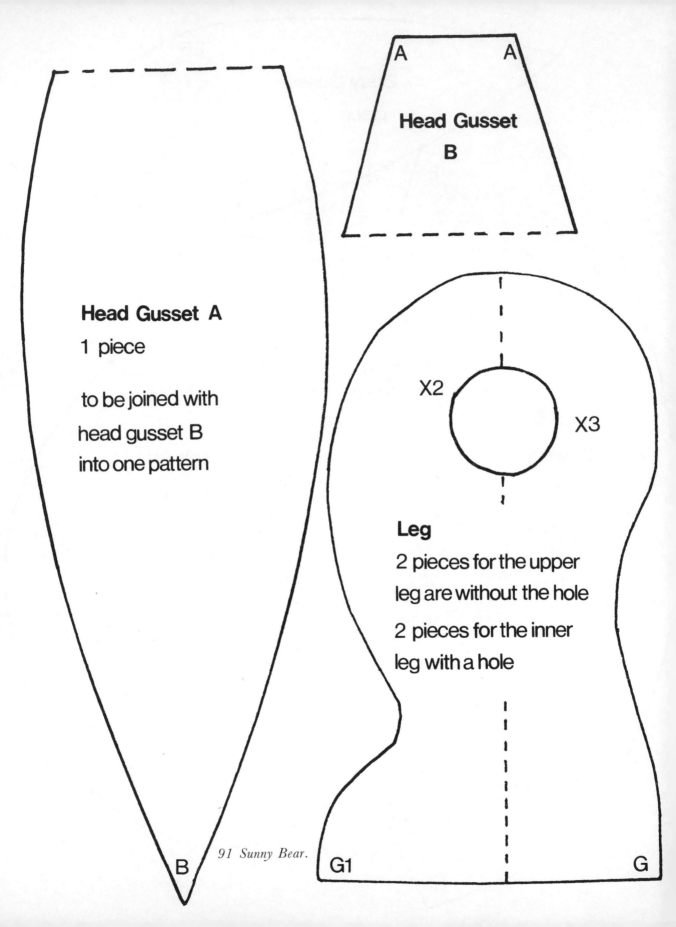

Head Gusset B

A   A

Head Gusset A

1 piece

to be joined with

head gusset B

into one pattern

X2   X3

Leg

2 pieces for the upper

leg are without the hole

2 pieces for the inner

leg with a hole

B   *91 Sunny Bear.*

G1   G

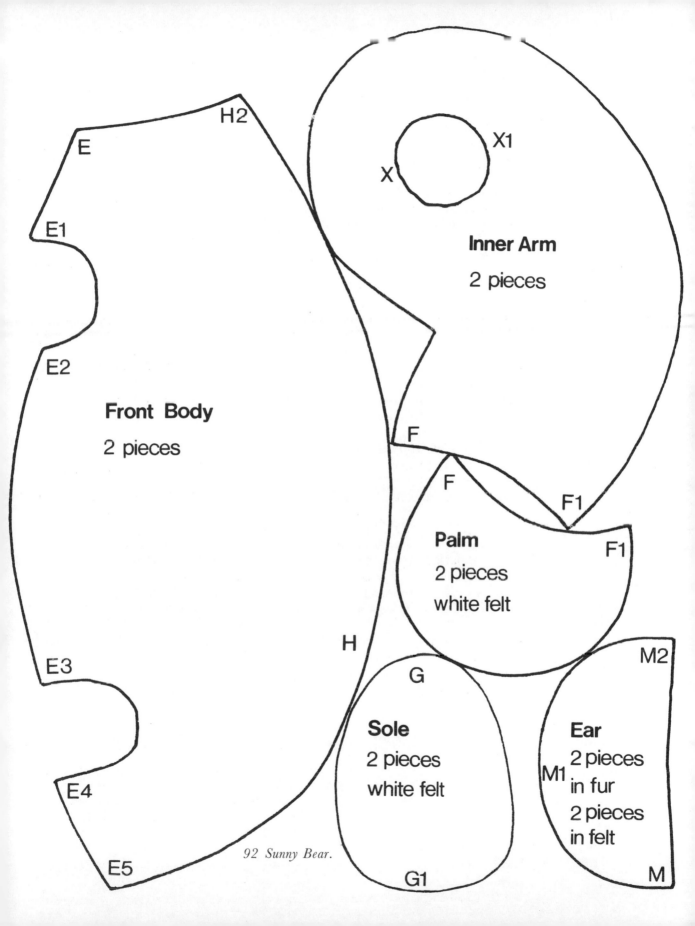

Inner Arm

2 pieces

Front Body

2 pieces

Palm

2 pieces

white felt

Sole

2 pieces

white felt

Ear

2 pieces
in fur

2 pieces
in felt

E

H2

E1

E2

E3

E4

E5

X

X1

F

F

F1

F1

H

G

G1

M2

M1

M

92 Sunny Bear.

Turn the head right side out and working through the opening in the neck catch the white felt inner jaws, and sew these together along the line D1/D3 to D2/D5. This line of sewing is better if started and finished on the fur fabric of the head. Put the head aside and start building the body.

Join the front to the back body from E to E1, leaving the gap between E1 and E2 for inserting the arms, then continue sewing from E2 to E3, leaving this open for putting in the legs and finish by joining the seams from E4 to E5. Work in the same way for the other pair of body pieces.

Sew on the white palm pieces to the inner arms from F to F1. Lay one of the body halves with the pile upwards. On this, pile down, lay the correct inner arm so that it faces forwards towards the front body. Check that X on the inner arm matches point E1 on the body and X1 joins with point E2. Machine round and repeat on the other half. Similarly work on the legs by laying the inner leg and fitting it round, starting at X2 on the leg and E3 on the body and finishing at E4 and X3 on the leg. Make sure that you work on the correct side of the body and that the pile of the legs and the body face each other. Sew round. Now pull the inner arms and legs through the holes in the body. Lay the upper arms on to the inner arms with the pile of both parts facing in, pin in place and sew. Work in the same way for the legs. Fit in the white sole pieces into the feet, starting at G and sewing to G1 finishing at G.

Pin the body gusset beginning from H through E5 and continuing up the back to H1 and sew to one half of the body. Now pick up the two body halves and pin them together with the pile facing in and starting at the neck at H2, passing H on the body gusset and the front body, going on to H1 and ending at H3. Machine.

Tuck the head, still right side out, inside the body matching H2 on the body to A3 on the head and sew round the neck. Close the back of the body from the neck down to H4 leaving a gap open from H3 to H4. Turn the whole toy right side out through this gap in the back.

Examine the work for any openings in the seams and mend these before you start stuffing.

Stuff with small pieces of cotton flock from the muzzle towards the head. Then fill the arms and legs and the rest of the body. Drive the flock well into the shape of the toy but avoid making the Sunny Bear too hard or lumpy. When finished the toy should feel soft and cuddly and light.

Close the stuffing opening with a ladder stitch, and using a strong needle remove any pile caught in the seams and give it a good brushing with a stiff brush, particularly along the seams to cover these over and so improve the whole appearance of the toy.

Start finishing with a shiny little nose made of black satin and shaped and worked on as shown in Diagram 36 and described on page 61. With black embroidery silk and using a small back stitch draw in the line of the upper lip and the division under the nose. Knot off firmly. Use large brown buttons or glass eyes mounted on black felt discs and insert these as shown in Diagram 9 and fully dealt with on pages 28 and 29.

Sew the white felt ear to the fur fabric ear with the pile facing in, from M to M1 and ending at M2. Turn inside out, sew and neaten the raw edges. Pin the ears to the head, experimenting with the placing till you find a position suiting the expression of the face. The approximate place is with the bottom of the ear in line with the top of the nose and eyes. Sew securely into place.

A gay flower as a finishing touch will certainly be very appealing, although it may not last long due to the "loving" attention bestowed upon the Sunny Bear.

If you prefer, the Sunny Bear legs can be put on in the standing position by marking X2 and X3 on the inner leg along the centre line of the leg. Line these marks with the body seam at E3/E4. (Dotted line on the patterns in Diagram 90.)

For the muzzle see Diagram 81.

PANDA

A natural substitute for a Teddy Bear is a Panda. A soft and cuddly toy and just as popular with children as a Teddy.

Materials

7″ × 48″ (18 cm × 1 m 22 cm) black fur fabric
7″ × 48″ (18 cm × 1 m 22 cm) white fur fabric
6″ × 6″ (15 cm × 15 cm) pink felt
2 buttons for the eyes each $\frac{3}{4}$″ (20 mm) in diameter
1 button for the nose $\frac{1}{2}$″ (13 mm) in diameter
14 ozs cotton flock for stuffing
Pink ribbon

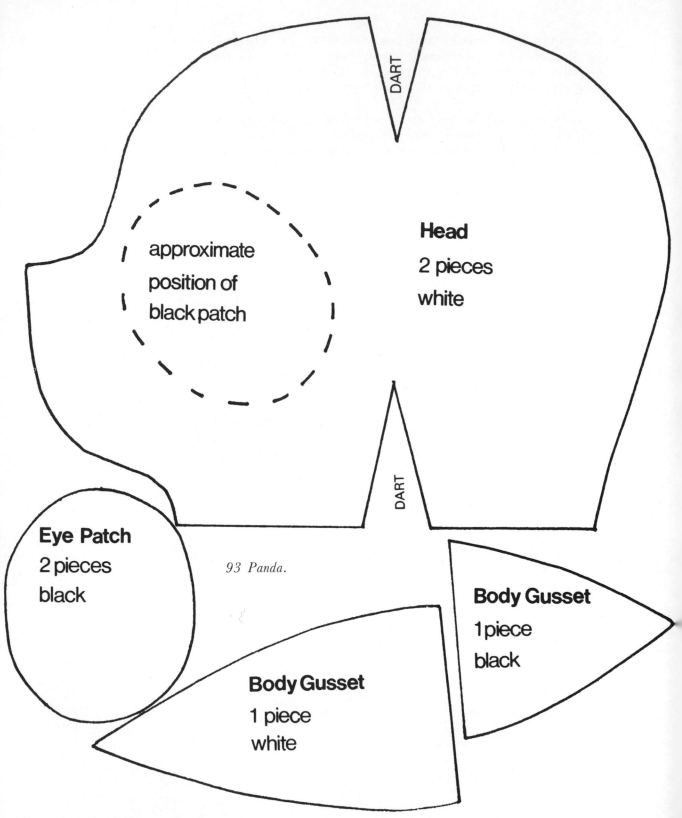

DART

Head

2 pieces

white

approximate

position of

black patch

DART

Eye Patch

2 pieces

black

93 Panda.

Body Gusset

1 piece

black

Body Gusset

1 piece

white

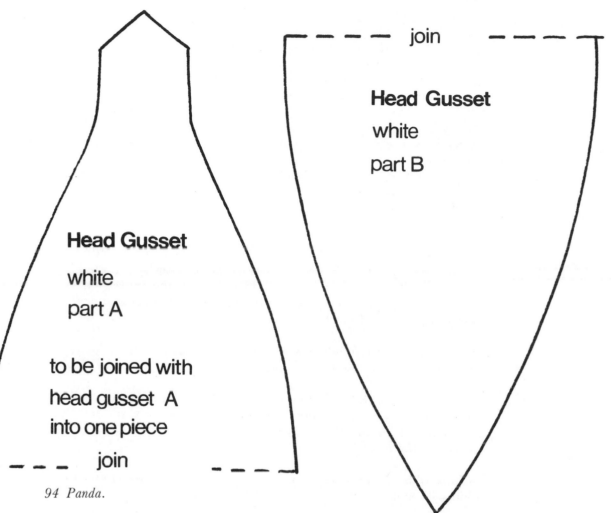

94 Panda.

The patterns for the Panda are the same as for Sunny Bear with slight variations only. The legs are fixed to the body in a standing position which is marked by a dotted line on the patterns for Sunny Bear, Diagram 90. The body gusset is divided into two sections, the black one fitting to the back body and the white one fitting into the front body.

The head has a closed mouth with a head gusset which runs from the tip of the nose to the back of the head. It is drawn in Diagram 94 in two parts but I strongly recommend to trace it as one piece on to a thin card.

Instructions for making

The cutting out of patterns and sewing is the same as for Sunny Bear. When the patterns are traced and cut out there should be thirteen pieces in all. In material there should be fifteen pieces in black fur fabric, six pieces in white fur fabric and six in pink felt.

It must be mentioned at this point that the measurements for the fur fabric indicated above are given in case these have to be purchased from a shop. In fact one will cut to waste but the leftovers can be stored and used for another toy.

Assemble the body parts, arms and legs as described for Sunny Bear. The head gusset is worked as the head on Little Bunny Cottontail.

The head, arms and the body are to be stuffed lightly but the legs are filled firmly in order to make them strong enough for the Panda to stand.

Before starting finishing, pin the black patches to the face. An approximate position is shown on the head pattern by a dotted line in Diagram 93. Pin the eyes and ears and when the expression looks pleasing, mark the place for the patches, the eyes and ears and remove them from the head.

Neatly stab stitch round each of the black patches turning the raw edges in and then sew them on to the face.

Work the eyes as described on page 28 and the ears as given for Sunny Bear. With embroidery silk stitch on the outline of the nose and mouth and then, sew on a shiny black button to represent the nose.

A pink ribbon round the neck finished into a large bow under the chin will enhance the looks of the toy.

BEGGING POODLE

This toy has a body, head and paws made in grey velvet and the legs and arms in grey fur fabric. If choosing velvet, it is important to use cotton-backed velvet or milliner's velvet as this does not stretch under the pressure of stuffing.

Begging Poodle is designed on the same principle as the Sunny Bear and the Panda with arms and legs set into the body.

Materials

9″ × 18″ (23 cm × 45 cm) velvet
7″ × 48″ (18 cm × 1 m 22 cm) fur fabric
1 pair of eyes $\frac{3}{8}$″ (1 cm) in diameter
12 ozs cotton flock for stuffing
Ribbon

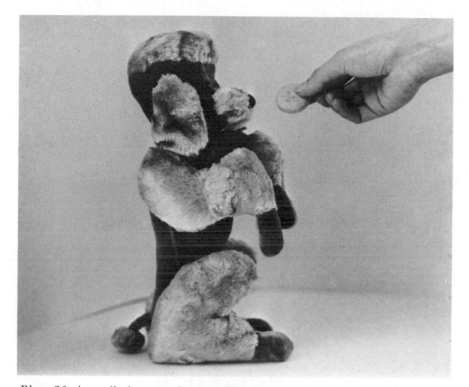

Plate 20 A poodle is a popular pet. This Begging Poodle made in pale grey velvet with matching fur legs, ears and pom-pom is no exception. This can also be made in black, white or apricot.

Instructions for making

Treat patterns as described on page 21. There should be thirteen pieces of patterns. The patterns for the tail and the fur pom-pom for the top of the head are marked in Diagrams 96 and 97 with a fold. To avoid mistakes trace and cut out the patterns in full size.

For marking on materials and sewing follow instructions as given for Little Bunny Cottontail on page 131. Then cut out. There should be sixteen pieces in velvet and seventeen pieces in fur fabric.

Assemble the head by sewing the head gusset to one side of the head from A to A1 and ending at A2. Work in the same way on the other side of the head. Then sew the gusset from A to A3 to one part of the head and then to the other section ending at the neck, A4. Put head aside and work on the body.

Like for Sunny Bear join each of the front to each of the back body pieces from B to B1 and from B2 to B3 and from B4 to B5.

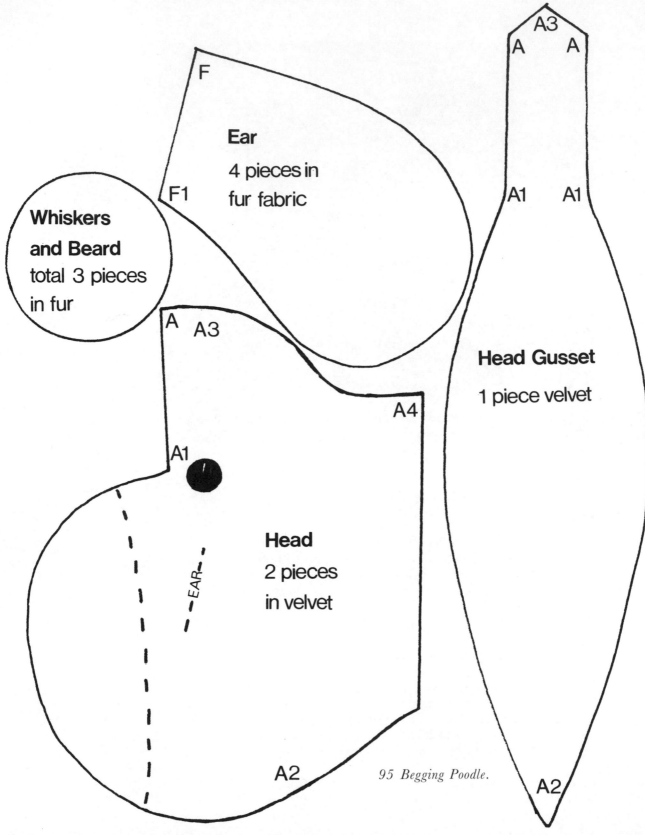

A3
A   A

A1   A1

F

Ear

4 pieces in
fur fabric

F1

Head Gusset

1 piece velvet

**Whiskers
and Beard**
total 3 pieces
in fur

A
A3

A4

A1

EAR

Head

2 pieces

in velvet

A2

95 Begging Poodle.

A2

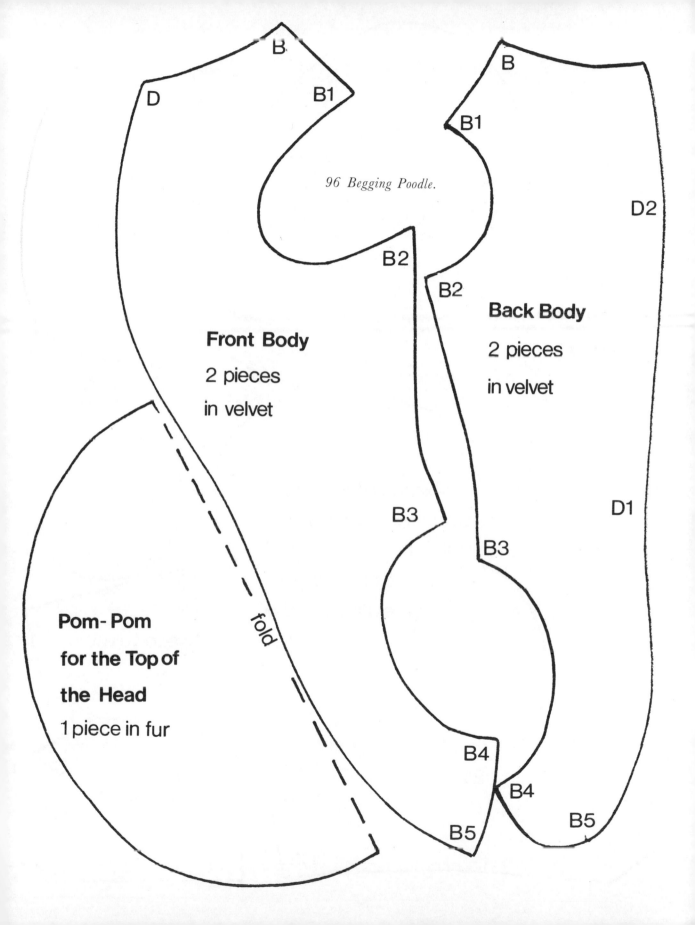

B

D

B1

B

B1

96 Begging Poodle.

D2

B2

B2

Back Body

2 pieces

in velvet

Front Body

2 pieces

in velvet

fold

Pom-Pom

for the Top of

the Head

1 piece in fur

B3

B3

D1

B4

B4

B5

B5

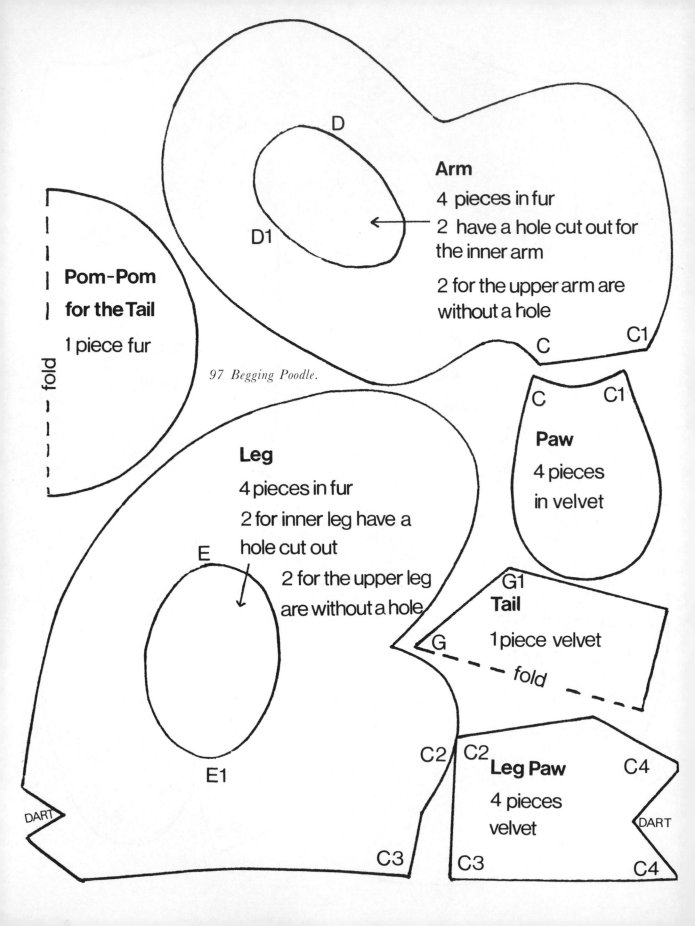

D

D1

Arm

4 pieces in fur

2 have a hole cut out for
the inner arm

2 for the upper arm are
without a hole

C   C1

**Pom-Pom
for the Tail**

1 piece fur

fold

97 Begging Poodle.

C   C1

Paw

4 pieces
in velvet

Leg

4 pieces in fur

2 for inner leg have a

hole cut out

2 for the upper leg

are without a hole.

E

E1

G1

Tail

1 piece velvet

G

fold

C2   C2

Leg Paw

4 pieces
velvet

C4

DART

DART

C3   C3

C4

Next close the darts in the legs and the darts in the leg paws, then join the arm paws to the arms from C to C1 and the leg paws to the legs from C2 to C3. Lay one of the body halves with the right side of velvet facing upwards. On this, <u>pile down,</u> lay the correct inner arm with point D on the arm matching point B1/B1 on the body and D1 corresponding to B2/B2 on the body. Arms are to point forward towards the front body. Machine round and repeat on the other half.

Use the same method for completing the arms and sewing on the legs as for Sunny Bear. Note that point E on the inner leg fits B3/B3 on the bodies and E1 matches B4/B4, and that the pile of the velvet and the inner leg face each other with the leg paw pointing forward. Pull the inner leg through the hole in the body and pin on to it the upper leg with the pile facing down. Sew round starting at the back dart and sewing round the curve of the leg to C2. Continue sewing the leg paw passing C4 and going round to C3 finally ending at the closed dart at the back of the leg. Work in the same way on the other leg.

Pin the two halves of the body with legs and arms attached. Begin at the neck, at D and work down the front of the toy passing B5/B5 and finishing at D1 at the back.

Tuck the head, still right side out, inside the body with A4 on the head corresponding to D on the body. Sew round the neck. Close the back of the head from A2 to the neck and beyond to end at D2 on the back body. Leave a gap between D1 and D2 for turning the toy right side out and consequently for stuffing. Inspect the seams for any gaps in the sewing. Repair these before turning the toy right side out.

Stuff, using small amounts of flock. Drive stuffing well into the legs and the leg paws. The legs are to be firm enough for the toy to sit on them without losing balance. Fill the toy to the waist and then proceed to stuff the head working from the nose and filling the rest of the head. Stop at the neck.

Stuff lightly the paws in the arms and the arms and continue filling the rest of the toy. Pin the stuffing opening and leave the toy to stand for several hours for the stuffing to "settle". It may be necessary to put some more stuffing in before closing the opening. Sew the opening with a neat ladder stitch.

Finishing. Start by pinning the eyes, ears, nose and the pom-pom for the top of the head. When pleased with the looks of the toy, mark the places and then work out the nose in a black satin disc as described on page 61 and in Diagram 36. Use glass eyes or

155

buttons and mount these on royal blue felt discs. Insert eyes as shown on page 28 and in Diagram 9.

Stab stitch round the pom-pom for the head turning the raw edges in and pull on the thread to gather slightly. Stuff in the front and sew neatly into place on the head.

Arrange the ears in pairs and sew round with the pile facing in and leaving an opening from F to F1. Turn ears right side out and neaten the raw edges. Pull slightly on the thread to gather. Sew the ears to the head.

Work the pom-poms for the whiskers and the beard by sewing round and turning the raw edges in. Pull on the thread and if necessary stuff lightly. Pin first and then sew into place on the muzzle.

Sew the velvet part of the tail and stuff. The end marked G–G1 is fitted to the body while the other end has a fur pom-pom stitched round it.

Approximate positions for placing eyes, ears and the pom-pom on the head are marked by a dotted line on the head pattern in Diagram 95.

Remove any fur pile caught in the seams and brush the toy well with a wire brush. A ribbon round the neck tied into a bow will finish the Begging Poodle. The time taken to make this toy should not exceed 4 hours.

4 Toys for 3- to 5-year-olds

In children of about three, signs of social games involving other children, take place. At first, a child is a bit apprehensive of the new experience of sharing with others of his own age, but soon they will overcome the difficulty and enjoy the games.

The Mummy and Daddy play comes in, with the imitation of all domestic activities, even the movements and sayings of both parents. With the development of imagination and the acquisition of a larger vocabulary, nursery stories are in great demand. And it is often noticed that, although children cannot read, they manage to memorise visually the text which corresponds to a picture in a book.

The best toys for this age are the ones to be dressed and undressed and also objects connected with domestic equipment. Books with large colourful pictures and stories describing animals in a "human" way are particularly enjoyed. Children are absolutely delighted by a puppy or a kitten being naughty and disobedient. This appeals to their parental instinct and makes them slightly superior by identifying themselves with the feelings of a parent.

As for fairy stories, one has to be very careful in choosing the right ones. Emotionally a child develops a great deal from the age of four and it often reacts with deeper intensity to these stories than is realised. Still having very limited experience of life, these uncanny witches can frighten a child for ever.

Animals, particularly dogs, also frighten some children. The reason is the sudden loud noise of barking which they cannot explain to themselves, and they cannot distinguish between a joyful or an angry bark. As a matter of fact a dog will never attack a small child unless it is provoked beyond endurance. I have seen my own dogs letting my grandaughter sit in their bed and eat their biscuits. She also cuddled and fondled them to "death" and although they were most uncomfortable with all this love, they never turned on her, except a slight warning growl when they really had had too much of it.

To help children with the emotional difficulty, it is a good thing to see that they have a little dog or a kitten, failing this a soft animal toy. It is also advisable to take them for a visit to the zoo and to a circus. A pantomime is a pleasant entertainment for children where their fears can be turned into laughter and so disappear completely.

The habit of play changes in the pre-school days. Boys will not play with girls. They seek the company of other boys and believe in organised gang games, like soldiers, Indians, explorers. They often form themselves into "secret" societies, invented and known only by the gang.

A tent, an Indian outfit, a cowboy suit, various weapons will be greatly appreciated at this time. For indoor activities, train sets, racing car games, a bus conductor set, with particular stress laid on tickets and toy money. The importance of "being in charge" delights little boys.

Girls also become clanny and they too feel only comfortable with other girls. The game of little mothers is very popular, with all the feminine activities it entails. They try to cook, and make cakes for tea parties, and even make or knit clothes for their dolls.

An elegant pram for the dolls, a dolls' house or a large wardrobe would be a splendid gift for them. There are some very fine sewing outfits available and lock stitch sewing machines. A nurse's dress and a toy set of first aid equipment will give a little girl the feeling of being important.

On the day a child enters school, the idea of play is absorbed into learning. A completely new world opens up where play is painting, modelling, making things to represent things. New materials are discovered and used, words are read and figures added. As far as soft toys are concerned, these cease to exist, except the "first friend" which, even if by now somewhat used up, will still give comfort in times of distress.

PRUNELLA A SOFT DOLL

A doll is one of the best toys for a three-year-old girl but even little boys will be interested and will take an active part in the Mummy and Daddy games.

Patterns in Diagram 55 and instructions on pages 81 to 82 can be used as they are, to make up a doll with non-moving arms and legs. Should you, however, feel a bit more ambitious the following section deals with modifications required to make a doll which, although it will not stand, will sit and has arms and legs which are not stiff.

Plate 21 Two dolls sunbathing in the garden. They are both based on the same pattern. Prunella, a doll with rigid limbs, is fair with golden hair and dressed in a blue-and-white striped cotton frock and red felt sandals. Red also appears on the dress in the line of ric-rac and in two red bows in her hair.
Cookie, a floppy doll, has short brown hair and wears a pink-and-white gingham dress (very small check) with a row of pleated nylon frilling round the skirt and at the neck.

COOKIE A FLOPPY DOLL

The design is based on the soft doll and the time taken to make this doll and her clothes should not exceed five hours.

Materials

8″ × 36″ (20 cm × 91 cm) pink calico or pink felt
2 buttons $\frac{1}{4}$″ (0·5 cm) in diameter in black
$\frac{1}{4}$ ozs rug wool for hair
6 ozs cotton flock for stuffing

Dress

$6\frac{1}{2}'' \times 36''$ (16 cm $\times$ 91 cm) gingham
$4'' \times 4''$ (10 cm $\times$ 10 cm) red felt
$20'' \times 1''$ (51 cm $\times$ 2 cm) white nylon frilling
$16'' \times \frac{3}{8}''$ (41 cm $\times$ 1 cm) red ribbon

Instructions for making

Work on patterns as described for previous toys, page 21. When "fold" is indicated, trace and cut out patterns in full size thus avoiding mistakes, and there should be fifteen pieces including the dress patterns. (Diagrams 98, 99 and 100.)

Lay patterns on materials, mark and cut out. There should be fourteen pieces for the body, six for the dress and four for the sandals.

Sew throughout on the wrong side of materials. Turnings of $\frac{1}{4}''$ (0·5 cm) are allowed for in the patterns.

Start working by sewing the darts round the face and then attach the face to the front body from A to the centre marked "fold" on the pattern and finish on the other side in a position corresponding to A.

Sew on the front legs to the front body from B to the centre and B on the other half. Pin the front feet to each of the front legs from B1 to B2, and sew. Put the front body aside, and work in the same way on the back.

Attach the head gusset to one half of the back head from C to C1 and then to the other half passing point C1 and ending at the neck, at C2. Flatten the back head and sew it to the back body at the neck starting at D passing the centre line of the back body C2 and ending at D on the other side of the neck.

Close the darts in the back body and then sew on the back legs starting at E working to the centre and ending at E on the other half. Fit in back feet to the back legs from E1 to E2.

Pick up the completed front body and pin it to the back body. Start at the centre of the face, point F and match this to F on the head gusset. Pin round the face to the neck and continue along the outer edge of the arm, round the hand, under the arm, along the body, down the leg to the feet. Sew along this pinned line and remove pins. Work in the same way on the other side. Then close the edge of the inner feet and legs. Insert soles matching G on the soles to G on the front feet and G1 to G1 on the back feet.

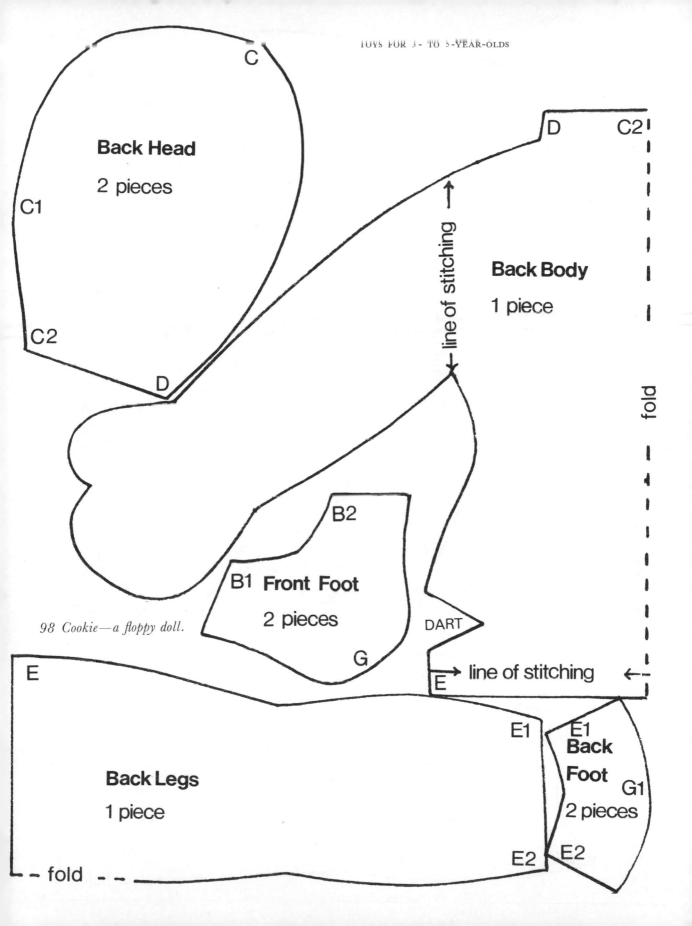

Back Head

2 pieces

C

C1

C2

D

D

C2

Back Body

1 piece

line of stitching

fold

B2

B1 **Front Foot**

2 pieces

G

DART

98 Cookie—a floppy doll.

E

line of stitching

E

E1

E1

Back Foot

G1

2 pieces

Back Legs

1 piece

E2

E2

fold

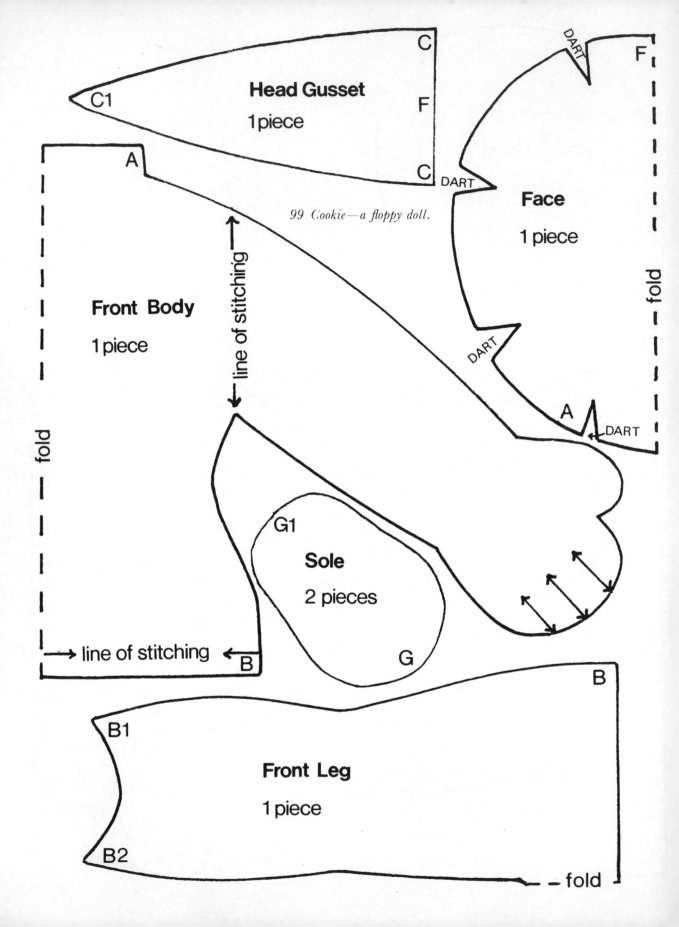

Head Gusset
1 piece

C

F

C1

C

A

DART

DART

Face
1 piece

F

fold

99 Cookie—a floppy doll.

line of stitching

Front Body

1 piece

DART

A

DART

fold

G1

Sole

2 pieces

G

line of stitching

B

B

B1

Front Leg

1 piece

B2

fold

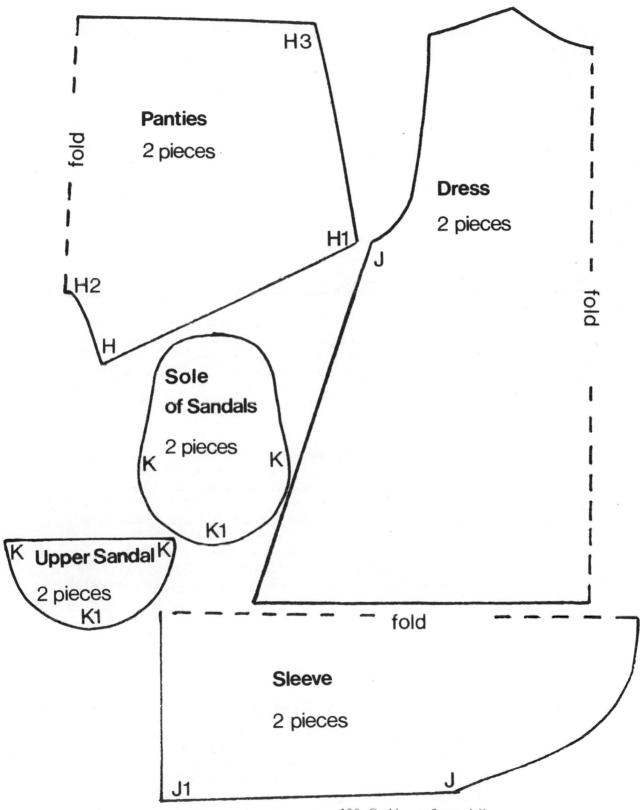

Panties

2 pieces

fold

H3

H1

H2

H

Dress

2 pieces

J

fold

Sole of Sandals

2 pieces

K

K

K1

K

Upper Sandal

K

2 pieces

K1

fold

Sleeve

2 pieces

J1

J

100 Cookie—a floppy doll.

Cut a slit in the back body about 3″ (8 cm) long, starting about 1″ (2 cm) below the neck. Inspect work for any gaps in the sewing and repair these before turning the doll right side out.

Stuff the feet to shape but not too hard and fill the rest of the legs reaching the line marked on the pattern as the "line of stitching". Machine along this line. Fill the hands very lightly as far as the wrists. Sew the fingers as marked on the pattern with arrows. Stuff the rest of the arms to the place marked "line of stitching" and sew along this line.

Work on the face carefully using small amounts of cotton flock and stuffing the darts so that the face becomes round with a good chin showing above the neckline. Fill the rest of the body and sew the stuffing opening with a neat ladder stitch.

Make up the clothes. Working on the panties, neaten the edge round the legs from H to H1 by turning it in about $\frac{1}{4}$″ (0·5 cm) or finishing off with a row of lace. Then sew from H to H2 and end at H on the other leg. Close the sides from H1 to H3 and turn the waist in, either by sewing a row of bias binding or by feeding in thin elastic thread.

The dress is in two parts. Sew the front part to the back at the shoulders and then along the sides. Cut an opening in the back about $3\frac{1}{2}$″ (9 cm) long and trim the fraying edges by turning these in and machining or by finishing with bias binding. Insert the sleeves. First sew each sleeve from J to J1 and then fit them into the armholes with J on the sleeves matching J on the dress. Any fullness in the sleeves gather in at the top so that they fit into the armholes. Turn in the raw edges at the wrists and sew. Hem the bottom of the dress and sew on a row of nylon frilling $1\frac{1}{4}$″ (3 cm) from the edge of the dress. Sew a row of the same frilling round the neck.

Before making up the sandals, sew on two strands of ribbon to the centre of the upper sandals and then sew the upper sandals to the soles from K to K1 and finishing at K on the other side.

With the clothes ready put them aside and finish off the face and the hair. Use carpet wool for the wig in reddish brown colour and work the wig as described on page 84 and in Diagrams 58, 59 and 61. Cookie has short hair worked into a wig in two parts. To cover the back of the head use a piece of tape $4\frac{3}{4}$″ (12 cm) long with strands of wool $3\frac{1}{2}$″ (9 cm) long and arranged as for the fringe in Diagram 61. The other part of the wig consists of a tape $3\frac{3}{4}$″ (9 cm) long with the strands of wool 9″ (23 cm) long and worked

as shown in Diagram 59 but bearing in mind that the parting is
on the side of the head.

The arrangement of the features and sewing these into place is
fully explained on page 82 and on page 83.

Make the eyebrows by placing two stitches in black embroidery
silk above the eyes. For the mouth cut out a small red circle or a
square and stick it into place and then sew neatly round. The nose
is made on the same principle as a nose for the animal toys shown
in Diagram 36 and described on page 61 with the only difference
that the disc for the nose of a doll is $\frac{1}{2}''$ (1 cm) in diameter and is
not worked into nostrils but sewn on just like a button.

Dress Cookie in her gingham clothes and red sandals and she will
be ready for play.

MINNIE—LITTLE BEAR GIRL

*Plate 22 Minnie, the little Bear girl, and Brock the Badger are toys with
floppy arms and legs. Minnie wears a printed cotton dress (very small
motif) and a white linen apron with lace straps. Her ears are lined in the
same cotton as her dress. A ribbon round her neck, wrists and ankles tied
into a generous bow picks up the pink in the pattern of the dress.*
*Brock has a cotton shirt and a pair of felt trousers. The colour of the felt
matches one of the motifs on the shirt.*

The patterns for this little Teddy Bear are taken from Cookie. This particular toy is dressed like a little girl but by making up a pair of trousers it can well portray a boy.

When finished Minnie is about 15″ (38 cm) long and time for making should not take longer than four hours.

Materials

10″ × 36″ (26 cm × 91 cm) gingham
8″ × 16″ (20 cm × 40 cm) fur fabric
2½″ × 3½″ (6 cm × 9 cm) white linen for the apron
18″ × ¾″ (45 cm × 2 cm) lace trimming
36″ × ¼″ (91 cm × 6 mm) ribbon
16″ × 1″ (40 cm × 2 cm) white bias binding
28″ × 1″ (71 cm × 2 cm) bias binding for the hem
2 glass eyes ½″ (13 mm) in diameter
1 black button ½″ (13 mm) in diameter for the nose
6 ozs cotton flock.

Instructions for making

Work on the patterns as described for previous toys, page 21. It is important, however, when "fold" is indicated to trace and cut out the patterns in full size, so avoiding any mistakes. No extra turnings to be added to the lines marked "fold".

There should be ten pieces of patterns. Lay these on the materials, mark round and cut out. There should be five pieces in gingham and thirteen in fur fabric. (Diagrams 101, 102 and 103.)

Sew throughout on the wrong side of fabric. Turnings of ¼″ (0·5 cm) are allowed for in the patterns.

Assemble the head by first sewing the darts in each half of the head and then pinning and sewing the head gusset to the two sections of the head. Use the same method as described for the Teddy Bear, page 118. Put head aside.

Next close the darts in the two halves of the back body and then sew together the two sections from A to A1, making it into one piece. Pin the front to the back body, starting at the neck and pinning along the outer edge of the arms from B to B1 and sew. Remove pins and flatten the arms at the wrists and then attach the fur hands to each of the arms with point B1 matching B1 on the arms and working outwards to end at B2 on the front arm and B3 on the back arm.

Sew on the front feet to the legs from C to C1 and the back feet to the back legs from C2 to C3.

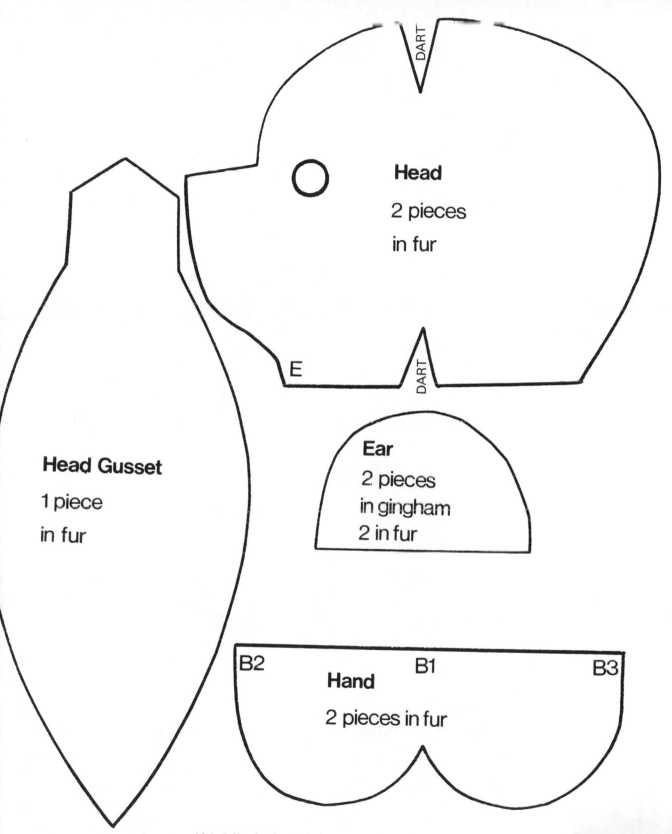

Head

2 pieces

in fur

DART

E

DART

Head Gusset

1 piece

in fur

Ear

2 pieces

in gingham

2 in fur

B2　　　　　　　　B1　　　　　　　　B3

Hand

2 pieces in fur

101 Minnie the little bear.

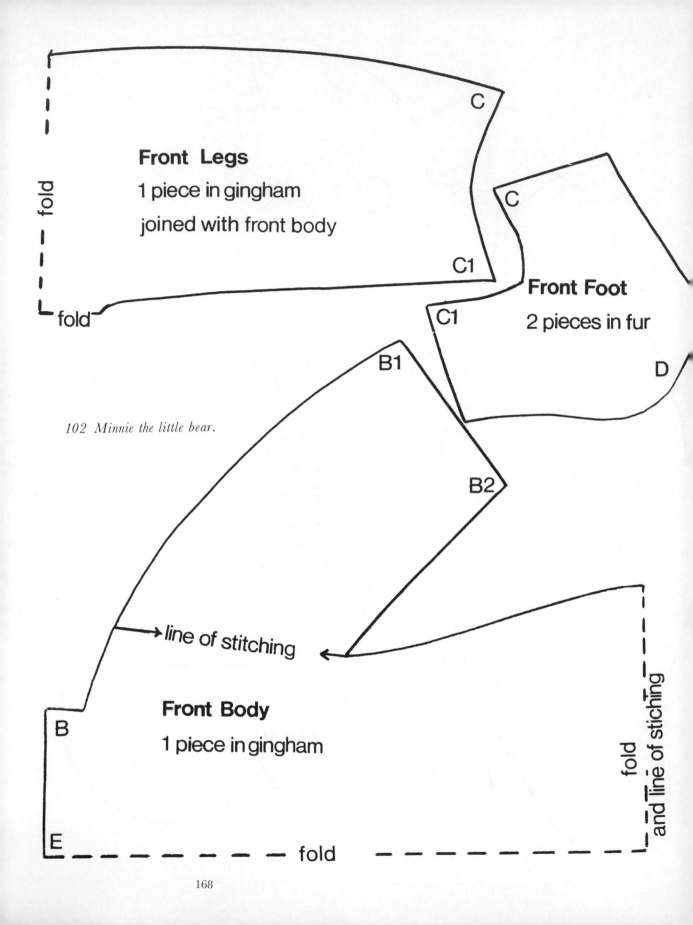

Front Legs

1 piece in gingham

joined with front body

fold

fold

C

C

C1

C1

Front Foot

2 pieces in fur

C1

D

B1

B2

102 Minnie the little bear.

→ line of stitching ←

Front Body

1 piece in gingham

B

E

fold

fold and line of stiching

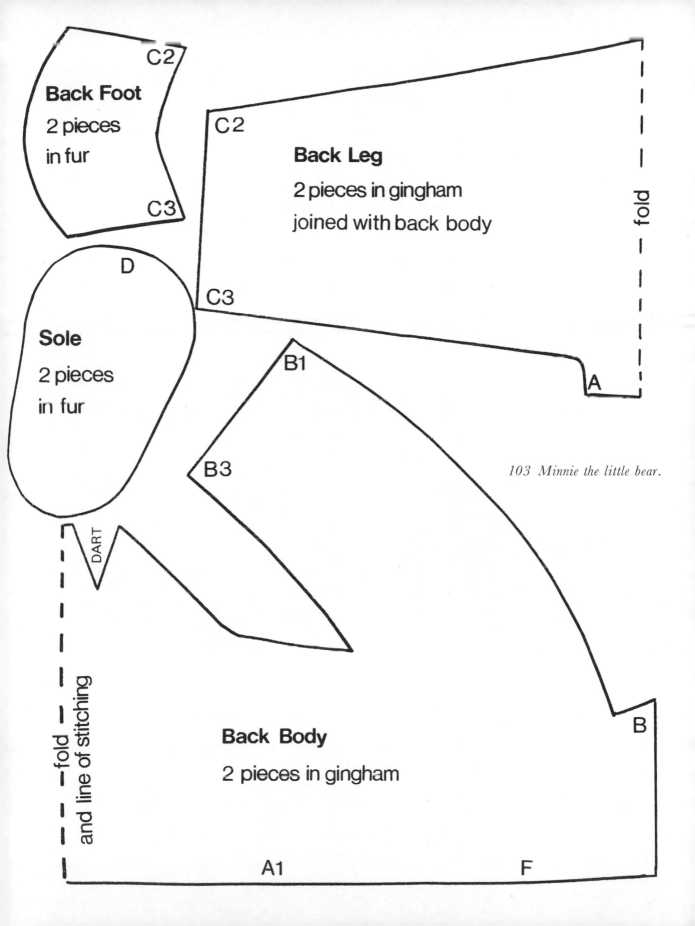

Back Foot

2 pieces

in fur

C2

C3

C2

Back Leg

2 pieces in gingham

joined with back body

C3

fold

A

D

Sole

2 pieces

in fur

B1

B3

103 Minnie the little bear.

DART

B

fold
and line of stitching

Back Body

2 pieces in gingham

A1

F

Then finish the sewing of the bodies by continuing round the hands, under the arms, along the body, and ending at the end of the front feet. Close along the edge of the inner feet and legs and insert soles matching the centre point of the soles to the front feet, marked D. Sew round.

Turn the head right side out and insert inside the body. Pin at the centre of the head E and match this point to E on the front body. Sew round. Close the back of the head and continue sewing on the back body to F.

Inspect work for any openings in the seams and repair these before turning the toy right side out.

As for stuffing follow instructions as given for Cookie, a floppy doll, on page 164. Close the stuffing opening with a neat ladder stitch.

Finishing is of course the most enjoyable part of toymaking and the character of Minnie can be changed into a boy or she can become a Panda or a little dog. This depends entirely on the type of head used and the imagination of the worker. The face is finished just like the face of the Teddy Bear, page 118.

The skirt is made in the same gingham as the rest of the body. To make the pattern for the skirt cut out a circle $8\frac{1}{2}''$ (21 cm) in diameter. Mark another circle in the centre of this which measures $2\frac{3}{4}''$ (7 cm) in diameter. Cut out the inner circle and a slit of about $1\frac{1}{4}''$ (3 cm) long running from the centre circle towards the edge of the outer circle. The outer circle is the hem line of the skirt, and the smaller one runs round the waist. Sew a row of bias binding round the hem of the skirt picking a colour in contrast to the gingham skirt. Cut out a rectangular piece of linen $2\frac{1}{2}'' \times 3\frac{1}{2}''$ (6 cm × 9 cm) to be used for the apron and gather it along one of the long edges. Sew on round the waist and then sew a row of white bias binding round the waist leaving extra length for tying the skirt on. To make the apron look pretty and girlish, finish it off by machining white lace round it and continue using the same lace for shoulder straps.

A ribbon tied into a bow under the chin and round the hands will add more colour to the toy.

BROCK THE BADGER

This toy is yet one more variation derived from the patterns originally designed for Minnie the little bear girl. By making up a head of a badger, and dressing the toy in a pair of trousers, collar and tie, Brock becomes a new character in the collection of soft toys. (Diagram 104.)

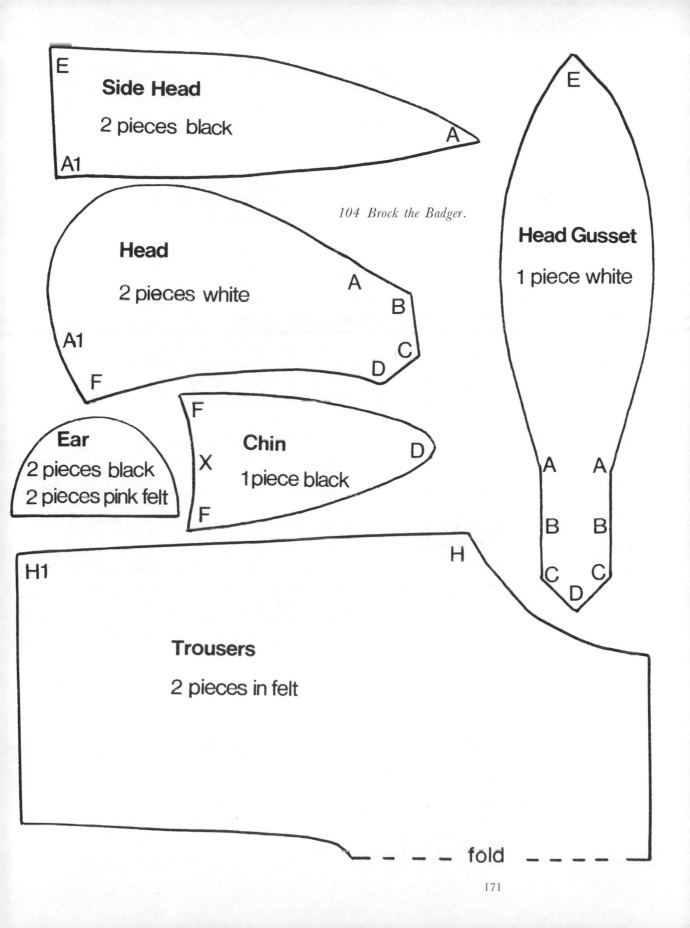

Side Head

2 pieces black

E

A1

A

104 Brock the Badger.

Head

2 pieces white

A1

F

A

B

C

D

Head Gusset

1 piece white

E

A   A

B   B

C   C

D

Ear

2 pieces black
2 pieces pink felt

Chin

1 piece black

F

X

F

D

Trousers

2 pieces in felt

H1

H

fold

171

Instructions for making

For making up the body follow instructions as given for Minnie on pages 166 and 170.

To assemble the head pin each black side of the head to each section of the head cut out in white fur fabric. Pin from A to A1 on the head and A to A1 on the side of the head. Machine along these lines. If necessary gather the head to fit into the side pieces.

Pick up the white fur head gusset and pin it to one part of the head, starting at A on both the gusset and the head and working in the same way to B/B and C/C. Pin along the curved edge of the black side head ending at E on the gusset and E on the side head. Machine along this line and repeat the same on the other part of the head. Then sew the tip of the gusset to the two sections of the head, matching D on the head gusset to D on the heads. Pin the black chin piece with point D on the chin corresponding to D on the head and F matching F on the head. Sew round from F on one side of the head to D and end at F on the other half of the head.

Insert the head into the body as described for Minnie the little bear girl on page 170. Make sure that point X on the chin falls in the centre of the neck on the body and that points F on the head correspond to the side seams.

Stuff and finish the toy in the same way as Minnie. No embroidered nose is necessary.

Machine the two parts of the trousers along the side seams from H to H1 and along the inner edge of the legs. If one uses felt for the trousers, it is always a good idea to match the colour of the felt to one of the colours in the motif of the body. This will contribute a touch of gaiety to the general appearance, a quality most essential in soft toys.

MR AND MRS DUCK

Both toys are made by using the same patterns. The only difference between them lies in the positioning of the wings, the type of the beak and the final finishing touches.

Mrs Duck has her wings pointing towards the tail and an open beak, and she wears a gay bonnet with ribbon bows down the front of her body, while Mr Duck has a collar and tie and a neat brown hat made in coarse linen.

Plate 23 A family of cuddly ducks ready for an outing. The father wears his best brown hat in coarse linen with a long feather and a special green-and-white cotton tie.

The mother has put on her best bonnet in white and royal blue glazed cotton, finished off with dainty white lace, while the daughter has a pink dress. This is made in pink-and-white gingham (very small check) with a nylon frill round the bottom of the body and round the neck and green bows.

With their yellow-and-orange felt beaks, large orange feet and cuddly white bodies, they will be accepted anywhere.

When finished the toys stand about 9½″ (24 cm) high and they take about three hours each to complete excluding the hat and the bonnet.

They first appeared in the magazine *The Lady* in one of the spring issues.

Materials required for each toy

7″ × 48″ (18 cm × 1 m 22 cm) white fur fabric
6½″ × 8″ (16 cm × 20 cm) orange felt
4½″ × 5″ (10 cm × 13 cm) yellow felt
2 buttons or glass eyes 13 mm in diameter
7 ozs cotton flock for stuffing

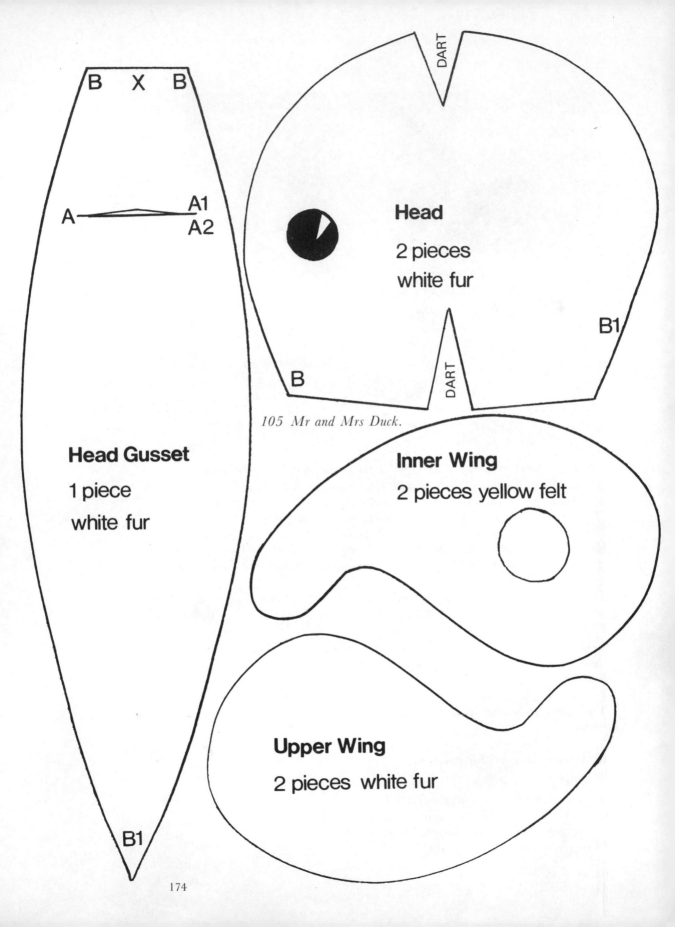

B X B

A — A1
A2

Head

2 pieces

white fur

B1

B

DART

DART

105 Mr and Mrs Duck.

Head Gusset

1 piece

white fur

Inner Wing

2 pieces yellow felt

Upper Wing

2 pieces white fur

B1

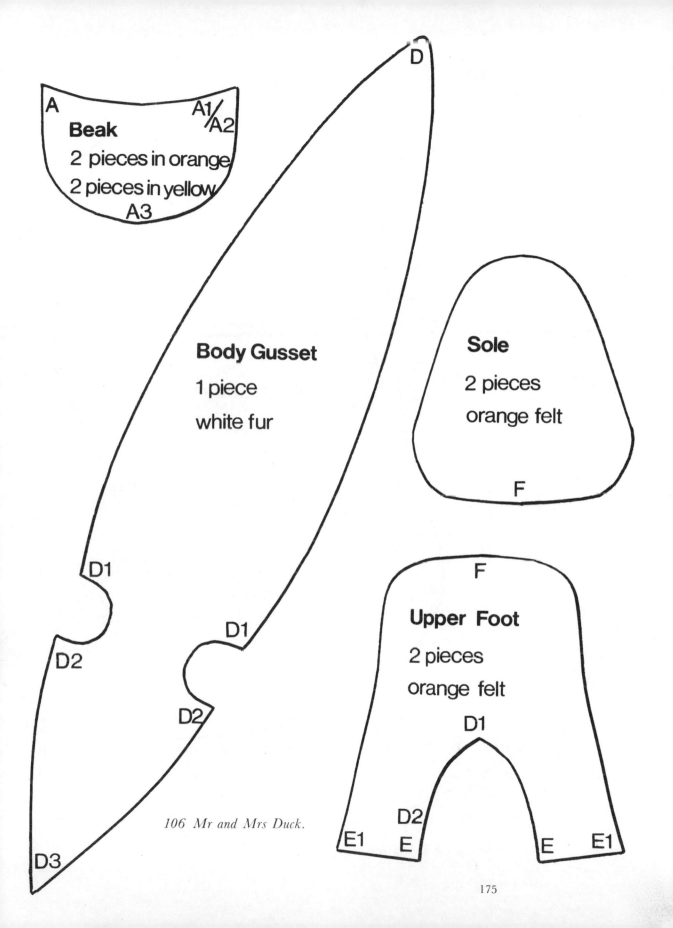

Beak

2 pieces in orange

2 pieces in yellow

A   A1
     A2

A3

D

Body Gusset

1 piece

white fur

D1

D1

D2

D2

106 Mr and Mrs Duck.

D3

Sole

2 pieces

orange felt

F

F

Upper Foot

2 pieces

orange felt

D1

D2

E1   E   E   E1

175

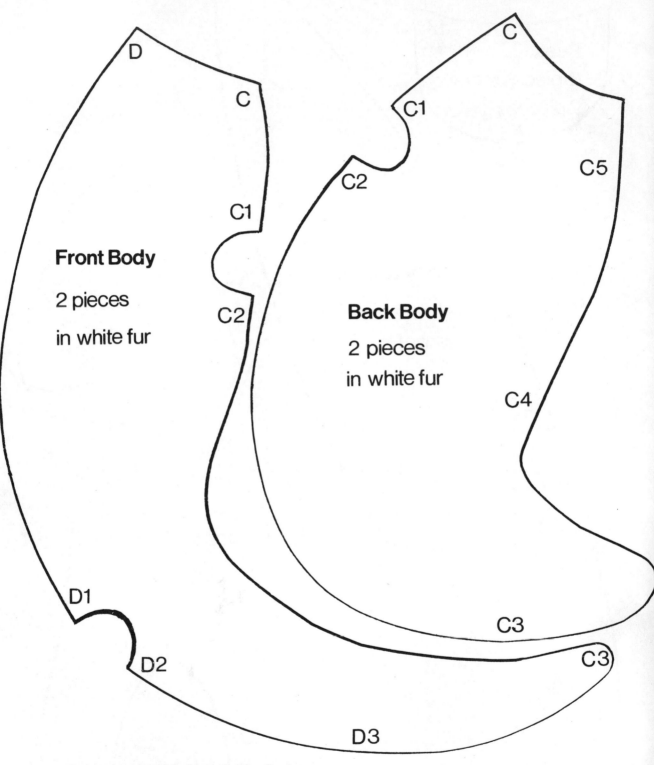

Front Body

2 pieces

in white fur

Back Body

2 pieces

in white fur

107 Mr and Mrs Duck.

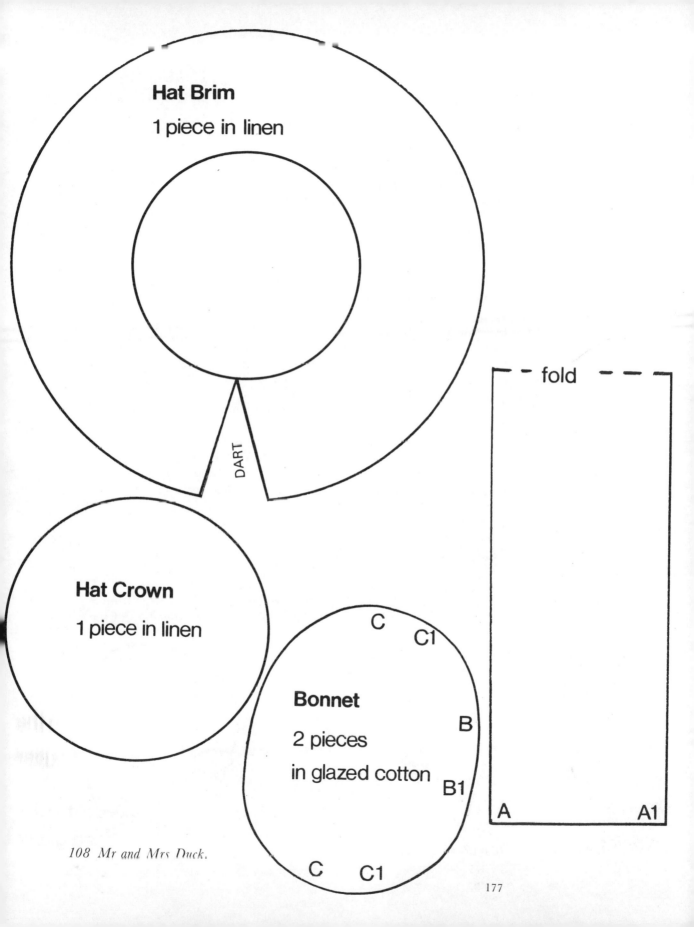

Hat Brim

1 piece in linen

DART

Hat Crown

1 piece in linen

Bonnet

2 pieces

in glazed cotton

C

C1

B

B1

C

C1

fold

A

A1

108 Mr and Mrs Duck.

Instructions for making

To trace and cut out the patterns follow instructions as given on page 21. There should be ten pieces of patterns for body and four for hat and bonnet. Lay these on the wrong side of the chosen fabric, mark round and cut out. There should be ten pieces in white fur fabric, six pieces in orange felt and two pieces in yellow felt for the lining of the wings. (Diagrams 105, 106, 107 and 108.)

For an open beak, remember to cut out two extra pieces in yellow felt for the inside of the beak.

Sew throughout on the wrong side of fabric. Turnings of $\frac{1}{4}''$ (0·5 cm) are allowed for in the patterns.

Before assembling the head, sew the darts in each section of the head. Then cut out a slit for the beak which is marked on the head gusset A to A1/A2. Sew one part of the beak to the slot starting from A to A1 and the other part from A to A2. To enhance the appearance of the duck, insert a strip of black felt between the two sections of the beak and then sew along the line A to A3 and finish at point A1/A2.

Next fit the head gusset to one side of the head from B going round the curve of the head and end at B1. Repeat on the other half of the head. Leave the back of the head open from point B1.

To make up the open beak work as follows.

Take up one yellow felt beak and lay it on to one of the orange felt beaks and machine round some $\frac{1}{8}''$ (3 mm) from the edge starting at A going round to A3 and finishing at A2. Turn the work inside out and machine again round the curved edge from A along A3 to A1. Work in the same way for the other half of the

head gusset

head

slit in the head gusset marked A to A1/A2

black felt piping

109 Closed and open beak for the duck.

slit in the head gusset

beak and when the two halves are completed lay them, one over the other, yellow sides together, and fit them into the slot in the head gusset marked A to A1/A2. Bring the raw edges of the beak to the inside of the gusset and machine along the slit, catching together the fur fabric of the gusset and the two halves of the beak. Diagram 109 shows clearly an open and a closed beak.

Put head aside and begin to work on the body.

Join each of the front to each of the back body pieces by machining from C to C1 and from C2 to C3. Lay yellow felt wings on the right side of the body with the hole in the inner wings fitting the hole in the body. For Mr Duck arrange the wings so that they point forward and for Mrs Duck point them towards the back. Sew round the hole. Pull each wing through the hole, flatten it and pin to it a fur upper wing with the pile facing in. Machine round, then remove pins and work in the same way on the other wing. Pin the body gusset to one section of the body from D to D1 and from D2 to D3 and machine. Remove pins and repeat the same on the other half of the body continuing the sewing to point C3, and further on up the back of the body to end at C4.

Pick up the upper feet and sew each of the pieces from E to E1 and then fit them into the holes in the body matching D1 and D2 on the body to D1 and D2 on the upper feet. Sew round. Pin the soles with the centre of the soles F corresponding to F on the upper feet. Machine round. Make sure that the feet point forward.

Place the head, which is inside out, into the body which is also inside out, so that point D on the front body matches point X on the head gusset, and sew from here all the way round.

So far you have been working with the right side of the fabric facing in, so now turn the work inside out through the gap between C4 and C5. Examine for any openings in your sewing and remedy these before starting to stuff. This is most important as if the sewing is too close to the edge of the fabric, the seams are likely to burst open when stuffing.

Cut two pieces of card for the soles, $\frac{1}{4}''$ (0·5 cm) smaller than the sole pattern, and very carefully insert these into the feet by bending them slightly.

Stuffing instructions are given in full on page 23.

This toy should feel light and firm, but above all cuddly, so be careful not to over-stuff which would make it too solid and hard. The wings are not stuffed. Stuffing completed, close the gap between C4 and C5 with a ladder stitch. Remove any pile caught in the seams while sewing and brush well.

Finishing. Pin the eyes to the head mounting them on felt discs. Use either black or dark blue felt for the discs. The approximate position for the eyes is marked on the head pattern. Insert the eyes as described on page 29 but work from the neck.

Finally make up a hat for Mr Duck and a bonnet for Mrs Duck. Patterns for both are featured in Diagram 108.

The hat. Cut out the brim and sew the dart. Then machine round the brim a row of bias binding to prevent it from fraying. To make the crown, first join the rectangular piece of linen from A to A1 and then fit it round the disc of the crown and sew into place. Pin the completed crown into the hole in the brim and machine round.

The bonnet consists of two pieces in glazed cotton. Lay one part on top of the other with the right sides of fabric facing in. Sew round leaving a gap between B to B1. Turn right side out, and pin round a row of nylon lace. Machine round closing the gap between B and B1 and remove pins. Sew two pieces of ribbon as marked on the pattern C to C1. Place the bonnet on the head and tie the ribbon into a bow under the beak.

Decorate the body by giving Mr Duck a collar and colourful tie and a few ribbon bows for Mrs Duck.

DONALDA

This is yet another example how by using basically the same patterns one can make a toy different in character and appearance.

Donalda has arms and hands instead of wings and is made in gingham (Diagram 110.)

Materials

9″ × 36″ (23 cm × 91 cm) pink gingham
9″ × 9″ (23 cm × 23 cm) pink felt
15″ × 9″ (38 cm × 23 cm) white nylon fur fabric
3½″ × 3½″ (9 cm × 9 cm) white felt for the lining of the beak
27″ (30 cm) white nylon frilling
18″ (46 cm) ribbon
1 pair of eyes 13 mm in diameter
7 ozs of cotton flock for stuffing

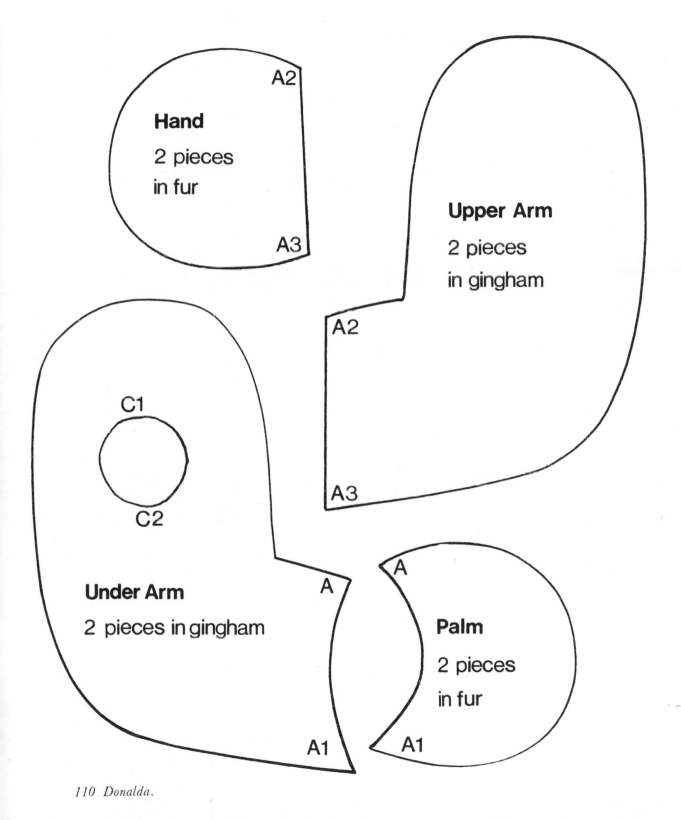

Hand

2 pieces

in fur

A2

A3

Upper Arm

2 pieces

in gingham

A2

A3

C1

C2

A

Under Arm

2 pieces in gingham

A1

A

Palm

2 pieces

in fur

A1

110 Donalda.

Instructions for making

Work in the same way as for Mrs Duck. But instead of using wings, sew on a pair of arms in gingham fabric with white fur hands attached. First machine the palms to the under arms from A to A1 and the hands to the upper arms from A2 to A3.

Fit the under arms into the holes in the body sections from C1 to C2, marked on the body and the arm patterns. Sew round and pull them through the hole. Lay the upper arms on to the under arms with the pile of palms and hands facing in, pin in place and sew. Remove pins.

Since Donalda is made in gingham, there is little she needs in the way of dressing up. It is sufficient to sew a row of nylon frilling round the body and another row round the neck. Finish with a large bow under the beak and one above the tail.

5 Animals from a zoo

The first visit to a zoo is a great event in the life of a child and although at the beginning some youngsters are a bit apprehensive, they soon learn to enjoy themselves there. They cannot resist the baby elephant or the whole atmosphere of the zoo.

It is interesting to note that zoos have existed in the form of collections of wild animals for a very long time. The ancient Egyptians had such collections, and a menagerie was attached to the Court of one of the Chinese Emperors as long ago as 1000 B.C. It was known that kings kept their own menageries, and there was one kept in the Tower of London for royal use from the thirteenth to the nineteenth centuries.

The scientific interest in collections of wild animals was inspired by a French naturalist, Buffon, who re-organised the royal menagerie at Versailles on a scientific basis. This collection was, however, destroyed during the French Revolution. But, later on, Buffon's ideas were taken up by the English when, in 1826, the Zoological Society of London was founded, with the London Zoo opening to the public in 1828. A year later a charter was granted to the Society by King George IV in which the aims of the Society were described as "the advancement of the Animal Kingdom". In spite of their scientific value and importance, zoos are places of entertainment for both children and adults.

From the large selection of animals in a Zoo, I have chosen to make an elephant, a camel and a giraffe. An elephant is always dear to a child—somehow its bulk gives an impression of good humour and helplessness. A giraffe with a long neck, tiny face and good-natured eyes hiding behind long eyelashes is also appealing, and for personal reasons I could not resist making up a camel. I have seen camels in the desert as working farm animals, as leaders of caravans and as carriers of exceedingly heavy loads, but whatever man asked them to do, they never lost their dignity and the expression of superiority on their haughty faces. Young camels, like most young creatures, are particularly enchanting with their large pink noses and soft, pinkish hooves, and I would love to have kept one of them as a pet.

ELEPHANT

The elephant is made in grey moquette, but can look equally good in grey felt. The approximate time required for making this toy should be about four hours. The height of the elephant when

Plate 24 *A piece of grey moquette left over from making a large horse came in useful for this elephant.*

finished is about $9\frac{1}{2}''$ (24 cm) and the span from the end of the trunk to the tail about $11\frac{1}{2}''$ (29 cm).

Materials

$12'' \times 36''$ (30 cm $\times$ 91 cm) grey felt
alternatively $10'' \times 54''$ (25 cm $\times$ 1 m 37 cm) grey moquette
$9'' \times 9''$ (23 cm $\times$ 23 cm) pink felt
13 mm brown glass eyes or buttons
10 ozs cotton flock

Instructions for making

Tracing and cutting out of patterns is given on page 21.

The body with the trunk attached is marked in Diagrams 111 and 112. Make sure that when traced, these three parts make up one body piece. This applies also to the body gusset, drawn in two sections in Diagram 113 but should be traced as one piece. No turnings to be added to places marked fold.

A total set of patterns for the elephant consists of twelve separate pieces. Mark each pattern with the information and letters given on the original piece. Working in moquette, mark the patterns on the wrong side of the fabric and make sure that you have the left and the right side of the body, the under front and under back legs and the ears. Cut out. There should be eleven pieces in grey, eight in pink felt and four in white felt.

Work on the wrong side of the fabric throughout.

Start sewing by closing the two darts on the trunk, on both sides of the body. Then join the two halves of the body from point A on the forehead to the end of the trunk A1. Match A on the body to A on the head gusset and sew along this curved line to point B on the head gusset. Repeat the same on the other half of the body. Next join the mouth, in pink felt, to the trunk along the line C/C and sew. Pin the mouth to the body gusset on the line D/D and sew. Close the two darts in the body gusset. Join the two under back legs to the body gusset from E to E1 and the two under front legs from F to F1.

Take the whole underpart and fit it between the two sides of the body. Start pinning, and working from the end of the trunk at G, pin along to match point C on the body to C on the trunk/mouth joint, continue to D, along D1 on to D2. Make sure that point F1 on the gusset corresponds to point F1 on the body. Sew along this line. Repeat the same on the other half of the body.

Proceed to work on the legs. Starting at F1, pin along the front edge of the front leg to F2 and sew. Pin from F3 on the body and

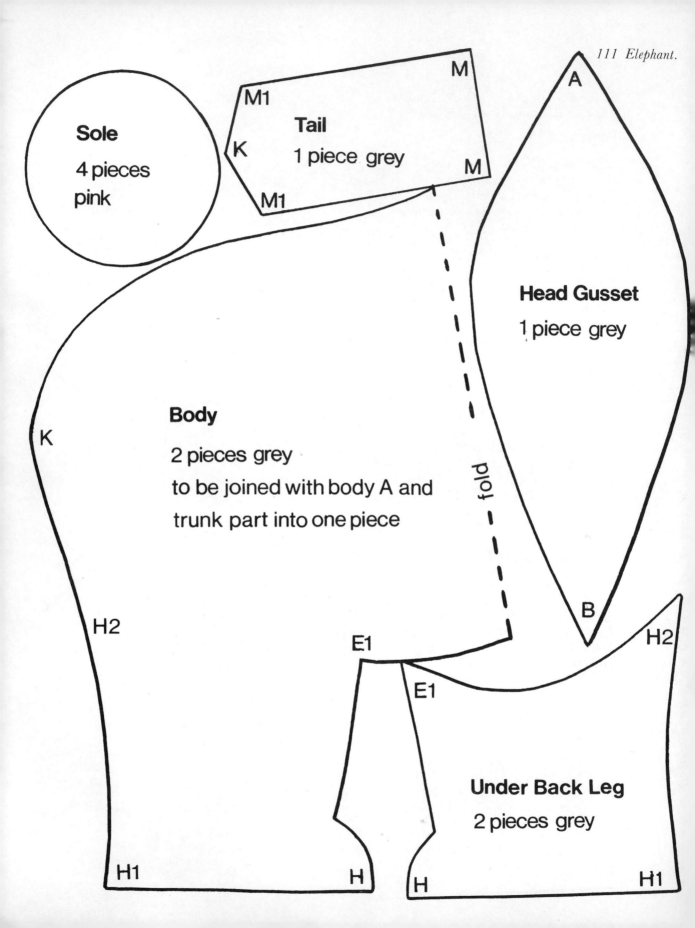

Sole

4 pieces
pink

Tail

1 piece grey

M1

M

K

M1

M

M

A

Head Gusset

1 piece grey

Body

2 pieces grey

to be joined with body A and

trunk part into one piece

K

fold

H2

E1

E1

B

H2

Under Back Leg

2 pieces grey

H1

H

H

H1

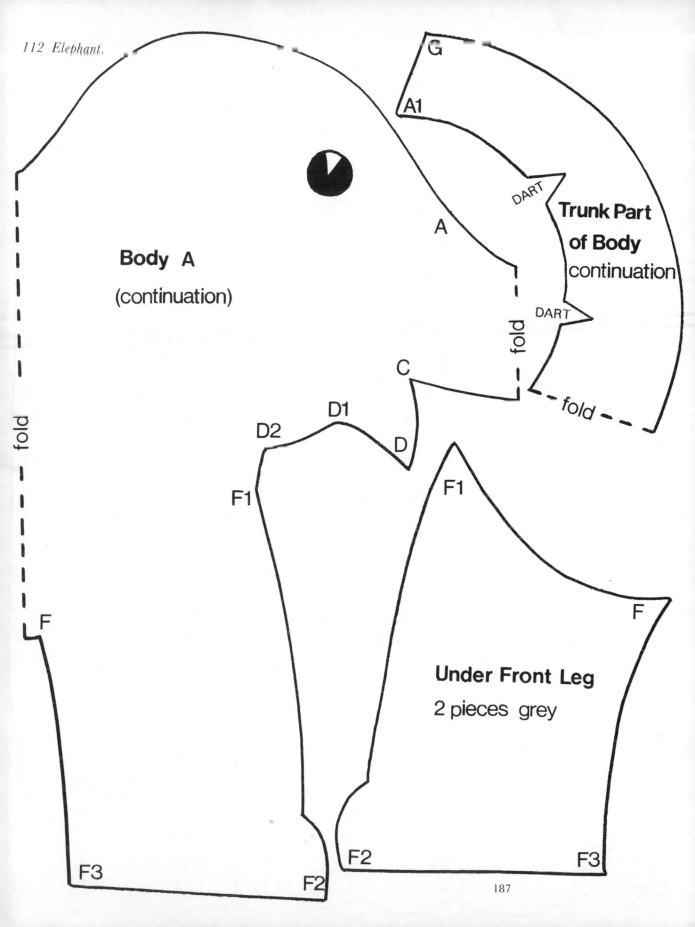

Body A

(continuation)

fold

G

A1

DART

DART

A

Trunk Part
of Body
continuation

fold

fold

C

D1

D2

D

F1

F1

fold

F

Under Front Leg

2 pieces grey

F

F3

F2

F2

F3

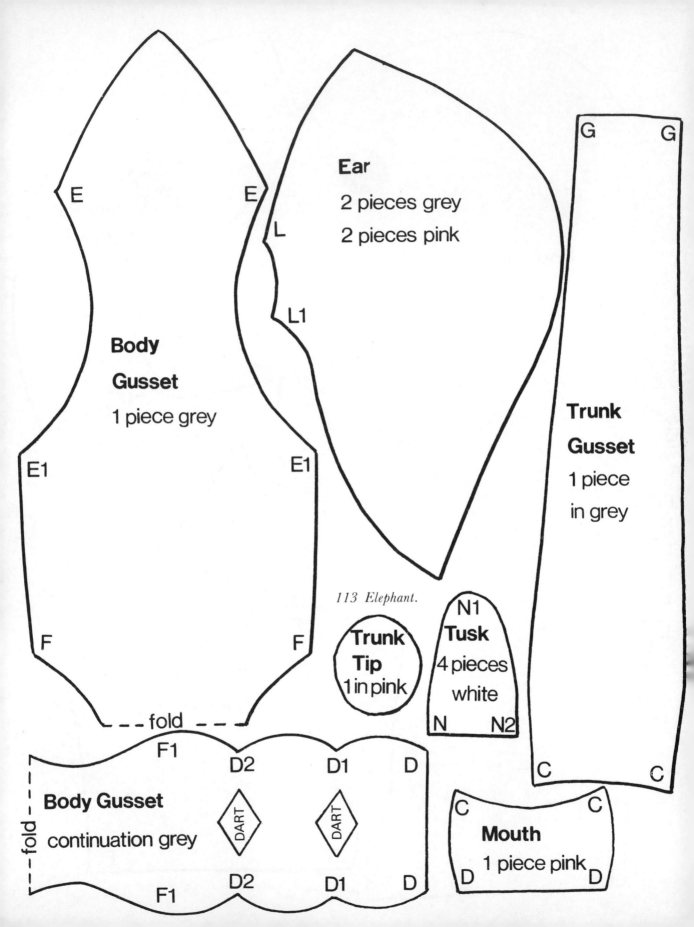

Body

Gusset

1 piece grey

E

E

E1

E1

F

F

Ear

2 pieces grey

2 pieces pink

L

L1

G   G

Trunk

Gusset

1 piece

in grey

113 Elephant.

Trunk

Tip

1 in pink

N1

Tusk

4 pieces

white

N   N2

- - - fold - - -

F1

D2   D1   D

fold

Body Gusset

continuation grey

DART

DART

F1   D2   D1   D

C   C

C   C

Mouth

1 piece pink

D   D

on the under front leg and work to F on the leg and the body, along to E1 and ending at H. Sew and repeat on the other half. To finish the back legs, pin from H1 to H2 and sew, repeating the same on the other back leg but continue the seam to point K.

Fit in and sew into place the pink felt soles and the small disc at the tip of the trunk. Inspect for any unwanted openings in the seams and then turn the work right side out through the gap K to B.

Start stuffing with small amounts of cotton flock from the end of the trunk, packing the stuffing well and working towards the head. Stuff the mouth, making sure that it is stuffed to shape and then work on the rest of the head from the forehead towards the neck.

Next fill the legs very carefully with small amounts of cotton flock, packing the filling very firmly but avoiding lumps. Then continue stuffing the rest of the body working from the neck towards the waist. Holding the toy in the waist turn to the back of it and stuff the back part before finishing the centre.

When the elephant looks well stuffed, close the gap K to B, adding small bits of cotton flock while sewing the opening with a ladder stitch. Start finishing.

Make up the ears by sewing the pink inner ears to the grey outer ears and turn right side out through the gap L to L1. Flatten the ears and make sure that they are sewn to shape. Sew the tail along the line M to M1 and turn right side out. Insert a bit of fur fabric or trimming at the end of the tail at M/M before closing the opening. Sew the pair of white tusks working on each from N to N1 and ending at N2. Turn right side out and stuff very firmly. With all the parts ready start working on the eyes.

Use large glass eyes mounted on royal blue discs, slightly larger than the eye. Work in the same way if buttons are substituted for glass eyes. Find the position of the eyes, as only approximate places are marked on the pattern. When satisfied with the expression, mark the positions on the head and delicately work round the marks with blue or brown eye shadow. Work from the eye towards the forehead. Insert the eyes as described on page 28.

Then pin the ears, again experimenting with the placing and when the right position is found, sew them on by turning the raw edges at L/L1. Pin the tusks facing outwards alongside the trunk and on the edge of the mouth and turn the raw edges in and sew very firmly into place. Pin the tail to the back body with the base of the tail point K matching K on the body. Sew the tail firmly to the body for about $\frac{1}{2}$" (1 cm), leaving the rest hanging loose.

CAMEL

This camel is made in camel-coloured felt with a slightly darker fur neck, a fringe between the ears and a beard. When finished the camel stands about $12\frac{1}{2}''$ (32 cm) high and is about $11''$ (28 cm) long. It will take about five hours to make.

Plate 25 A camel is an animal of the desert. His sandy body makes him blend with the surrounding countryside of his habitat. This camel is made in felt with fur neck, hump and fringe matching the body in tone.

Materials

9″ × 36″ (23 cm × 91 cm) felt
$3\frac{1}{2}$″ × 4″ (9 cm × 10 cm) brown felt
4″ × 18″ (10 cm × 45 cm) nylon fur fabric
13 mm glass eyes
9 ozs cotton flock for stuffing

Instructions for making

Work on the tracing and cutting out of patterns as for the previous toys. The body pattern is in one piece including the hump as described in Diagrams 114 and 115. After cutting out there should be fourteen pieces of pattern.

Lay the patterns on the felt and mark round. If you use fur fabric for the entire toy, then mark the patterns on the wrong side of the fabric and make sure that there are left and right parts for the body, the neck, the head and the back and front under legs. Cut out.

There should be thirteen pieces in camel-coloured felt, four soles in dark felt and six parts in fur fabric.

Work on the wrong side of the fabric throughout the sewing of this toy. Start with one side of the body by joining on the neck part from A to A1. Then sew the corresponding side of the head to the neck easing in the head between B to B1. Repeat the same on the other half. Join the two bodies at the neck from C to A1 and from C1 on the nose to B. Take the head gusset and pin it to the head beginning at C1 working along to C2, continuing past point C3 to B1 finishing at C on the head gusset and on the neck. Repeat the same on the other part of the head and sew the gusset round. Put work aside and take up the under legs.

Sew the darts on all four under legs. Pin the two under back legs to the body gusset along the curve D to D1 and the two under front legs along E to E1. Sew the four under legs into place. Ease in the neck gusset to the body gusset from F to F1 and sew. Put the work aside.

Fit in and sew the hump gusset to <u>one side</u> of the body with the pile facing in. Now pin the whole of the body gusset and the neck gusset with the under legs attached to the body, starting at the neck with the pile of the fur and seams facing in. Match B on the neck to B on the neck gusset. Pin along the curve of the neck to A and some $\frac{1}{2}$″ (1 cm) below this to F1 on the neck gusset, continuing along the edge of the front leg to G and over the foot to G1. Repeat the pinning on the other side of the body and sew

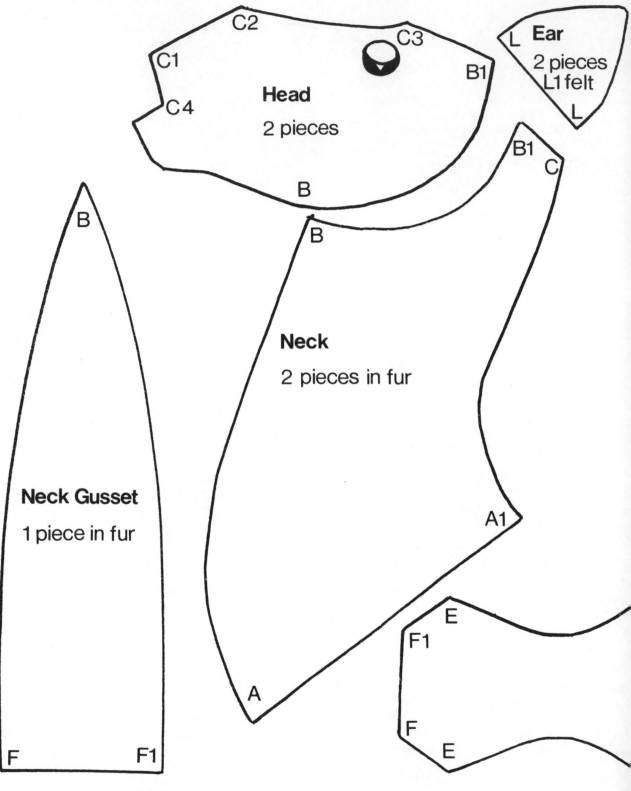

Ear
2 pieces
L1 felt

Head
2 pieces

Neck
2 pieces in fur

Neck Gusset
1 piece in fur

114 Camel.

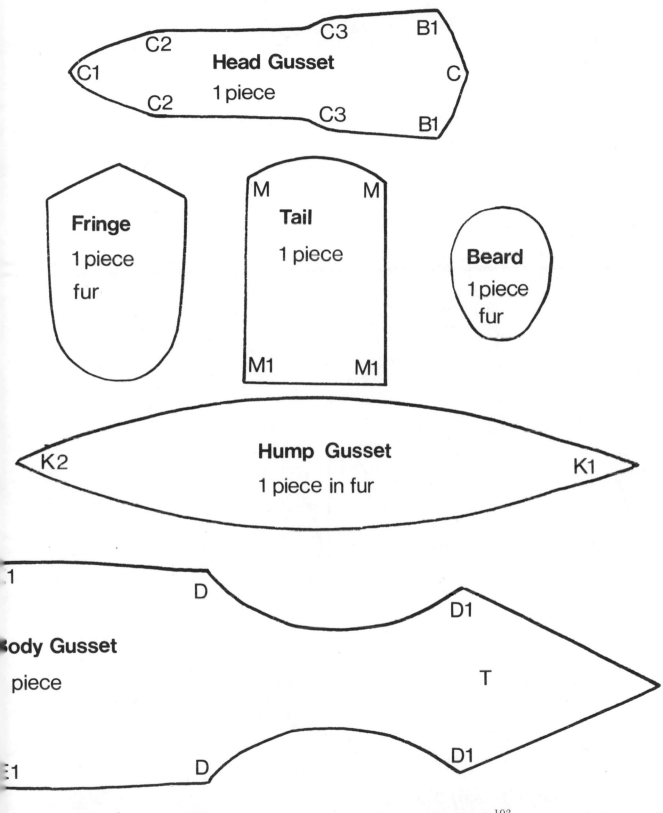

Head Gusset

1 piece

C1 C2 C3 B1 C C2 C3 B1

Fringe

1 piece

fur

Tail

1 piece

M M M1 M1

Beard

1 piece

fur

Hump Gusset

1 piece in fur

K2 K1

Body Gusset

piece

D D1 T D1 D

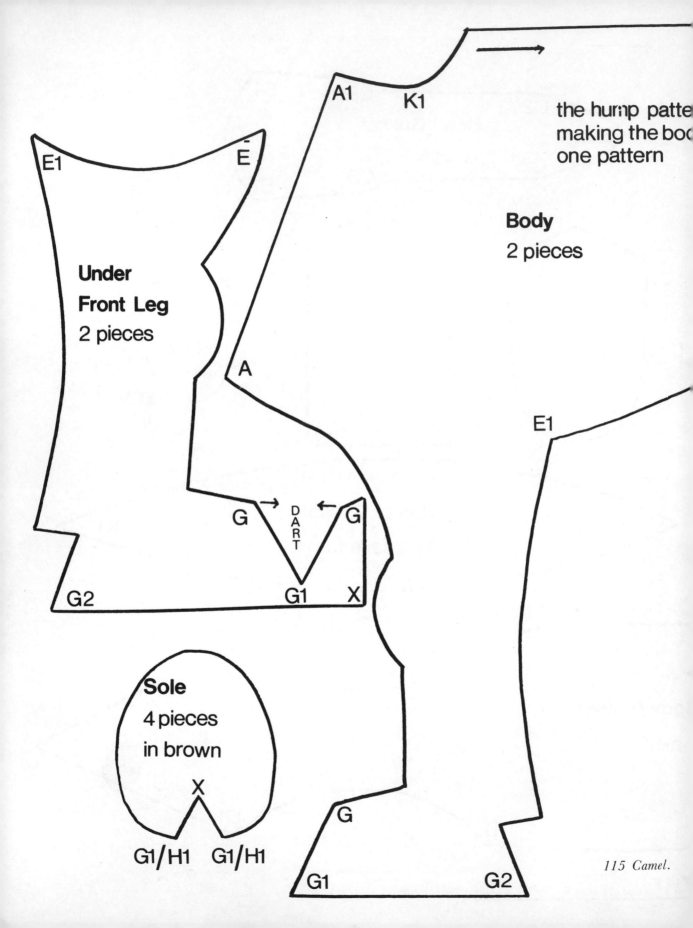

A1 K1

the hump patter
making the bod
one pattern

Body
2 pieces

E1   E

**Under
Front Leg**
2 pieces

A

G   → D   ← G
            A
            R
            T

G2   G1   X

E1

Sole

4 pieces

in brown

X

G1/H1   G1/H1

G

G1   G2

115 Camel.

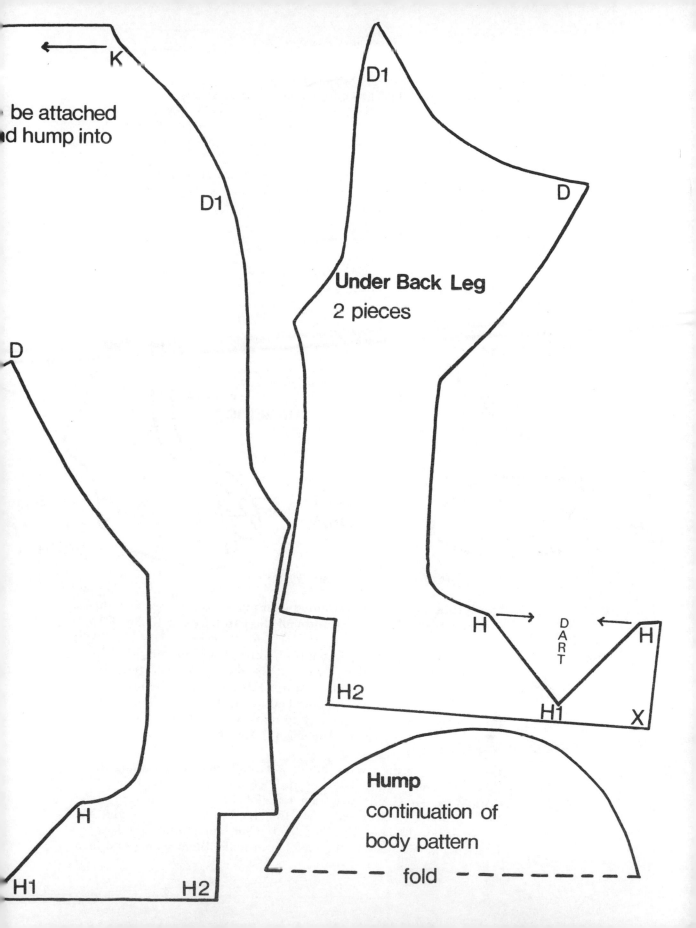

K

be attached
d hump into

D1

D

H

H1   H2

D1

D

Under Back Leg
2 pieces

H

D
A
R
T

H

H2

H1   X

Hump
continuation of
body pattern
— — — fold — — —

the two seams. Then fit and pin the under front leg from G2 to
E going along the body and the body gusset to D, down the front
edge of the back leg to H, over the foot to end at H1. Repeat the
same on the other half of the body and sew along these lines.

To close the back legs, pin and then sew from H2 up the back of
the back leg finishing at D1. Work in the same way on the other
back leg but continue the seam from D1 to K.

Close the seam from point A1 to K1 on the body and neck to K.

Fit the soles starting on the front leg at G1, working to X on the
sole and X on part of the toe, sewing right round to end at G1 on
the other toe. Repeat the same work on the other three feet,
Diagram 116.

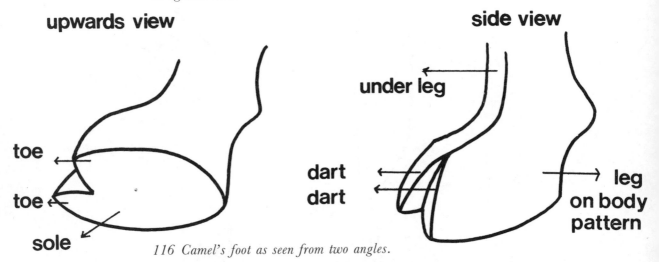

upwards view

side view

under leg

toe

dart
dart

toe

leg
on body
pattern

sole

116 Camel's foot as seen from two angles.

Inspect the toy for any unwanted openings in the seams, and then
turn the work right side up through the gap between K and K1.

Start stuffing with small amounts of cotton flock, shaping the chin
and then the nose, making sure that the nose slopes and that the
chin protrudes forward to form a lip. Fill the rest of the head,
giving the camel slightly bulging cheeks but be careful not to stuff
the head too hard and therefore to make it too round. A camel's
head is narrow (except for the cheeks) and oblong.

Fill the neck to the end of the fur part and then start stuffing the
legs. Push small amounts of cotton flock into the toes to form
distinct gaps in the hoof characteristic of the camel, Diagram 116.
While stuffing the feet make sure that the line between G1 and X,
the centre of the hoof is pushed back. Continue stuffing the legs
to shape, particularly at the knees, and make them strong and firm.

On reaching the body go on stuffing from the neck to the beginning of the hump, filling the neck well to shape.

Holding at the waist, fill the back part of the toy, starting from the toes and continuing into the feet and the legs towards the haunches and the centre of the body. Stuff the legs very firmly but avoid lumps. When the toy feels firm to the touch, stands well and is a good shape, close the stuffing opening with a ladder stitch and if necessary keep on adding small amounts of cotton flock whilst sewing.

Although the camel is very easy to sew, great care must be taken in stuffing, as stuffing to shape will enhance its appearance and make it look like a real camel. The strength of this toy would be improved by inserting a wire frame as described on page 50 and in Diagrams 25 and 26.

To finish, work in the nose and mouth with black embroidery cotton starting at point C2, the approximate position for the nostrils, and work to C2 on the other side. Catch the long stitch in the centre, C1 and bring down in a V shape to C4, then work the mouth.

Eyes are set well back on a camel's face. Use glass eyes with eyelids and eyelashes as shown in Diagram 35 and described on page 61. Insert them using the method discussed on page 28.

The ears are small and are made of single pieces of felt without a lining. Bring both points, marked L to the centre L1 and sew the ears on to the head, employing strong cotton and sewing them on very firmly. Finally cut out a fur fabric fringe and beard and pin these into their respective places. When satisfied with the position, turn the raw edges in and sew firmly into place.

Sew the tail from M to M1, turn right side out and flatten it. Add some fur fabric at the M1/M1 end and close the opening. Place the tail on the body gusset at a point marked T on the gusset and sew firmly into place, leaving about half of the tail hanging loose.

Remove any pile caught in the seams and brush. Using dark brown eye shadow work round the feet to give the impression of hooves.

GIRAFFE

The giraffe in this book is easy to make but like the camel it must be properly stuffed. The strength of this toy would be improved by inserting a wire frame as described on page 50 and in Diagrams 25 and 26.

It is made in golden yellow felt with dark brown patches and a black fur mane. The height of the toy when finished is about $16\frac{1}{2}''$ (40 cm) and the length about $7''$ (18 cm), and should take about five hours to make.

Plate 26 A giraffe's face is one of her most charming features. With long eyelashes, an inquisitive look, slightly smiling mouth, she is a very attractive creature. The small horns are made of rolls of felt.

Materials

12″ × 36″ (30 cm × 91 cm) golden yellow felt
3½″ × 2½″ (9″ cm × 6 cm) dark brown felt
8½″ × 1½″ (21 cm × 4 cm) black fur fabric or lampshade trimming for the mane
13 mm glass eyes
8 ozs cotton flock for stuffing

Instructions for making

Trace the patterns on to a thin card and transfer all the letters and information given on the original pieces (Diagram 117 and 118). The body and body gusset consist of one part and when tracing make sure to join them on the line marked "fold" on the pattern. No turnings for sewing to be added. The patterns when cut out comprise of eleven pieces in all. Lay the patterns on the doubled

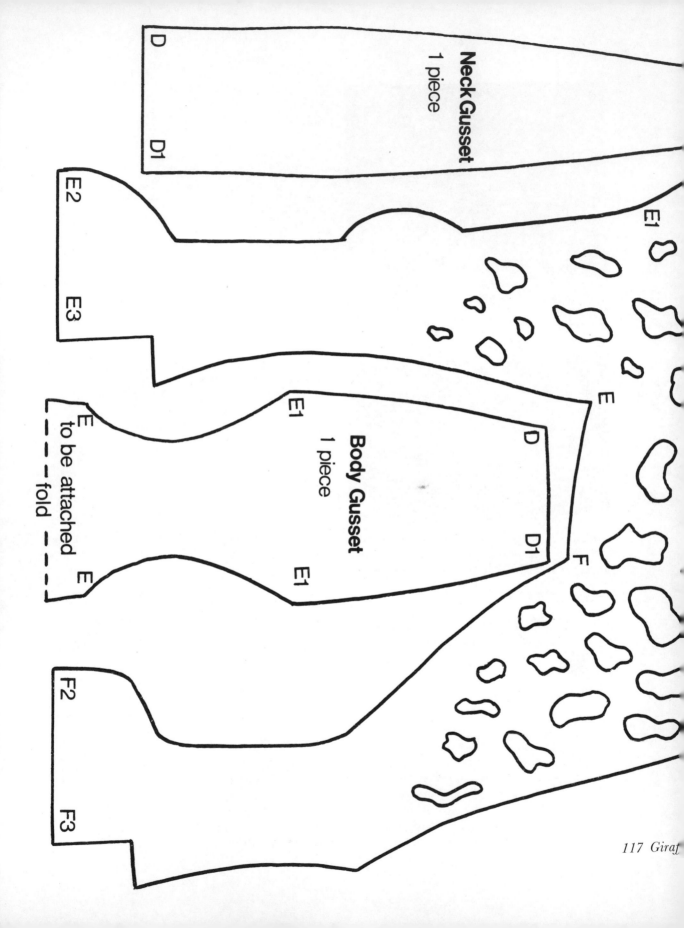

Neck Gusset
1 piece

D

D1

E2

E3

E1

E

Body Gusset
1 piece

E1

D

D1

E1

E1

E

F

E

to be attached

fold

E

F2

F3

117 Gira

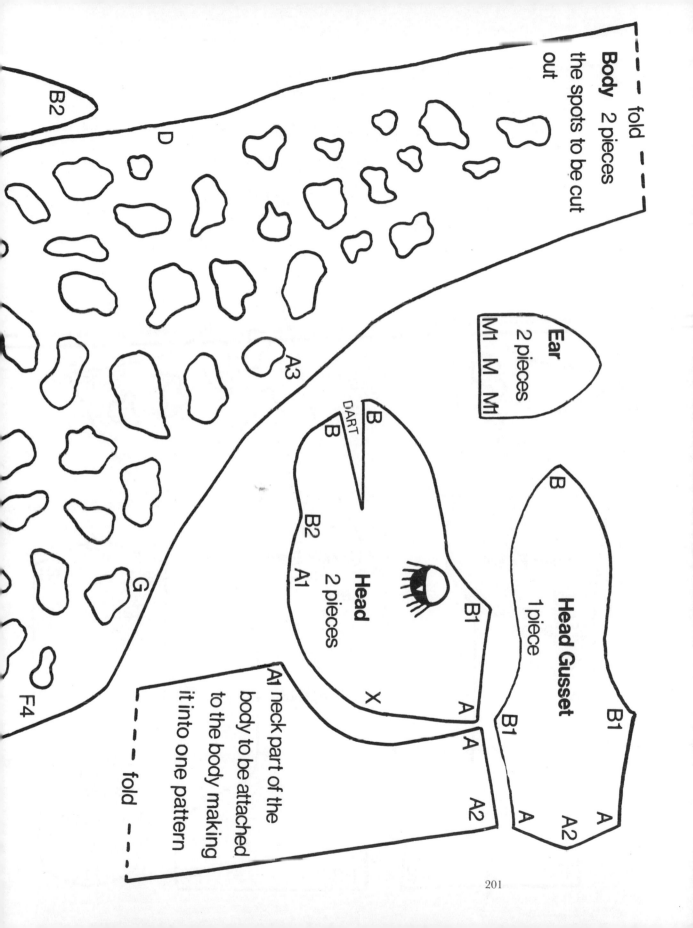

fold

Body 2 pieces
the spots to be cut
out

B2

D

A3

Ear
2 pieces

M1 M M1

B
B
DART
B
B2
A1

Head
2 pieces

B1

X

A

A

A2

B

Head Gusset
1piece

B1

B1

A

A2

A

A2

G

F4

A1 neck part of the
body to be attached
to the body making
it into one pattern

fold

201

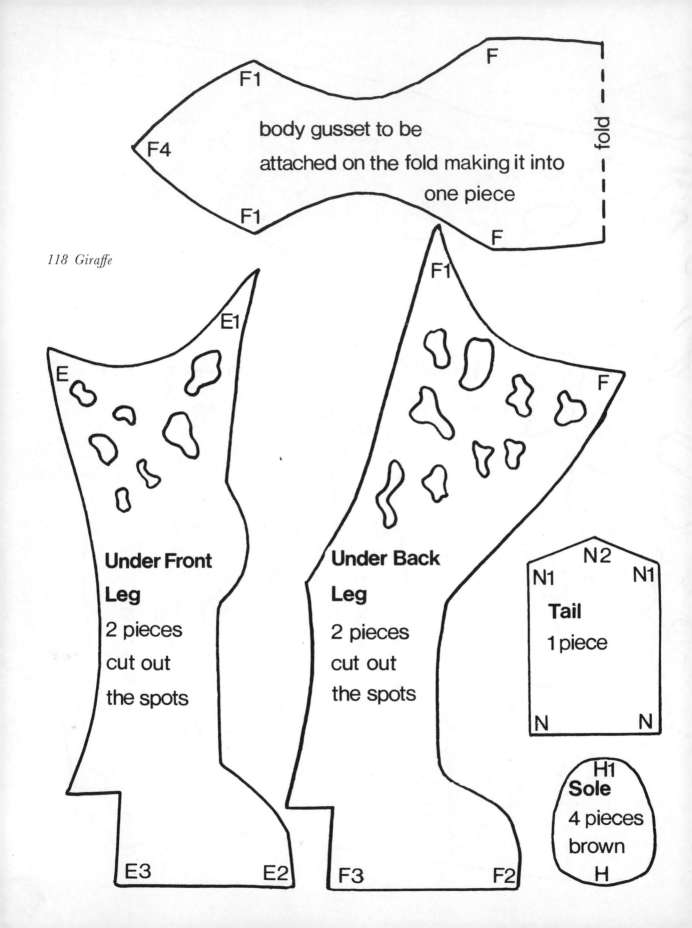

F1
F

body gusset to be
attached on the fold making it into
one piece

fold

F4

F1
F

118 *Giraffe*

F1

E1

E

F

**Under Front
Leg**
2 pieces
cut out
the spots

**Under Back
Leg**
2 pieces
cut out
the spots

N2
N1   N1
Tail
1 piece
N   N

E3   E2

F3   F2

H1
Sole
4 pieces
brown
H

piece of felt and mark round, bearing in mind that there are four single pieces, the neck gusset, head gusset, body gusset and tail. When working on a single thickness of felt make sure that there is a left and right side of the body, the head and the back and front under legs. There should be fourteen pieces in yellow felt, four soles in brown felt and a strip for the mane either in fur or some other trimming, such as a black fringe used in making lampshades.

Before sewing, paint the markings on the body sections. The best method is to cut out the body pattern again in card, and then transfer and cut round the markings as given in the original pattern. Lay the left and the right side of the body flat on a sheet of paper. To prevent the fabric from moving under the stencil pattern, secure it with weights. Use dark brown poster paint, without mixing it with water and dip the brush right into the pot of paint and apply the spots. Leave to dry.

Work throughout sewing on the wrong side of the fabric. Start sewing by closing the darts on each head piece then fit the head pieces into the neck. Begin by working on each part of the head separately and pinning it to the neck between A and X, with the remaining part of the head gathered to end at A1 on the head and the neck. Sew into place. Repeat the same on the other side.

Fold in half the mane with the black fur pile facing out.

Then close the neck from A2 to A3 inserting, at the same time, the mane with the pile facing in. Sew together the front parts of the head starting at the end of the dart at B and going to point B2. Pin the head gusset matching B on the gusset to B on the nose and work to B1, along to A and end at A2 on the head gusset and A2 at the back of the neck. Continue pinning on the other side of the head and then sew along this line. Put this part of the work aside and take up the body gusset.

Join the neck gusset to the body gusset from D to D1, if necessary ease the neck gusset to fit the body gusset. Pin and sew the under legs into place. Start with the front legs, sewing the under legs along the curve E to E1 and the back under legs from F to F1.

Take up the body and fit in and pin the body gusset with the neck gusset and the under front and back legs attached. Start at point B2 on the head and B2 on the gusset, work past A1 to D. Now go along the leading edge of the front leg to point E2 and sew along this line. Work in the same way on the other section of the body. Then fit and pin the under front leg from E3 to E, continuing on the body and on the gusset to F and down the leading edge of the back leg to F2. Sew along this line and repeat the same on the other half of the body.

To close the back part of the giraffe, begin by pinning the under back leg to the back leg at F3, end at the point of the gusset F4. Sew along this line and repeat the same on the other back leg but continue the sewing beyond point F4 to finish at G.

Insert the soles matching H on the soles to E2 on the front feet and H1 to E3. Sew the soles into place. On the back feet match points H on the soles to F2 on the feet and H1 to F3. Sew round.

Make sure that there are no openings in the sewing and turn the work right side out through the gap between G and A3.

Stuffing, as I have already mentioned, is most critical and important for this toy. Start with stuffing the nose with small amounts of cotton flock and working it in so that the nose protrudes forward above the lip. Continue stuffing the head, giving the giraffe good wide cheeks, as the head of this animal should be almost triangular. Fill the head and the neck to the end of the neck gusset, stuffing very firmly. Then fill the front feet, driving small amounts of cotton flock, to shape a well-modelled foot with a high instep. Work on the legs, stressing the knees till you reach the body. Go on stuffing the front part of the body till it feels firm and solid but is not lumpy. Holding the toy at the waist, fill the back feet, carefully shaping the instep and working up the legs to the haunches. Remove your hand and holding the toy by the chest fill the middle section. When satisfied with the shaping and the giraffe feels firm and stands well with an erect head and solid legs, start closing the stuffing opening with a ladder stitch and while doing so, keep on inserting small bits of cotton flock so that it does not sink in the saddle.

To finish, work in the mouth and the nostrils. The mouth consists of a strip of black felt $\frac{1}{8}''$ (3 mm) by $2\frac{1}{4}''$ (6 cm) long. Lay this piece along the line of the dart in the head and stick on first and then sew firmly into place with a stab stitch. The nostrils are made of two tiny discs in black felt about $\frac{1}{8}''$ (3 mm) diameter. Pin them on first and when in the right place, stick them on and sew in firmly.

Next work in the eyes using large glass eyes with yellow lids and lashes $\frac{5}{8}''$ (1 cm) long. To do this see instructions on page 61 and Diagram 35. Fit the eyes into the head as discussed on page 28 and Diagram 9.

The ears are made of single pieces of felt without linings. It is advisable to shade in the inner side of the ears with dark brown eye shadow to give them depth. Fold the two outside points marked M1 to meet in the centre of the ear at M and then pin them on to the head. When satisfied with the position sew into place.

The horns are made in yellow felt in two strips each 1″ (2·5 cm) long and ¾″ (2 cm) wide. Roll these strips up to give two cylinders ¾″ (2 cm) in height and sew them along the raw edge on the side so that they will not unroll. Pin the horns on the head in front of the ears, stick them on first and then sew round the base with a firm stab stitch, with the side seams facing at the back.

The tail is made of a piece of yellow felt. Sew along the line N to N1 and turn right side out. Insert black fur fabric or a bit of lampshade trimming at the N/N end of the tail and sew it firmly into place closing the opening at the same time. Pin the tail with the point N2 on the tail resting on F4 on the body gusset and sew very firmly into place leaving half of the tail hanging loose.

For the final touch, lightly rub brown eye shadow from the nostrils spreading it towards the horns and almost covering the head gusset. Also rub in eye shadow round the feet to give an impression of hooves.

6 Circus toys

Circuses, with their marvellous acts of skill and daring have always fascinated old and young alike. The circus has a long history and some of its many performers have earned as much fame as kings, politicians and warriors.

In England, it is believed that the "father of the circus" was Philip Astley who as long ago as 1768, took a bit of waste land in Lambeth, known as Halfpenny Hatch, now covered by Waterloo station, and there made his ring, surrounding it by covered seats for the public. He was an experienced soldier and an excellent horseman, an ex-Sergeant Major of His Majesty's Regiment of Light Dragoons, and he built up his circus around equestrian displays. Performing on his splendid charger Duke, he was admired by many Londoners, including King George III, who was an excellent horseman and therefore appreciated Astley's act. In spite of other establishments of this kind—one in Islington and the other in Mile End—Astley's circus was the most popular and soon he had to move to a larger site near Westminster Bridge to accommodate the audience. There he perfected his ring, the audience enclosure, and also his act. What was originally only a show of trained horses became the Astley Amphitheatre with different performers, such as acrobats, clowns and a variety of animals.

But it is said that the greatest of all English showmen was George Sanger. He adopted the title of Lord to keep up with his American rival Buffalo Bill who called himself "the Honourable"!

After Astley's death, George Sanger bought the Amphitheatre from Astley's widow, paying her the sum of £11,000. When business was flagging, he was adept at putting on publicity stunts to draw the crowds, for instance, his famous "tame oyster that sits by the fire and smokes his yard of clay". He was also known for organising most colourful and impressive circus parades to announce the arrival of his circus in towns and villages.

Although he was doing extremely well at Astleys, the continual demands and restrictions of the London County Council were crippling his business and so he took to the road, setting up his show under canvas. His show was reputed to be "The Greatest Show on Earth", and was greatly admired by Queen Victoria and her Prime Minister, Disraeli.

His most spectacular display was his "Congress of Monarchs" with

200 horses, 1,200 costumes, and the best acrobats and performers, costing him some £30,000, which he later sold to a man named Barnum for a good profit.

Phineas Taylor Barnum was, without doubt, the most colourful character of the circus world. He was an American, born in 1810 in a small town, Bethel, in Connecticut. He was a clever business man and also his very best public relations officer, aptly describing himself as the "Prince of Humbug".

In his autobiography he tells of many amusing tricks by which he used to entice people into his tents. One was the Fejee Mermaid—a complete fake, the other the "one-hundred-and-sixty-one-year-old negress", also a fake.

He always had an eye for the spectacular and his launching of the midget Tom Thumb and its consequent popularity, brought him a fortune. Barnum was known to do everything on a large scale. For example, he once engaged Jenny Lind the Swedish singer, who was then completely unknown in America. Her arrival in New York was a monumental display of colour and magnificence, and the publicity proceeding her visit was so successful that "people scrambled and fought to buy tickets at fabulous prices to hear her sing". For her ninety-three concerts given in collaboration with Barnum's circus she received 93,000 dollars and it was estimated that Barnum made nearly 200,000 dollars on this deal, during the years 1850–51.

Barnum's private residence on Long Island Sound was in keeping with the character of the man. While visiting England he liked the look of the Pavilion in Brighton and, as he could not buy it to transfer to America, he went one step further—he had one built, but his was even richer and more exotic! This he called "a home for comfort only" and in fact it was a vast and weird mansion called "Iranistan".

The twentieth century brought new ideas into entertainment. The great attractions of the day were music halls and the bioscope shows, the latter being a glorified magic lantern display. Astley's was completely demolished, George Sanger was dead, and Henglers, a small Victorian circus in Argyll Street changed into Palladium—now the London Palladium—so the circuses found themselves in a bad way. It was then that an ex-Army Captain named Bertram Mills injected new life and spirit into the circus world.

In London, back from the First World War, he visited a circus at Olympia with a party of friends. It is said that for a bet of £100 he decided to put on a show himself, and so Bertram Mills became a man of the circus. Although he knew no artists and had no previous experience or any contact with the circus, he managed to achieve great results, and to appear with the Bertram Mills Circus became the ambition of the best performers in the world. He too, was a great showman and the pageantry and pomp which each year marked the opening of his season were an exciting event for newspapers and in later years for the television.

Since animals form the largest part of a circus and since there is still, among some people, a strong belief that cruelty is employed in training them, one must dispel this theory by introducing the name of Gottfried Hagenbeck, the greatest reformer in this field. He was born in the early part of the nineteenth century in Germany. Although he started business life as an owner of a fish shop in Hamburg, his passion for dumb animals, which he bought from all over the world and housed in his menagerie, earned him the name of "the Gentler". He was the first to devise humane methods of transporting animals to and from various parts of the world and to treat them with kindness and care. His son Carl, inherited this compassion for animals from his father and he built up the Hagenbeck menagerie into the world-famous Hagenbeck Circus which still operates in Hamburg. "Like children"—Carl used to say—"they need petting and encouraging", and this is now the recognised method of training.

The court jesters, over the years, have become clowns. To entertain their masters the clowns like the jesters, performed clever acrobatics, or sang songs or were given to reciting poetry. William Frederick Wallett for instance, used to recite long passages from Shakespeare to amuse Queen Victoria.

But it was Tom Belling, a member of the Berlin Circus Renz who in 1889 created an "auguste"—a modern conception of a clown.

The story goes that one day he was amusing himself in the dressing room trying on an old wig and tying his hair into knots and putting his coat on inside out, when he was seen by Renz who thought him extremely funny and pushed him into the ring. Tom arrived in front of the public sprawling in the sawdust and then trying to get to his feet, he tripped and tumbled again. This was simply too much for the audience, they rocked with laughter because never before had they seen anything so grotesque and pitifully clumsy. When amid cheering and applauding a cry "Auguste" was heard, this cry was taken up by all and a completely new idea of clowning was born.

His style was adopted by many clowns and the most famous of

these were the Four Bronette Brothers. By fooling around with water and an assorted selection of musical instruments they were filling the circuses and earning themselves about £600 per week. Two of the brothers are still alive and they are now the owners of the most modern circus in Europe, the Swedish Circus Scott.

The Fratellini Brothers commanded great audiences and were the only clown act to receive a most remarkable recognition of their talents—an invitation to perform at the Comédie Française, the highest honour paid to an artist in France.

The immortal Grock, a son of a Swiss watchmaker, was the last of the great clowns to have the ring entirely to himself, and his act was a masterpiece in timing, skill and clowning. To day we have Coco the clown who, like his predecessors, is beloved by children.

The Americans had their famous clown Slivers Oakley, whose private life was typical of the romantic stories of a clown with a broken heart. Their other great clown was Dan Rice, who too came to a tragic end, dying penniless and unknown in an attic in New York.

It is true to say, that when one reads the life stories of clowns, one realises that they are in their private life often shy and reserved people. Sometimes philosophers, widely travelled and often extremely well-educated. Indeed, through the ages clowns have been drawn from theologians, students of Greek literature and collectors of rare books.

There were many other personalities and great circus families besides those mentioned here, but to tell the story of their lives would require a book of its own.

Instead we will pass on to the making of circus toys starting with the clown, the greatest performer of them all—the one who makes us laugh.

CLOWN

This clown's body is made in white calico with felt shoes and hands, a black and white costume in glazed cotton and white felt hat. The hair is made of red double knit wool. The ruffle round the neck and ankles is the type used for lampshade trimmings. The features consist of a red felt mouth and nose, black felt eyes with four sequins, two of which are fixed into each eye. The patterns are based on the design used for Cookie, a floppy doll, page 159, and are featured in Diagrams 119, 120 and 121.

Plate 27 When making a Clown, let yourself go and choose gay, bright colours and exciting trimmings. This Clown is dressed in a black-and-white spotted costume made in glazed cotton, with white frill round his neck and ankles. His red wool hair is matched by his bright red nose and mouth. Eyes are made in sequins which add to his general mood of careless gaiety.

When finished the clown measures about 16″ (40·5 cm) without the hat. The time for making including the costume takes about six hours. He was first designed for *Homes and Gardens*.

Materials

18″ × 36″ (45 cm × 91 cm) white calico
7″ × 36″ (18 cm × 91 cm) white felt (cutting to waste)
9″ × 9″ (23 cm × 23 cm) red felt
1 oz wool in double knit
Small bits of black felt for the eyes and eyebrows
4 sequins
27″ (68 cm) white lampshade trimming
27″ (68 cm) $\frac{1}{2}$″ wide (1 cm) white bias binding
18″ × 36″ (45 cm × 91 cm) glazed cotton for the costume
7 ozs cotton flock for stuffing

Instructions for making

If you want to make a larger toy, to measure 21″ (53 cm) when finished, then enlarge the patterns by the method discussed on page 17. The length of the front body pattern for the clown featured here reads 15$\frac{3}{4}$″ (40 cm) and when enlarged it should be 20$\frac{3}{4}$″ (53 cm) with the remaining pieces to correspond.

The front body piece should be cut out in one piece, joined on the lines marked "fold" in Diagram 119. This also applies to the front part of the costume and the sleeves, Diagram 120, and to the hat in Diagram 121.

Trace the patterns, mark on them the letters and the information as given on the original patterns. Cut out, and there should be a set of patterns comprising thirteen single pieces. Lay the patterns on the material, mark round and cut out. There should be five pieces in calico, seven in white felt including the hat, seven in red felt including the disc for the nose and five pieces in black and white glazed cotton for the costume.

Sew throughout on the wrong side of fabric. Start sewing the darts on the head, joining the two last darts to the neck at point A.

Close the darts in each section of the back body, and join each section of the back head to each section of the back body from B to B1. Then join the two sections of the back body with heads attached, starting at B2, on the head, going along the curve of the back of the head, passing B1 and ending at C. Start sewing again at point C1 to D, leaving C to C1 open for stuffing.

Sew the hands to the arms on the front and the back body parts,

211

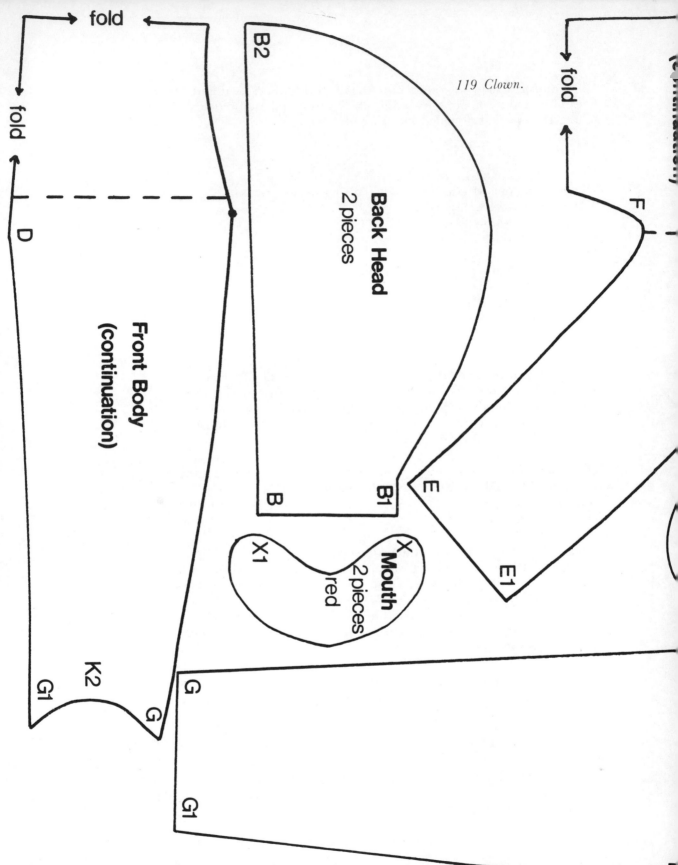

fold

fold

fold

B2

119 Clown.

Back Head
2 pieces

fold

F

D

Front Body
(continuation)

B

B1

E

X1

**X
Mouth**
2 pieces
red

E1

K2

G1

G

G

G1

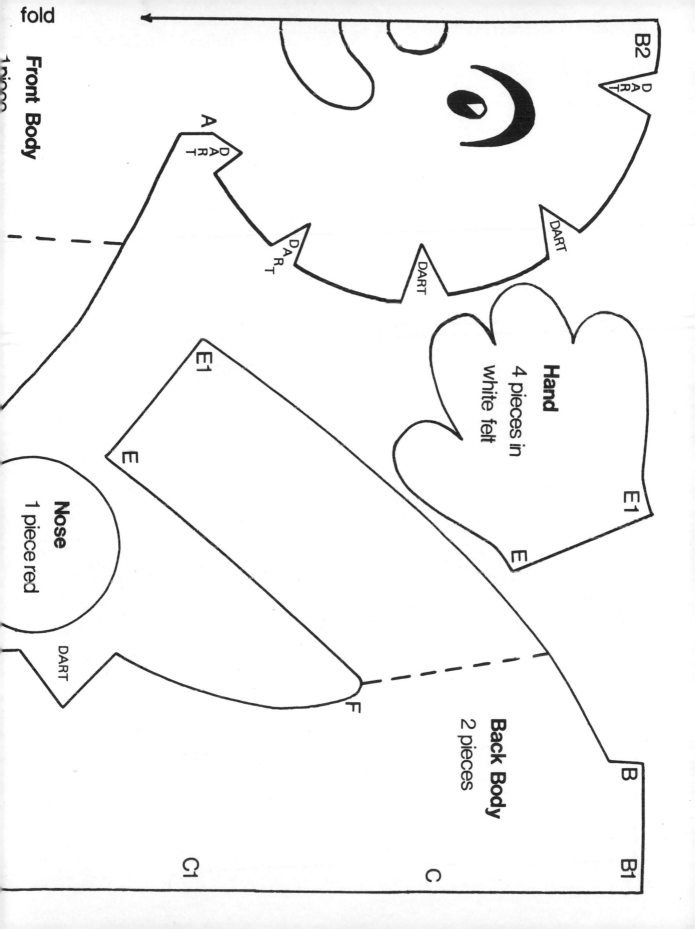

fold

Front Body

B2

DART

A
DART

DART

DART

DART

Hand
4 pieces in
white felt

E1

E

E1

E

Nose
1 piece red

DART

E1

F

Back Body
2 pieces

B

C1

C

B1

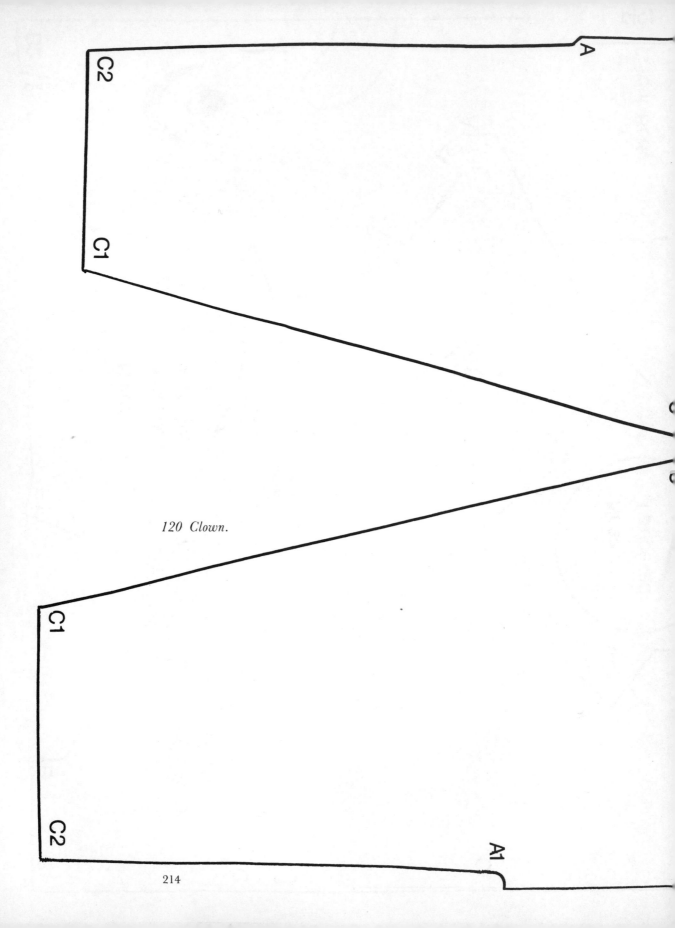

120 Clown.

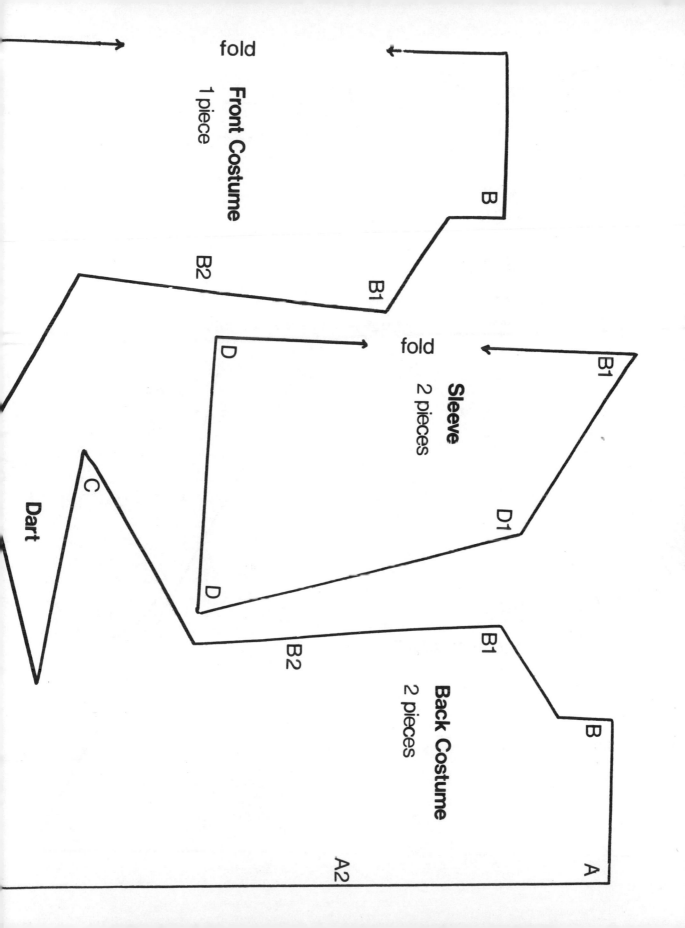

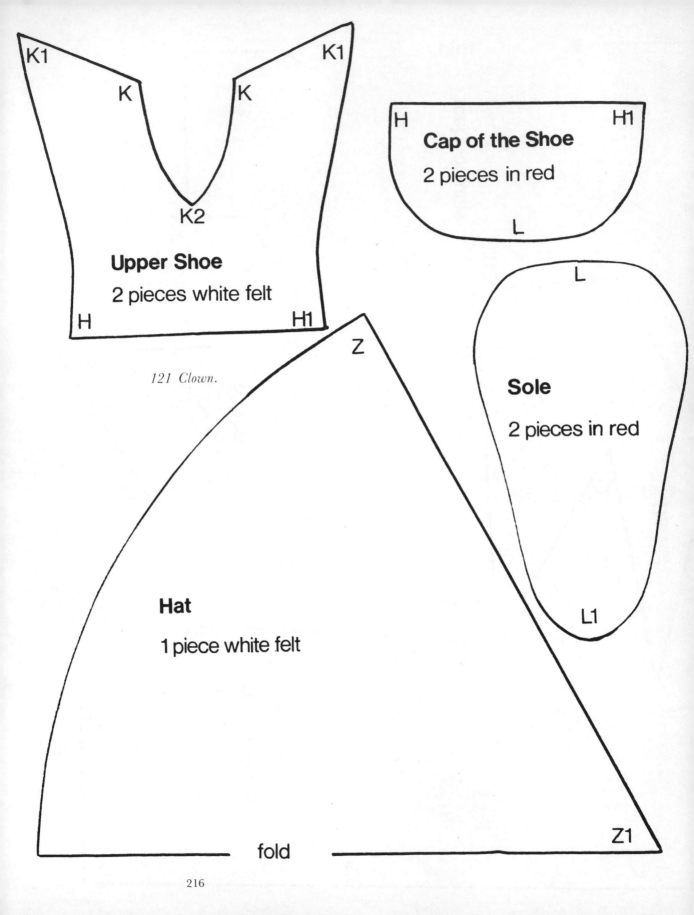

Upper Shoe

2 pieces white felt

K1 K K K2 K K1 H H1

Cap of the Shoe

2 pieces in red

H H1 L

Sole

2 pieces in red

L L1

121 Clown.

Hat

1 piece white felt

Z Z1

fold

216

with the shortest of the four fingers facing towards the body and starting at E to E1. Repeat the same on the remaining three hands.

Then fit and pin together the front and the back bodies with the heads attached, beginning with point B2 on the back head, matching the centre on the front head B2, and working round the head, passing point A, and continuing along the shoulder, the outer edge of the arm, round the felt hand to E, and further on to point F on the front and the back body. Go on fitting the sides of the bodies gathering the "seat" in the back body to fit the front body, ending at G on the ankle. Sew along this line and repeat the same work on the other side of the head and the body. Fit and pin the legs of the back to the front body from G1 to D, finishing at G1 on the other leg.

Take the two caps of the shoes and sew them along to the upper shoes from H to H1 and then close the backs of the upper shoes from K to K1. Fit and pin the shoes to the legs, starting at the centre of the curve on the front leg K2, matching K2 on the shoe and work round. Pin the soles from point L on the sole corresponding to L on the cap of the shoe, passing H and going to L1 which matches K1 on the upper shoe and work round to L. Sew along this line and remove pins.

Make sure that there are no openings in the sewing except the stuffing gap and turn the work right side out through the gap between C and C1.

Start stuffing the feet with small amounts of cotton flock, working from the cap towards the shoes, the ankles and the rest of the legs. Stuff to shape but not too hard, reaching the dotted line marked on the pattern. Machine along this line.

Fill the hands, working the fingers with small amounts of cotton flock, then the arms to the dotted line marked on the pattern. Machine along this line on both arms.

Stuff the head shaping the face and the head, then the neck and finally the rest of the body. Make sure that the neck feels firm and is not floppy.

Close the gap between C and C1 with a ladder stitch, and put the toy aside and start working on the costume.

Machine the two darts on the back body of the costume, beginning at the outer edge of the costume. Join the two back body sections from A2 to A1. Fit and pin the front to the back of the costume, beginning at the neck at B, continuing over the shoulder to B1 and then from B2 to C. Leave B1 to B2 open for inserting of the sleeves. Continue fitting and pinning from C down to the end of the leg to C1. Sew along this line and repeat the same on the other half of the costume. Pin the leg from C2 to A1 and down the other leg to C2 on the other side.

Lay a $\frac{1}{2}''$ (1 cm) wide bias binding along the leg openings at the ankles, facing inside the leg, parallel to the line C1 to C2 ending at C1 and sew in place. Insert an elastic thread into each of the legs. Using bias binding neaten the opening of the dress from A to A2 and run a row of bias binding on the inside of the neck. Insert a thin thread of elastic round the neck.

Before sewing the sleeves into the dress, run a row of bias binding along the edge of each sleeve, working on the inside along the line D/D. Sew each sleeve from D1 to D and fit them into the dress with point B1 on the dress corresponding to B1 on the sleeve and working round. Thread elastic through the bias binding in each sleeve.

Sew by hand the ruffle (lampshade trimming) round the neck and round each bottom opening in the trouser leg of the costume.

The features are marked only approximately on the face, so complete them first and then experiment with their placing before sewing them on to the face.

Take the two pieces of felt for the mouth and sew them together along the curved edge of the mouth starting at X and ending at X1. Turn the work through the gap between X and X1 and stuff lightly to shape. Close the opening and run a line in white felt to indicate the two lips. Make sure that this is sewn firmly into place.

Make up the nose as described on page 61, Diagram 36. Of course no nostrils are necessary and when the disc is made into a red felt ball stitch it to the face and sew round.

The eyes are made of two oblong pieces of black felt and the eyebrows of two black felt arches. Before sewing the eyes on to the face, insert two sequins into each eye. You can buy these in a chain store, complete with proper fittings for insertion. When a satisfactory place is found for the features, sew them on <u>very</u> firmly with a stab stitch, going over twice if necessary.

The hair is made in red wool and there are two methods of sewing it on to the head.

Method one: cut the wool to equal length of 2″ (5 cm), (rug-making wool comes already cut). Sew this wool by spreading it evenly on a piece of tape measuring 10″ (25 cm) and going over it several times for firmness. Place the tape round the head starting on a level with the top end of the eye and going round ending on the other side. Turn in the raw edges of the tape and sew securely into place on the head, leaving the top of the head uncovered.

Method two: fold the wool into curls working directly on the head and following the line from the level of the top of the eye, round the head, ending on the other side of the head. Pin each of these curls into place and if necessary make a second row of curls just above the first. Now sew by catching each strand of wool along this line. The top of the head is uncovered to give the clown a bald head surrounded by a thick red "fringe".

Sew the hat along the line Z to Z1 and turn up the edge to form a ½″ (1 cm) wide brim.

MONKEY

This monkey dressed in her best party frock, can be made in white and lime-coloured checked gingham, with red felt collar and shoes, decorated by a row of gathered lace. The head is in black fur fabric and the beard in white fur. The face, the ears and the hands are in flesh-coloured felt.

Plate 28 The body and dress of this monkey is in lime-and-white gingham. The brightening touches come with the addition of a large pink felt collar, pink felt shoes and rows of dainty white lace round the wrists.

The body and the legs are worked on the same principle as the body and the legs for the Sunny Bear, Diagrams 89 to 92. The legs, therefore, can be adjusted to make a standing monkey. Use the same method as for Panda.

The time for making either the sitting or a standing monkey, need not exceed four hours.

Materials

12″ × 36″ (30 cm × 91 cm) gingham
10″ × 9″ (25 cm × 23 cm) red felt
9″ × 9″ (23 cm × 23 cm) flesh coloured felt
3″ × 9″ (7 cm × 23 cm) black fur fabric
$2\frac{1}{2}$″ × 4″ (6 cm × 10 cm) white fur fabric
8 ozs of cotton flock
1 pair of eyes either glass eyes or buttons 13 mm in diameter
$\frac{3}{4}$ yard $\frac{1}{2}$″ wide (68 cm, 1 cm wide) white lace

Instructions for making

Work on the patterns as described for the previous toys, and cut out. Remember to trace the front body gusset as one piece joining on the line marked "fold" on the patterns in Diagram 124 (the remaining patterns are featured in Diagrams 122, 123, 125 and 126). There should be seventeen single pieces of card patterns. Lay these on the materials, mark and cut out, making sure that there is a left and a right side to each of the front and back pieces of the head, the front and the back body, the under and the upper legs and the under and the upper arms. There should be fifteen pieces in gingham, including the skirt which measures 18″ × 3″ (46 cm × 7 cm), eight pieces in red felt, nine pieces in flesh-coloured felt, four pieces in black fur fabric and one piece in white fur.

Work throughout on the wrong side of the material.

Start by closing the darts, one in the face and one in the beard. Join the beard to the face from A to B. Then sew the left to the right side of the front head from C to D, pile facing in. First fit and then sew the face to the front head by matching C on the front head to C/C on the face, continuing to C1 on both the front head and the face, passing B/B and ending at B1. If necessary gather the beard to fit to the front head part. Repeat the same on the other half of the face. Sew the two back parts of the head together from D to D1 and fit and then sew the back head, now one piece, to the front head, beginning at D/D working along to D2 and ending at D3. Repeat the same on the other side of the head. Put the head aside and start working on the body.

Join the front to the back body from E to E1, leaving a gap to E2. Continue from E2 to E3, leaving a gap to E4 and work from E4 ending at E5. Work in the same way on the other half of the body parts.

Sew on the shoe to the under leg from F to F1 and work in the same way on the other three leg pieces.

Take an under leg and lay it flat on half of the body with the shoe facing towards the front body. Match point E3 on the under leg to point E3 on the body and E4 on the under leg to E4 on the body, pin into place and then sew round. Make sure that the body is facing right side out. Pull the leg through the hole, take the upper leg and fit it with the wrong side of fabric facing out, to the under leg, starting at the shoe F2, passing F1 and going round the leg to F, finishing at F3. Work in the same way on the other leg.

Making a standing monkey, match the under legs with point X on the under leg corresponding to E3 on the body and point X1 to E4.

Sew the body gusset to one section of the back body from G, passing point E5 and ending at G1 at the neck. Do the same on the other section.

Now fit and sew in the soles to the shoes, matching F3 on the sole to F3 on the shoe, passing round F2 and finishing at F3. Put work aside and assemble the hands and arms.

Sew the hands to the arms along H to H1. Close the darts on the palms and sew on the palms to the under arms from K to K1. Join the arms and the under arms from L going down the leading edge of the arms to H1/K, round the thumb and the hands to H and continue sewing to L1. When completed fit the arms to the bodies at L, going round to E1 matching L1, end at L and sew. It may be necessary to gather the arms to fit them in.

Sew the back gusset to one side of the back body from M to M1 and from M to M2 on the other side, leaving the gap M2 to G3 open.

Turn the head right side out and insert it into the body with G1 on the body corresponding to B1 on the beard. Pin round and then sew into place.

Inspect the work for any unwanted openings in the seams, repair these before turning the work right side out through the gap M2 and G3.

Start stuffing the tips of the fingers with very small amounts of cotton flock working towards the hand. When the hands feel well stuffed but not too hard, pin the fingers along the dotted lines given on the pattern and sew right through the two thicknesses of the felt and the stuffing. This done, stuff the head well to shape but not too hard. Then stuff the arms and the rest of the body to the waist.

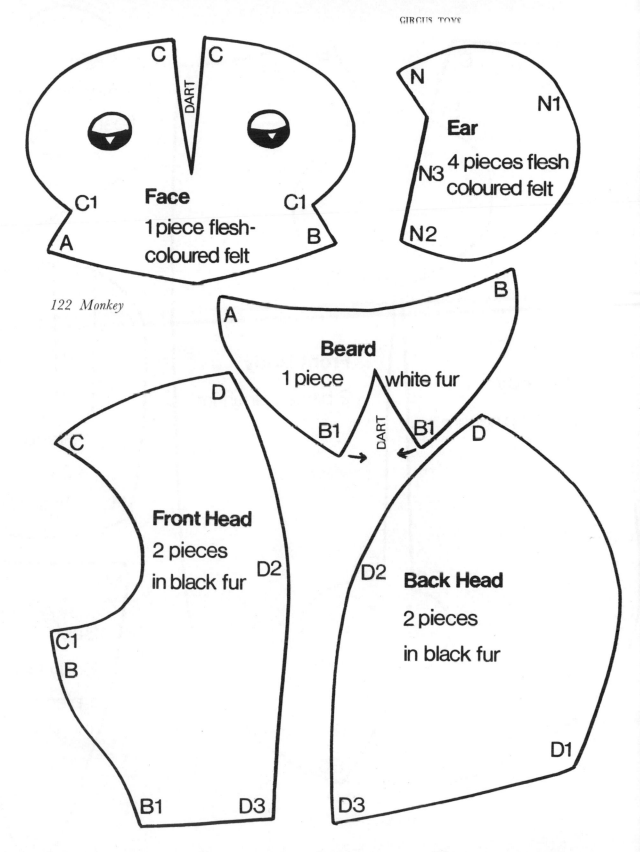

Face

1 piece flesh-coloured felt

DART

C   C

C1   C1

A   B

122 Monkey

Ear

4 pieces flesh coloured felt

N   N1

N3

N2

Beard

1 piece white fur

A   B

B1   B1

DART

Front Head

2 pieces in black fur

D

C

D2

C1

B

B1   D3

Back Head

2 pieces in black fur

D

D2

D1

D3

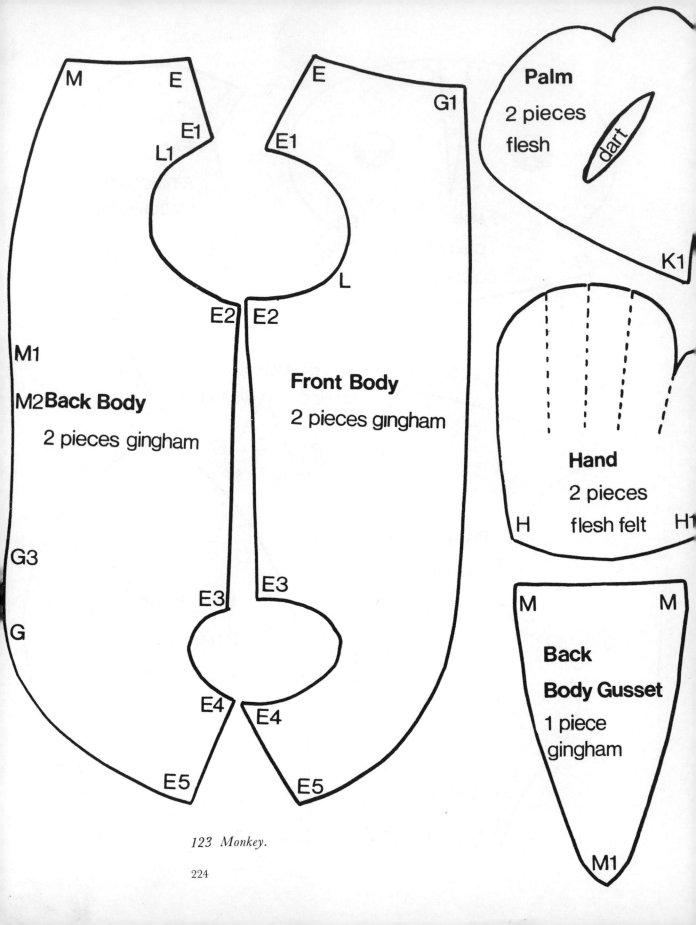

M E

E1

L1

E G1

Palm

2 pieces

flesh

dart

E1

L

K1

E2 E2

M1

Front Body

2 pieces gingham

M2**Back Body**

2 pieces gingham

G3

Hand

2 pieces

flesh felt

H H1

E3 E3

G

M M

E4

E4

Back

Body Gusset

1 piece

gingham

E5 E5

123 Monkey.

224

M1

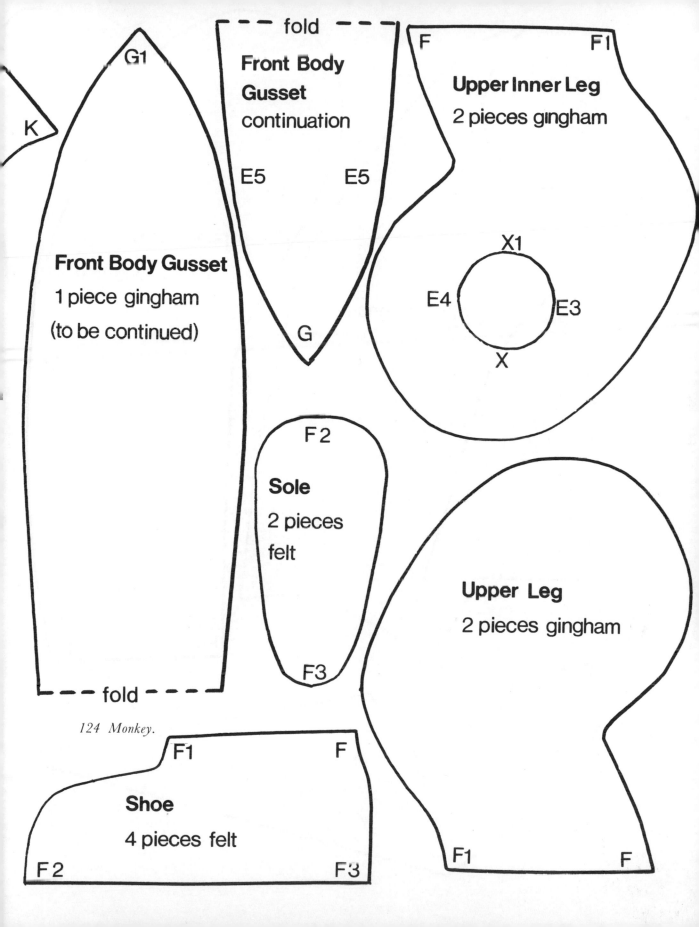

K

G1

Front Body Gusset

1 piece gingham

(to be continued)

fold

Front Body Gusset continuation

E5   E5

G

fold

124 Monkey.

F

Upper Inner Leg

2 pieces gingham

F1

X1

E4   E3

X

F2

Sole

2 pieces

felt

F3

Upper Leg

2 pieces gingham

F1

Shoe

4 pieces felt

F2   F3

F1   F

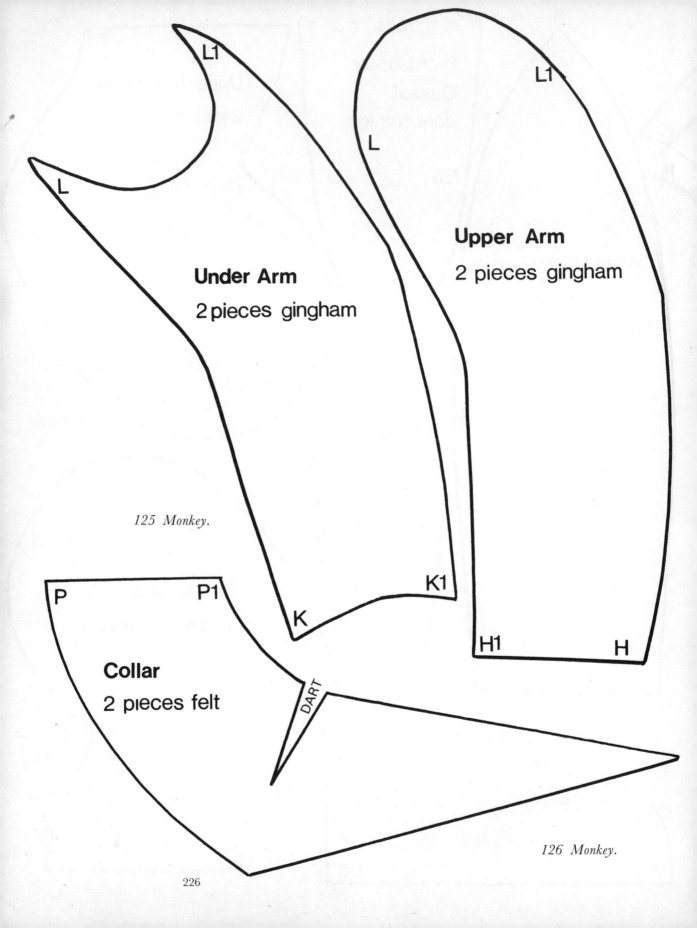

Under Arm

2 pieces gingham

Upper Arm

2 pieces gingham

L1

L

L1

L

125 Monkey.

K1

K

H1

H

P

P1

Collar

2 pieces felt

DART

126 Monkey.

226

Holding the toy by the waist, fill the tips of the shoes with small amounts of cotton flock, working towards the back of the shoe and continuing on to the legs. Remove your hand from the waist and fill the rest of the toy. When the monkey looks well stuffed, close the opening between M2 and G3 and remove any of the fur fabric pile caught in the seams and give the head a good brush.

To finish the dress, sew the darts on the two halves of the collar and then join the two sections between P and P1. Sew a row of gathered lace round the edge of the collar. Use two strips of felt in the same colour as the collar, each $3\frac{1}{2}''$ long and $\frac{1}{2}''$ wide (9 cm × 13 mm), sew a row of lace at one edge, gathering the lace while sewing. Fit these round the wrists with the lace hanging over the hands to give an impression of a lace cuff. Sew firmly into place.

Make the skirt by cutting a strip of gingham 20" long and 1" wide (51 cm × 2 cm) for the waistband, and a strip 18" × 3" (45 cm × 7 cm) for the actual skirt. Gather the skirt into a width of 10" (25 cm) and neatly sew the side edges. Turn up the hem and sew a row of ric-rac to the right side of the material to cover up the turnings. Mark the centre of the waistband and the centre of the skirt and pin together, right sides facing, some $\frac{1}{4}''$ (0·5 cm) from the gathered edge. Sew along this line. Fold the waistband over to the wrong side of the skirt, pin and sew, turning in the raw edge.

To finish the face use 13 mm glass eyes with felt eyelids using the method discussed on page 61. Shade the eyelids very delicately with blue-coloured eye shadow and insert the eyes following instructions on page 28. The position for the eyes is marked on the pattern for guidance only.

Stick and then sew a tiny triangular bit of black felt placing it directly under the dart on the face. Sew a red felt strip 2" long and $\frac{1}{4}''$ wide (5 cm × 0·5 cm) along the seam joining the beard to the face, giving an impression of lips. Sew the four felt ear-pieces into pairs, working on each pair by sewing along N to N1 and ending at N2. Turn right side out through the gap N to N2, flatten the ear and give it a row of sewing repeating the same line, some $\frac{1}{8}''$ (3 mm) from the edge. Lightly work in red rouge on the inside of each ear, then fold each ear with point N resting approximately on point N3 and pin them on to the head with point N2 on the ear touching point D2 on the head. Sew securely and firmly into place.

Place the collar round the neck and catch into place with a bow in red ribbon.

Put on the skirt and tie the loose ends of the band into a bow and the monkey is finished.

CIRCUS DOG

Trained dogs make excellent circus performers and dressed up they
delight children with their almost human tricks. This circus dog is
dress in a red felt coat, black and white gingham trousers, white
spats and a little red pill-box hat. He first appeared in a
Christmas issue of the magazine *The Lady*.

*Plate 29 This Circus Dog is particularly gay. He wears black-and-white
checked gingham trousers and a bright red felt jacket with a couple of
gold buttons on the back. Gold braid holds his pill box hat in place and a
red bow at the base of his tail finishes off his dress.*

The length of the circus dog is 16″ (41 cm) and the height 9″
(23 cm). To make this toy will take about five hours.

Materials

6″ × 36″ (15 cm × 91 cm) red felt
9″ × 36″ (23 cm × 91 cm) gingham, cutting to waste
5″ × 6″ (13 cm × 15 cm) black felt
5″ × 6″ (13 cm × 15 cm) white felt
1 lb of cotton flock
1 pair of glass eyes or black buttons, 13 mm in diameter
2 gold buttons
$\frac{1}{4}$ yard (23 cm) red ribbon
10″ (25 cm) gold braid

Instructions for making

Trace the patterns on to a thin card as described for previous toys
and cut out. Make sure that the body gusset is cut in one piece,
joining it along the line marked "fold" on the pattern in Diagram
128. Also cut the hat band in one piece, joining it along the line
marked "fold" in Diagram 129.

There should be seventeen single pieces of pattern. Lay these
patterns on the materials, making sure that the head has a left and
a right side. Mark round and cut out. There should be six pieces
in red felt, five parts in black and white checked gingham, six
pieces in white felt of which two are the inner ears, four in black
felt and nine pieces in white fur fabric including the tail.

Work throughout on the wrong side of the materials.
Start sewing by assembling the head. Pin the head gusset to one
side of the head, from A to A1 round the curve to A2 and sew
along this line. Repeat the same on the other side of the head.
Pin the gusset from A to A3 on the nose and sew. Do the same on
the other part but continue by passing point A3 and finish the
sewing at B. Put the head aside and work on the body leaving the
back of the head open from point A2.

First of all close the darts, two in each part of the upper body, and
then cut along the "cut" marked on the pattern. Take the under
arm and lay it to correspond with the arm on the upper body,
matching point C on the under arm to C on the upper body.
Sew along this line to C1. Work in the same way on the other arm.
Take each of the white hands, close the dart in each and sew the
hands to the arms along the lines C2 to C1 and to C2 on the other
half, with the pile of the fur facing inwards. Close each arm by
sewing from C2 to C3. Sew along the line marked "cut" on the
pattern from C to B1 on both the upper body and the under arm.
Fit and then sew the palms into the hands, from D going round to
D1 on the palm matching C2 on the hand and finishing at D.
Put the work aside and assemble the lower body.

229

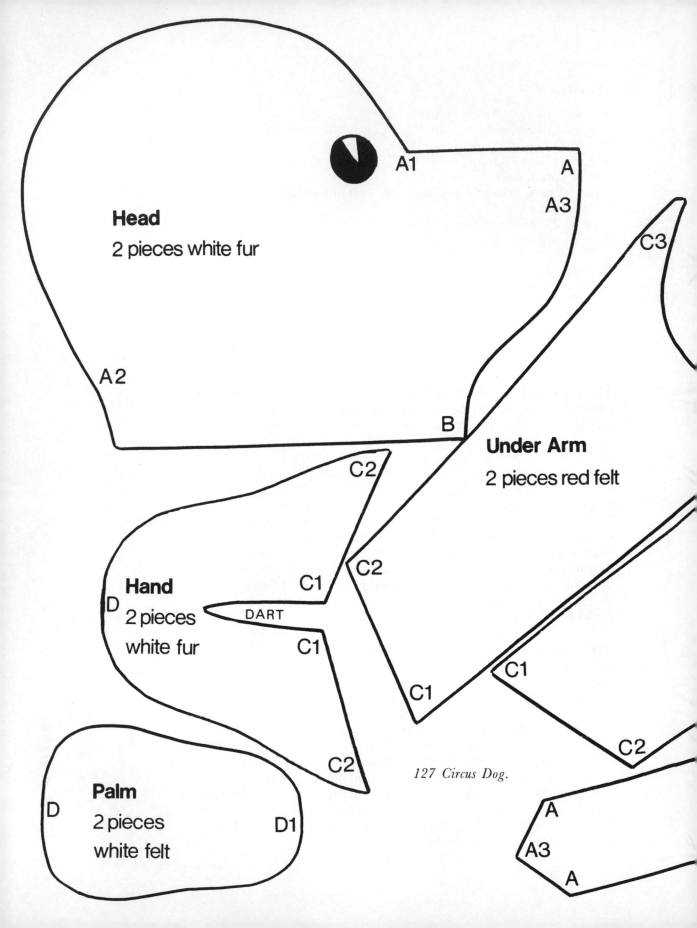

Head

2 pieces white fur

A1

A

A3

C3

A2

B

Under Arm

2 pieces red felt

C2

C2

C1

C2

Hand

D

2 pieces
white fur

C1

DART

C1

C1

C2

C1

C2

127 Circus Dog.

Palm

D

2 pieces

D1

white felt

A

A3

A

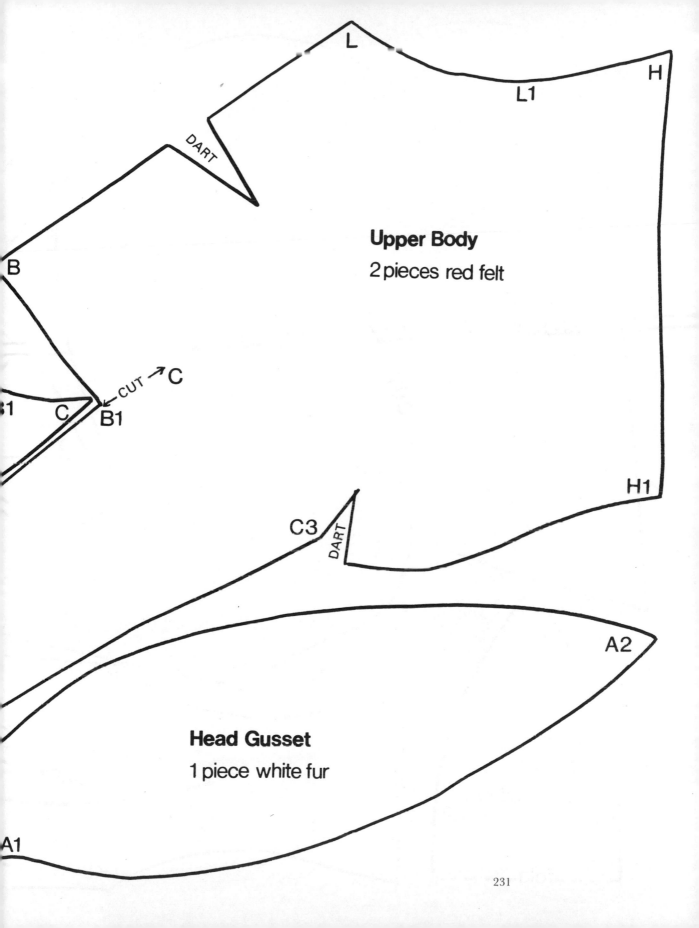

L

H

L1

DART

B

Upper Body

2 pieces red felt

CUT → C

B1   C   B1

H1

C3   DART

A2

Head Gusset

1 piece white fur

A1

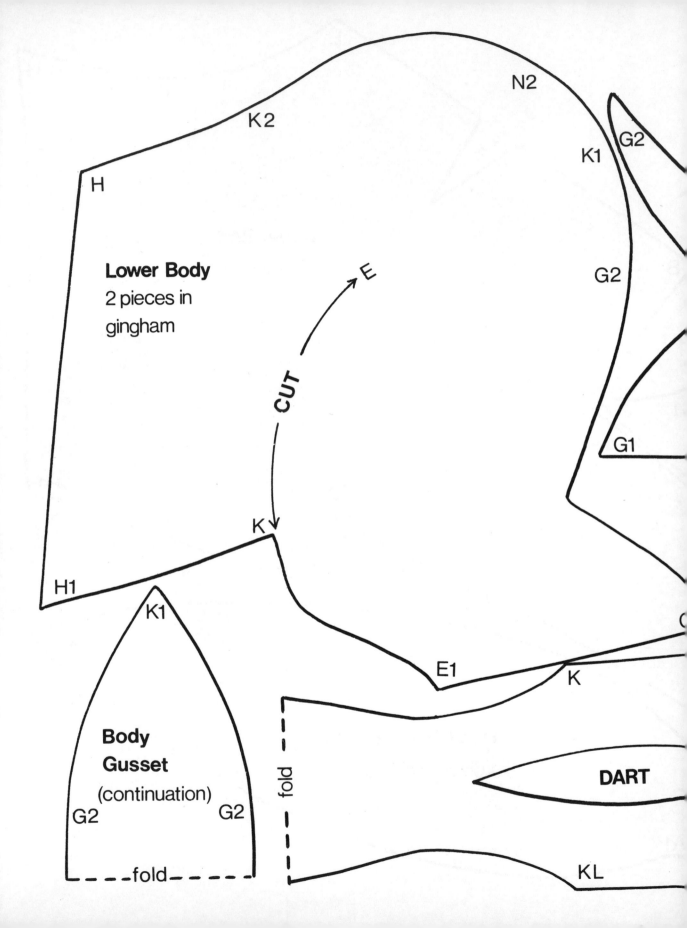

Lower Body

2 pieces in gingham

CUT

H

K2

N2

K1

G2

G2

G1

E

H1

K1

K

E1

K

Body Gusset

(continuation)

G2

G2

fold

fold

DART

KL

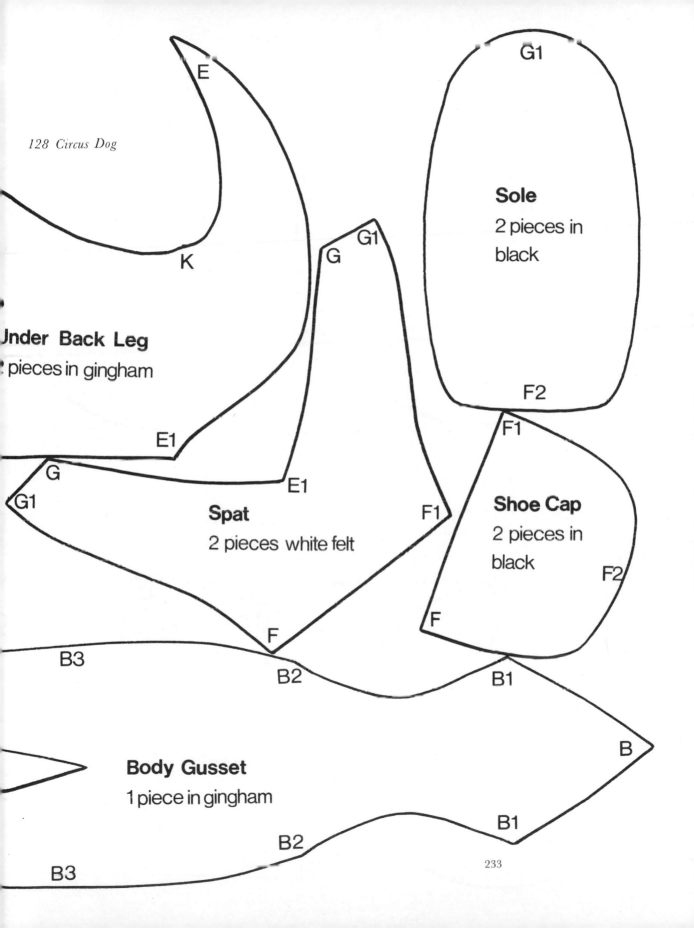

E

G1

Sole
2 pieces in
black

K

G
G1

Under Back Leg
pieces in gingham

E1

F2

E1
F1

G

Spat
2 pieces white felt

G1

F1

Shoe Cap
2 pieces in
black

F2

F

F

B3

B2

B1

B

Body Gusset
1 piece in gingham

B1

B2

233

B3

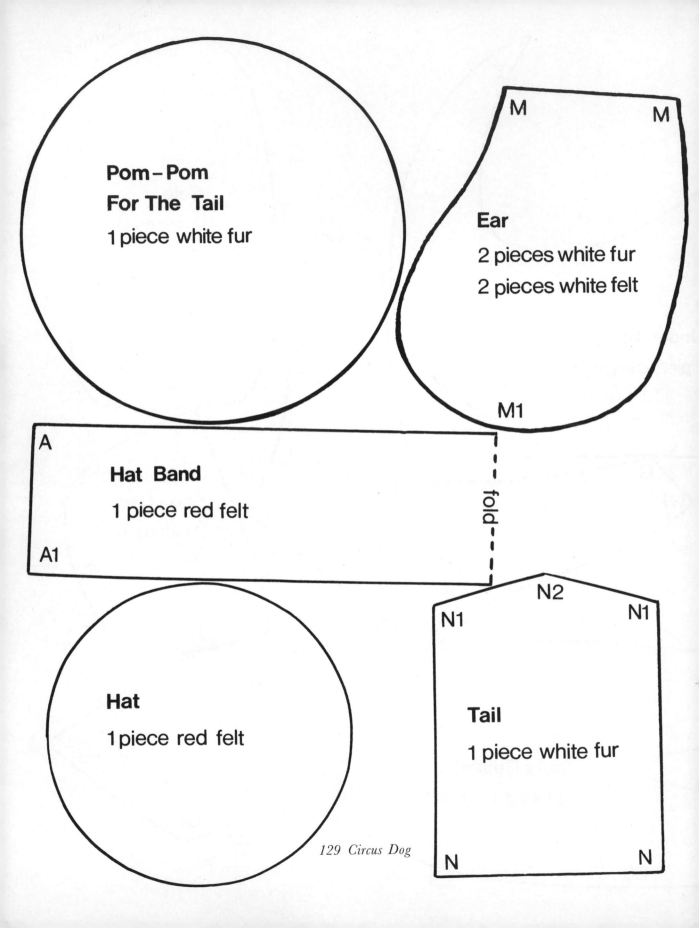

**Pom – Pom
For The Tail**
1 piece white fur

M   M

Ear
2 pieces white fur
2 pieces white felt

M1

A

Hat Band
1 piece red felt

A1

fold

N2

N1   N1

Hat
1 piece red felt

Tail
1 piece white fur

129 Circus Dog

N   N

Cut along the line "cut" as marked on the pattern and sew each of the under back legs to the lower body parts from E to E1. Join the black felt shoe caps to the spats from F to F1 and each of the completed shoes to the under back legs starting at G passing point E1 on both pieces and ending at G on the other side. Then pin and sew each of the under back legs to each of the lower body and sewing to K on the under back leg and K on the lower body, leaving the rest of the under back leg open. Close the back legs along the back edge of the legs, sewing from G1 on the spat, passing G/G and ending at G2 on both the under back legs and the lower body pieces. Fit and sew the soles to the shoes, beginning on the spat with G1 matching G1 on the sole and going round to F2 on the sole and shoe cap finishing at G1. Join each of the lower body parts to the upper body section from H to H1.

Pick up the body gusset and close the dart. Pin the body gusset to one side of the completed body section, starting at B on the body gusset matching B on the upper body, pinning to B1 on the under arm, then alongside the curve of the under arm to C3 continuing along the chest to B3 which corresponds to H1/H1. Go on pinning to point K on the body gusset and K on the under back leg to point G2 on the back leg and G2 on the body gusset finishing at K1 on the lower body piece and K1 on the body gusset. Sew along this line. Repeat the same on the other half of the body but continue sewing after passing point K1 and ending at K2.

Turn the head right side out and fit it inside the body with point B on the head corresponding to B on the upper body. Pin round and sew into place. Close the back of the head from A2 passing L on the upper body and ending at L1 leaving the gap L1 to K2 open. Inspect for any openings in the seams and turn the work right side out through the gap L1 to K2.

Sew the felt ear to the fur fabric upper ear, with the pile facing in. Start from M to M1 and continuing to M on the other side. Turn the ears right side out through the gap M/M.

Make the hat by sewing the two short edges of the strip together from A to A1. Fit the round disc, sew round and turn the hat right side out.

For the tail sew along the line N to N1, turn right side out and stuff firmly. Tack round the white fur disc with the pile facing out, about $\frac{1}{4}''$ (1 cm) from the edge and pull on the thread to form a pom-pom. Stuff lightly in the centre and turning in the raw edges, sew this pom-pom to the end of the tail round the opening N/N. The sewing completed, start stuffing the circus dog.

Begin by filling the head, working to shape, particularly round the nose and the forehead, and then stuffing the rest of the head to the neck. Then with small amounts of cotton flock stuff the hands filling towards the arms and the front body, stuffing the chest well to shape. Holding the toy at the waist turn round to fill the back body. Before stuffing the shoes, cut out two pieces in stiff cardboard in shape of the sole but $\frac{1}{4}$" (1 cm) smaller all round, and insert each of these pieces into the soles in the shoes. Then, stuffing with small amounts of cotton flock, work from the toe towards the ankle and the rest of the back leg, working in the same way on both legs. Keep on filling towards the waist, remove your hand and holding the toy by the neck fill the centre of the body. Close the opening L1 to K2 with a neat ladder stitch.

To finish the circus dog, dislodge any pile caught in the seams in the fur fabric and brush well. Make up a black satin nose and sew as instructed on page 61 and Diagram 36. With black embroidery silk work a mouth as for Sunny Bear, page 147. Use large glass eyes or buttons and mount them on black felt discs, each disc slightly larger than the eye and insert the eyes as described on page 28. The position for the eyes is only approximately marked on the pattern, so it is advisable to experiment before inserting the eyes.

Working very gently, rub some rouge on to the inner ears and pin them to the head pointing them backwards to make the circus dog look as if he is just about to make a sudden, quick movement. When satisfied with the position, sew the ears very firmly into place. Pin the tail with point N2 resting on N2 on the lower body and sew very firmly into place turning the raw edges inwards.

Three small white fur discs each about 1" (2 cm) in diameter and worked as for the Begging Poodle on page 156 will give the circus dog a beard and a furry muzzle.

Two gold buttons on the coat and two tiny black felt discs on each side of the spats will add the finishing touches. The hat placed at an angle is tied on with narrow gold braid. Red ribbon round the neck tied in a large bow under the chin and a red ribbon bow at the base of the tail will finish the toy.

Washing and repairing soft toys

WASHING SOFT TOYS

In choosing your materials make sure that they are washable. This also applies to the type of stuffing you buy. Cotton flock washes well as do most of the fur fabrics and ginghams.

After a toy has been washed, shake it well and dry either on a clothes line or in the airing cupboard, giving it an occasional shake to keep it in shape. If necessary after a toy is dry, re-open the stuffing seam and add extra stuffing. This may be needed for toy animals as the legs, particularly at the top, often collapse due to continual bending. This also applies to dolls when their heads get too floppy at the neck.

Wired and joined toys cannot be washed, but I have sponged them down using only detergent foam on a clean rag and changing the rag often. As a matter of fact you can treat wired toys as you would treat a carpet or an upholstered chair and some of the liquid furniture cleaners can also be used on toys.

REPAIRING SOFT TOYS

If you use strong material and cotton for making toys this will naturally prolong their life. Machining the seams at a steady $\frac{1}{4}''$ (0·5 cm) from the edge of the fabric will prevent them from splitting. Nevertheless, in time the favourite toy, in particular, will show signs of wear and tear. The ears and the tail are usually the first to go. As long as these are not lost, it is easy to sew them back into place.

Arms and legs are vulnerable at the joints, since children are inclined to drag them along by their hands or feet. Immediately a split appears, sew it firmly together with a ladder stitch, going twice over the split.

After a time and a few washings the fabric becomes thinner in places and the pile wears out. The only remedy to preserve the toy is to make some patches on the body or legs or wherever the bald areas appear.

Remember that when making a patch, and it is impossible to find the right fabric to match the original one, be bold and make the patches in bright colours, and if possible work them into some sort of trimming, such as pockets, a pair of trousers, a little jacket or a pair of boots.

A great deal of force would be necessary to pull out the eyes, but if this happens, do not use the same eyes again, particularly when the wire is bent or the loop open—sew buttons instead.

Remember that "a stitch in time saves nine" is never truer than with children's soft toys, and what would be a quick repair as soon as any damage is noticed, could turn into a lengthy job if this chore were to be postponed.

Note on Käthe Kruse

It is little realised that the type of doll impersonating a small girl was the invention of Käthe Kruse, born in 1883 in Breslau, East Germany. When 17 years old she married a well known German sculptor, Professor Max Kruse, and settled down in Ascona.

There her first two children were born and to amuse them she made them little dolls. Encouraged by her husband and his friends in 1910 she exhibited her dolls in Berlin and was immediately acclaimed as an outstanding designer.

From these small beginnings sprang a factory, now run by her daughter Hanne in Donauwörth, Bavaria. In spite of two major wars with the ensuing changes in Europe, the tradition of Käthe Kruse still exists and her beautiful dolls are even more popular today than they were in 1910.

These dolls have travelled far and wide, even to the White House in Washington when President John Kennedy of the U.S.A. gave one to his daughter Caroline.

Bibliography

Children's Toys of Bygone Days, Karl Grober.
The Psychology of early childhood, C. W. Valentine.
Modern Child Psychology, A. H. Bowley.
The Sawdust Ring, R. Croft-Cooke and W. S. Meadmore.
Anatomy of Drawings, V. Perard, Pitman, 1961.
Drawing the Head and Figure, J. Hamm, Studio Vista, 1963.
Drawing Children, G. Shimmer.
Animals of the World, Hamlyn.
Collins' Encyclopedia of Animals, Collins.
The Wonder Book of Animals, Ward Lock.
Modern Soft Toy Making, M. Hutchings, Mills & Boon, 1969.